Debt Politics after Independence

University of Florida Social Sciences Monograph 79

N. 922

REPUBLICA BOLIVIANA.

———◦——◦◦——◦◦◦——◦◦——◦

Empréstito interior de un millon de pesos
conforme á la ley de 16 de Noviembre de
1826 del Congreso Constituyente.

VALE DE CIEN PESOS.

Con la renta anual de seis pesos, pagadera por
tercios en Enero, Mayo y Setiembre.

Es negociable; y recibido en las Tesorerias de la Re-
pública por su valor nominal en la compra de propiedades
públicas y redencion de censos, segun los decretos de 12
de Junio de 1827.

PENA DE MUERTE AL FALCIFICADOR Y COMPLICES.

Chuquisaca á *veinticuatro* de *Julio* de 182*7*

El Ministro de Hacienda

Mudero

Departamento de   de 182
Décimo setimo de la Independencia.

A la órden   Anotado al folio N.

El Prefecto   El Administrador del Tesoro.

Gavino Muñoz

EMPRESTITO DE 1826.

Debt Politics
after Independence

The Funding Conflict in Bolivia

THOMAS MILLINGTON

University Press of Florida

Gainesville / Tallahassee / Tampa / Boca Raton
Pensacola / Orlando / Miami / Jacksonville

Frontispiece—

Bolivian treasury loan bond (vale) negotiable for purchase of state property and redemption of censos. This vale, dated July 25, 1827, has a face value of 100 pesos and 6 percent annual interest. It was issued at Chuquisaca over the signature of Madero as minister of hacienda just a month before his resignation. The vales were printed up after the June 12 decrees. They all bore the statement that they were receivable per those decrees in the departmental treasuries for their face value in the purchase of state property and redemption of censos. This one was apparently not yet in circulation, since the department, date of entry into circulation, and the name of the holder are blank. The signature at the bottom is that of Gavino Ibañez, a Bolivian-born military officer who served as prefect of Chuquisaca in 1827.

Source: Ministerio de Hacienda, Contaduría General, Vales, 1827–1828, t. 5, No. 3.

Copyright 1992 by the Board of Regents of the State of Florida

Printed in the U.S. on acid-free paper ∞

All rights reserved

The University Press of Florida is the scholarly publishing agency of the State University System of Florida, comprised of Florida A & M University, Florida Atlantic University, Florida International University, Florida State University, University of Central Florida, University of Florida, University of North Florida, University of South Florida, and University of West Florida.

University Press of Florida, 15 Northwest 15th Street,
Gainesville, FL 32611

Library of Congress Cataloging in Publication Data can be found on the last printed page of the book.

A Mis Cuñados, Los Hermanos Vivado Pizarro:
Raul, Manuel, Juan Carlos,
Alfredo, Fernando

Contents

Tables

Preface

THE SUBJECT OF Latin America's foreign debt dominated the headlines in the 1980s and shaped much of the academic and policy agenda. The same promises to occur in the 1990s.

How will this debt problem be resolved? We can expect more debt reduction schemes to be applied, with beguiling debt-for-nature swaps heading the list. In the meantime, the Brady Plan will eventually include all of the Latin American debtor states in one form or another. Latin Americans will continue the conversion of unpaid bank debt to longer-term treasury bonds as a means of reducing debt and postponing debt payments, thereby freeing up money to service new debt. Instead of relying on foreign banks, Latin American states and companies will raise the new loans by selling their bonds abroad. Since 1989 nearly $7 billion new debt has been floated this way.

Whatever merits they may have, these debt "reduction" approaches do nothing to broaden the domestic base of Latin American states. They perpetuate a politically disastrous historical predilection for foreign-held as opposed to domestic-held debt.

Another and better approach is to seek to fund the foreign debts domestically by allowing the Latin American citizenries to invest in them and receive from their states long-term annuity contracts. Latin American savings and capital flight could in this way be channeled into amortization of the foreign debt while, at the same time, accountable relations between the states and their citizenries—a bedrock for future democratic development—could be put into place.

The historical efforts made by Latin American states to fund their internal debts have not been systematically analyzed. Yet these efforts contain useful clues about the viability of domestic funding of foreign debt. Moreover, the study of the funding efforts can provide important insights into the origins of the predilection of Latin American states for foreign over domestic debt. Analysis of historical funding projects reveals a deep-seated political struggle between proponents of a funded state debt and proponents of a floating state debt. The latter won this struggle. Their victory eventually moved the state in the direction of foreign borrowing as a preferred substitute for funding the domestic debt with the broader and more accountable relations between state and citizenry that that effort entailed. Instead of the public debt constituting a national bond as it would have through legitimate funding, it became the basis for secretive and mutually manipulative relations between the state and its creditors. Creditor factions armed with floating debt paper used it to exercise a proprietary influence over state revenues, to purchase state property cheaply and gain tax relief, to influence state policy making in favor of their interests. When the state appeared to be performing the manipulation by imposing forced loans on creditors, the creditors began to shift state borrowing into the foreign sector in an effort to relieve state pressure on them and to convert uncollectible internal loans into collectible foreign loans.

Had the funding projects succeeded, state debt would not have been allowed to extend such a long shadow over the domestic political process. The underlying distortions in the economy and society that resulted from the circulation of nonfunded state debt paper would not have had to be built into the political systems. Nor would it have been necessary, as Carlos Marichal has said in reference to the later foreign borrowing by Latin American states, to build the deception of the public interest, upon which those loans were erected, into the political systems of the Latin American states. It is important therefore to learn why the funding projects failed in order to evaluate their chances of future success. I believe that unless Latin American debt, foreign and domestic, is moved from a floating onto a funded basis, it will be impossible to lay the foundations for a democratic development.

This book really began in the month of January 1977 in the National Archive in Sucre, Bolivia. During that time I was working as a budgetary analyst in the Ministry of Finance in La Paz. That work had stimulated my interest in the historical origins of the financial practices of the Bolivian state. I therefore arranged to do some research in the archives in Sucre on the financial policies of the Sucre administration in Bolivia (1825–28). I knew from reading William Lofstrom's pioneering work that the administration had been active and innovative in this area. During this research I began to notice that there were really two financial policies at stake, each involving debt management and the issuance of state debt paper. Lofstrom had dealt extensively with each of these policies, but he saw them differing only in technical terms. In contrast, I believed that each of these policies had different political, social and economic horizons. I felt that a useful analysis could be made by conceptualizing the difference between these two debt policies—what will be called the funded debt project as opposed to the floating debt project—and then proceeding to trace the roots of their joint appearance in the financial policies of the Latin American states in the early independence period. Within this plan, I decided to use the Bolivian case in order to explore, using mainly archival data, what seemed to me to be a striking case of an authentic funding project being undermined by an alternative policy of raising new short-term loans charged against state assets.

My purpose in chapter 1 is to introduce categories of debt management theory, particularly as they relate to the concept of a funded debt. This concept of funded debt is then traced in the early debt management practices of the Latin American states in the immediate postindependence period, with special emphasis placed on the European origins of the funding models that were current and on the nature of the difficulties in reproducing those models in a Latin American context. The Spanish funding model is introduced at the end of this chapter because of its special relevance to the Latin American funding experiments: to a great extent the Latin American fundings recapitulated the Spanish funding experience, especially in regard to the involvement of funding paper in the rural land markets that arose out of the dismantling of feudal and ecclesiastic mortmain.

In chapter 2, I describe the spread of church *censos* (property liens) as the main form of rural entailment in Bolivia, the appropriation of these censos by the Sucre administration, and the outlines of a market for state debt paper based on the use of that paper to redeem censos held against rural property. The funding project in Bolivia lost its integrity largely because of the pressures to make all state debt paper negotiable in this market or, more exactly, to give preference to state loan paper that was uniquely negotiable in this market.

In chapter 3, I analyse the efforts of Sucre to position treasury loan bonds (*vales*) in the disentailment market in order to increase their value to holders who were largely Sucre's own compatriot Colombians, while his minister of finance, Juan Bernabe de Madero, was trying to position the funding paper (*billetes*) of the Public Credit Administration in the

hands of holders of the existing internal debt. My purpose in this chapter
is to define the different constituencies and different agendas associated
with these two enterprises.

In chapter 4, I evaluate this conflict in favor of the funding project.
Focusing on the capital formation process in the rural sector, I show the
untoward effects that were caused by the role of nonfunded state debt
paper in the rural land market. I pursue a speculative line of argument
about how a more equitable result would have come about if funded state
debt paper had been relied on to organize rural savings.

In chapter 5, I intend to place the Bolivian case in perspective by examining some of the main lines of theory concerning internal state debt—
including the relevance to peripheral states of the normative argument
conducted in Europe and the United States in the last century over whether
internal state debt was a good or a bad thing. In the final section in this
chapter I review some of the main tendencies in fiscal historiography concerning Latin America as they bear upon the question of how the internal
state debt is best to be understood and evaluated.

Certain individuals played a key role in the progress of this book, and I
would like to mention them here. It was at the suggestion of James Wilkie
that I undertook a quantitative analysis of the Bolivian budget in 1977
that was published in 1983 by the UCLA Latin American Center of which
he was then and is now the director. That work initiated me into Bolivian
state finances and, as I indicated above, prompted me to do the historical
research that led to the present book. At the other end of the book, toward the completion stage, I would like to mention the generous guidance
and advice on scholarly technique supplied to me by my former professor
at Williams College, James MacGregor Burns, whose example was inspi-
rational to me.

Gunnar Mendoza, the great patriarch of the Bolivian Archives at Sucre,
provided wonderful support during my work there, as he has done for so
many others. One of those certainly was William Lofstrom, whose own
books on the Sucre administration's reforms in Bolivia were of immense
use to me, as were his suggestions concerning the manuscript of this book.
Robert Jackson convinced me of the referential value of the Spanish Consolidación de Vales Reales to my own thesis, as well as of the value of
linking Bolivian state finances to the whole question of rural society.
Those two directions in my book owe a lot to his suggestions. George E.
Pozzetta, editor of the University of Florida Social Sciences Monograph

Series, provided me with timely advice over the year-long period during which I was trying to respond to and evaluate the reviews of the manuscript. At the University Press of Florida itself, my thanks are also due to Walda Metcalf for editorial guidance and Judy Goffman for a very skillful job of copyediting.

At Hobart and William Smith Colleges, I would like to express my appreciation to the librarian, William Crumlish, for his multilayered and unstinting support, not only for this book but for my other projects as well. A library as well run and as accommodating as his is a boon to scholarly endeavor. The whole library staff has been a great help, but I would like to thank Kathy Knox and Michael Hunter in particular for helping me with sources. At a college like Hobart and William Smith, where faculty discourse leaps across departmental boundaries with comparative ease, it would be impossible for me to cite all of my interlocutors who have in some way contributed to this book; in some measure the interdisciplinary quality of my book reflects the interdisciplinary atmosphere of the colleges. I would like to mention Geoffrey Gilbert and Scott McKinney of the Economics Department for special stimulus and for reading the manuscript. Thanks are also due to James Crouthamel and William Atwell in the History Department. My current colleagues in the Political Science Department—Joseph DiGangi, Peter Beckman, Craig Rimmerman, Iva Deutchman, David Ost, Michcline Ishay, and Hamideh Sedghi afford me daily opportunities to test out some ideas. The departmental secretaries, Sue Yates and Dawn Feligno, have been helpful in manuscript management. Sarah Dollard, my former William Smith student, helped me immensely with the preparation of the manuscript for publication and made a lot of substantive suggestions on organization. Important secretarial and logistical support were provided by Ann Rago over a protracted period of time.

My brothers-in-law in Bolivia, to whom this book is dedicated, enormously facilitated my contacts there and immeasurably facilitated my research not only for this book but for other projects concerning Bolivia. My wife, Rosario, has suffered through the long gestation of this book as well as equally long periods for my other projects. Her support, interspersed with some veiled and not so veiled threats, was a constant inspiration. Our three boys, Tom, Ken, and Greg grew up with this project, and they each have their own particular roots in Bolivia. The two older boys, Tom and Ken, were with me in Sucre during one of my main research stints there.

1

Frames of Reference

UPON ACHIEVING INDEPENDENCE the Latin American states rushed to open their doors to foreign capital. The British investors in particular were anxious to accommodate them. The loan bonds of the new states and shares in companies organized in London to exploit the mines fueled the British bull markets of the period 1823–25. With the exception of Bolivia and Paraguay, all of the new states received considerable infusions of foreign capital from the London money market. In 1826, however, the London market began to crash, largely because of Mexican and Colombian defaults which were repeated by all of the other states in Latin America with the exception of Brazil. In most cases the full proceeds of the loans never arrived. Among the defaulting states only a few of the mining companies in Mexico avoided bankruptcy. Foreign loans to the Spanish American states disappeared for the next thirty years.[1]

During the first half of the nineteenth century, as a result of this early experience with foreign loans, the borrowing positions of the Latin American states developed exclusively in the domestic private sector. There, the virtual absence of central banks, or even commercial banks, in the first half of the century meant that the state borrowed directly from individuals and groups of individuals, particularly commercial groups. The need to place their new borrowings in the domestic sector, without any bank intermediation, impeded the states' concurrent attempts to fund their massive internal debts inherited from the colonial period and from the period of the armed struggle for independence. This inability to fund internal debts allowed the formation of a particular kind of state creditor class, composed of individuals who made new ad hoc loans to the state. Instead of being amortized out of funds created specifically for that purpose, these new loans were charged against state revenues, made negotiable for pay-

ment of import taxes and state-held mortgages, or accepted in the purchase of state-owned properties.

In contrast, the fundings were intended to transform the existing public
debt into a national bond by converting it to long-term, low-interest state
annuities held by a broad class of citizen savers and amortized out of a national sinking fund. The Latin American fundings thus were designed to
prevent the concentration of economic and political power in the hands of
a narrow range of public creditors using nonfunded short-term debt to
gain control over state revenues and property. Ultimately the nonfunded
state debt paper involved in these activities took precedence over the debt
paper involved in the funding attempts. Had the funding efforts been successful, the new states would have been shielded against the process of
presiding over the mortgaging of their own wealth, as well as the wealth of
their countries, to this intrusive creditor class.

We will examine here the struggle that took place in Latin America in
the early independence period between the advocates of funded debt and
the advocates of floating debt. Bolivia has been selected for detailed analysis because it offers a particularly vivid picture of a funding operation
under siege by an alternative debt policy that was geared to making new
borrowings from a rising commercial clientele and to the repudiation of
the existing internal debt. It also offers an example of how state debt management became linked (as it was in Spain at the same time) to the growth
of a rural land market in a way that led to the failure of the funding policy
and provided that failure with a particular domain of economic and social
consequences.

The Bolivian funding operation provided, theoretically, a means for
mediating an area of accountable "full faith and credit" relations between
state and citizenry. As it was, a more compromised role was imparted to
the state by the circulation of its nonfunded debt paper. The liberal cor-
rective to this situation was worse than the disease, at least as far as the rural Indian population was concerned. By shifting state debt from the rural
land market to the foreign sector as part of a program of extracting the
state from the functioning of the domestic economy, liberalism degener-
ated into a form of social Darwinism aimed at the elimination of "socially
unfit" portions of the population (the Indians). The problem was not,
however, the role of state debt paper in the rural land market; it was the
role of nonfunded (floating) debt paper at the expense of funded debt
paper. This then is a distinction that has to be considered before analyz-
ing the Bolivian case.

Debt Concepts and Terminology

Modern debt economics employs terms and concepts that were not current in the 1820s; many terms that were current then, such as public credit, are not current now. Furthermore, two modern conditions of state debt—a capital market and an institutionalized guarantee against repudiation—were not current in Latin America in the 1820s. Nevertheless, public debt economics was a nascent reality. The terminology and the concepts of modern debt economic theory are useful in providing a framework of reference for the analysis of state debt in this earlier period, particularly if they are attuned to the prevailing conditions and practices. They are also helpful in defining the funding question as it existed then.

PUBLIC DEBT AND PUBLIC CREDIT

Public debt designates those sums owed by the state in the forms of bonds, notes, and bills issued by the state and stipulating the payment of specified amounts of money to the holders at designated calendar dates. The term *public debt* was current in Latin America in the 1820s, within this modern definition. The more positive phraseology of public credit was also current, although its usage disappeared toward the end of the nineteenth century.[2] The term was imported from Europe, where it had come to mean the raising of loans on the state authority as opposed to the personal debts and credit of the princes, the former basis of "public" loans. The term *public credit* expressed the new and higher levels of internal authority and legal accountability achieved by the Renaissance states of Europe. Ideologically, public credit was bound up with the theory of the sovereignty of the state.[3]

In Latin America in the 1820s, the term *public credit* implied more than just the public debt; it was a belief that through public credit programs the new states could strengthen their accountability to the citizenry and solve their financial problems at the same time. Public credit represented, specifically, a plan to convert short-term debt (which was seen as destabilizing the state) into long-term funded debt which the state would amortize over time, thereby demonstrating its reliability to the citizenry whose money was entrusted to them. Public credit systems, as such, went hand in hand in Latin America with the introduction of direct tax systems, which were designed to replace the endemic indirect taxes of the colonial period. The idea behind direct taxes (taxes on property) was that, because they came proportionally out of each citizen's wealth, the citizens would demand accountability from the state concerning the use to which tax revenues were being put. Indirect taxes (taxes on sales and transactions) were seen as devices for extracting money from the people in a way that would avoid scrutiny on public matters. Public credit and direct taxation were thus seen as vehicles for building up an attentive citizenry, thereby allowing the mercantilistic state of the colonial period to be replaced by the modern representative state.

DEBT MANAGEMENT AND CHOICE OF LENDER

Like the fiscal processes of taxing and spending by the state, internal state borrowing provides a means to redistribute the wealth and income among individuals and groups. The virtue of placing the internal state debt on a funded basis is that it broadens the distribution of wealth by creating a large class of citizen savers who accumulate capital in the form of a steady stream of annuity payments from the state. In the last century, opponents of internal state debt, whether funded or not, argued that it constituted a regressive redistribution of wealth. In his analysis of the "social significance of public debts," Henry Adams wrote of public debts that "wherever existing, the citizens of a state are divided into two classes— those who pay taxes for the support of the debt and those who receive interest payments out of the proceeds of those taxes. It is not intended to imply that holders of bonds form a distinct class in the community, but rather that there always exists in a country burdened with debt an interest peculiar to the holders of bonds." Public debts were bad in Adams's view because they transferred wealth in a manner that reinforced class divisions in a society. Adams did not accept the argument that funded debt was any more progressive than nonfunded debt. In fact, funded debt was worse because it added the problem of big government bureaucracy, which he saw as antidemocratic; funded debt smacked of a European statism that was inimical to the needs of a "commercial democracy" such as the United States. We will return to some of Adams's arguments in chapter 5 in the light of the foregoing analysis of the Latin American funding experience.[4]

The question of whether the domestic holders of state debt paper are concentrated in certain sectors of society or whether they are broadly distributed depends, in the first place, on whether they are competing with foreign holders for the state's debt. Second, it depends on domestic "choice of lender" decisions made by the state. States can choose to borrow from central banks, the effect of which is basically to create new money. The state can also sell debt issues to commercial banks and exert pressure on them to buy. Or the state can sell the debt issue to individuals and restrict bank purchases.

The absence of central banks in Latin America in the 1820s, and even of commercial banks, meant that the state borrowed from individuals with capital, particularly those comprising commercial groups, foreign and domestic.

Given the range of lenders available, choice of lender issues are decided by debt management policies. The two basic policy areas concerning state debt management involve new borrowings by the state and the conversion (or refunding) of existing debt securities into new issues.

In Latin America in the 1820s, experiments in public credit were based on conversion of the existing debt. As such, they were challenged by groups wanting to shape the state's internal borrowing position through the floating of new short-term loans, and effectively to repudiate the existing debt. The struggle over debt policy, defined in these terms, was a struggle to control the choice of lender decision: it was a question of who the state's essential domestic lenders were going to be, those whose claims originated in the late colonial and revolutionary periods or those with fresh capital to offer the state. This struggle involved in turn an underlying issue of whether the public debt was to form a national bond institutionalized in the form of public credit administrations embedded in the state structure, or whether the debt was to be of the floating, short-term variety more amenable to the limited, laissez-faire state.

FLOATING AND FUNDED DEBT

The modern distinction between floating and funded debt originated in the practices of European princes in the late medieval period. Their credit was brought into play when their subjects granted money or services in return for promises of a princely service. Initially, loans were raised without pledging particular revenues to the payment of interest and principal. Services or money turned over temporarily with no specification of repayment terms were called a floating debt. Subsequently, the practice arose of mortgaging particular revenues for periods of time until the interest and principal of a loan were repaid. The turnover of services and capital was still regarded as temporary and still part of the floating debt. But finally, when money was turned over permanently in exchange for annuity payments made from permanent funds created for that purpose and extending indefinitely into the future, it became common to speak of a funded debt. For most of the Middle Ages, the floating debt remained much larger than funded debt. But with the rise of state structures, princes began to raise more of their capital by funded loans and the practice of converting floating loans into funded loans became common.[5]

But even as the European states undertook to rely more on funded loans, floating debt accumulated as the result of recurring needs to procure goods for military purposes. Likewise, periods of internal revolution generated large floating debt. In the periods following the Revolution of 1688, the Napoleonic Wars, and the American Revolution, England faced enormous procurement bills and claims. The same was true for the United States after its struggle for independence, for France in 1800 after its revolution and the onset of the Napoleonic campaigns, and for the Latin American states in the 1820s after their independence struggles. Victualing bills, ordnance debentures, forced loans, warrants, commissary certificates, orders from an army general on the treasury, expropriation edicts, and damage claims were all part of the floating debts that faced these states.

The paper of record that the suppliers of goods and services were left with under these conditions did not bear on its face the evidence of its genuineness and was not negotiable. It was like an itemized bill, each item of which could be contested, and normally the states reserved the right of investigation. In the case of funded debt, the paper of record (a bond) was itself evidence of a valid claim, bearing on its face the terms and extent of the claim. The state no longer retained the right of inquiry into the validity of the claim. In the periods following their military exertions, states in the modern period inevitably faced the problem of trying to fund some portion of their floating debts. Major funding enterprises were launched by Britain in 1693 and 1783, by the United States in 1790, by France in 1800, and by the new Latin American states in the 1820s.

Genuine funding was associated more with the concept of a public annuity than with the concept of a public loan bond. The key difference is whether a sum of money given over to the state is stipulated. In the case of an annuity, the language of contract takes the form of a pledge to pay periodically or annually a stipulated amount (the annuity). In the case of the loan bond a principal is stipulated, and the person who buys this contract buys the right to reclaim the principal at the end of a designated time period, along with the payment of interest.

With a loan bond, the state is helpless to change the time when the whole principal becomes due. The virtue of annuities, as a form of the state's debt, is that there is no principal as such to become due. In the case of terminable annuities that expire at some fixed point, a portion of the principal is paid with each interest payment until the principal is paid off in full. Annuities can be drafted to lapse at a specific time, to lapse at the death of the annuitant (life annuities), or to run permanently (perpetual annuities).

From the funding perspective, annuity debt is superior to loan debts with a principal that is repayable at a definite date because the state has the option of converting annuity debt to lower interest rates (or redeeming the contract) and using the savings to build up the amortization fund. Loan debt is less subject to conversion operations since it is characteristically short term and charged against specific state revenues. Perpetual annuities are the superior form of annuities from the point of view of funding the debt, because the debt is redeemable at the option of the state, thus allowing the state to engage in conversion operations that cannot be performed on terminable annuities, much less on debt repayable at a definite time. Perpetual annuities as the form of the public debt are in fact the key to genuine funding of the debt, in which the public creditors hold state loan stock that is redeemable only at the option of the state. This entails the placing of unconditional trust in the state; it positions the debt on a genuine fiduciary basis and opens the way to the institution of a sinking fund.

In Latin America in the 1820s, three kinds of state debt paper circulated: paper representing floating money claims against the state originating in the pre-independence period; the debt paper issued by the public credit administrations (*billetes de credito publico*) that took the form of terminable and perpetual annuities and was used to fund the existing debt; and new commercial paper and short-term loan bonds issued by state treasuries (*vales de tesoro*).

It was the British fundings, particularly the techniques employed in William Pitt's ministry, that were closely followed by the Latin Americans, especially the Argentines, as their congressional debates clearly reveal.[6] Pitt in the 1780s developed a more powerful concept of the sinking fund based on the principle of the accumulation of the fund through compound interest on stocks of the state's debt purchased by the commissioners appointed to govern the fund. Capitalized initially at a million pounds assigned by Parliament from revenues, the commissioners used it to redeem stock standing at or above par at par value. Alternatively, they purchased stock standing at below par at the market price. The interest earnings on the purchased stock were used to purchase fresh stock so that compounded interest earnings would permit rapid accumulation of the fund on a self-sustaining basis. The fund was enormously successful in redeeming existing bonded debt stock, permitting a large new issue of 5 percent stock which was used to fund the large floating debt held over from the American War of Independence. Pitt was successful therefore in funding the floating debt, restoring confidence in public credit, and pioneering new methods in the sinking fund operation, including ironclad arrangements that prevented raiding of the fund.

In addition to Pitt's financial achievement, the British experience clearly revealed that the development of a funding system produced more parliamentary control over finance, a desirable development from the point of view of the new Latin American states which were fighting to prevent executive dominance. Parliament's authority was required for the raising of loans and for earmarking duties and taxes to meet the interest on a debt that was becoming permanent. Before the first funding legislation in 1693, Parliament's involvement in public borrowing had been sporadic, mainly because most of the debt was floating.[7]

But the British experience in funding differed in one crucial respect from the Latin American situation. The British state was able to rely on its central bank to cash out its floating debt paper (mostly Exchequer bills) and to accept from the state annuity payments for the amount of capital retired. This ability allowed the state to concentrate on moving the whole of the debt over to an annuity basis and to legislate a sinking fund. In the meantime, the state relied mainly on the Exchequer bills (cashed out by the bank) as the main instrument used by the state to raise temporary loans in anticipation of revenue. No conflict of interest developed within the state between the Exchequer bills and the annuity paper.[8]

In Latin America there were no banks, much less central banks, to facilitate the funding operations of the state by absorbing its floating debt. As a result, the state had to market and service its own short-term treasury bonds and to become compromised, it might be added, by the holders of those bonds. The treasury loan bonds (vales) entered inevitably into competition with the annuity paper (billetes) issued by the public credit administrations. Servicing the loan bonds deprived the public credit administrations of needed revenues to pay amortization costs on the funded debt and, more significantly, created a narrow but politically powerful creditor class with privileged access to state revenues and policy making at the expense of the nascent class of citizen-savers holding the funded debt.

MATURITY AND MARKETABILITY

The maturity of a public debt issue is the date on which the state will pay the holder the face value (or par value) that the issue bears; the maturity date is the date of redemption. States typically set an interest rate on a debt issue that will allow the issue to sell in the market at par value. A lower interest rate would require it to sell at a discount. Modern state bonds are mostly salable (they have a daily market price at above or below par), but they are not redeemable until maturity. Like annuities, however, many savings bonds are not salable, but they are redeemable at will for a face value principal, although interest rates rise the longer they are held.

These considerations generally held good in the debt markets of Latin America in the 1820s. The funded billetes and the treasury vales had different maturity and marketability characteristics, although neither carried a specific maturity date (*fecha de vencimiento*). The treasury vales were usually auctioned off and were allowed to circulate as commercial paper, or they were retired when negotiated for tax or purchase of state property. On the other hand, funded billetes were assigned to the holders of the existing debt. They were intended to be held like a savings bond, drawing relatively low interest payments, like annuities, over an undefined period. The state could also amortize the funded billetes by purchasing them in the open market at the price of the day. These open market purchases were also known as *rescate de licitacion*. Buying back the billetes at discounted prices in the market enabled the state (theoretically) to reduce the interest payments on its outstanding paper, and with those savings, "rescue" more of its funded paper, raise its market price, and prepare the ground for new issues. The key to public credit programs was the existence of a sinking fund, *capital amorzante*.

In the 1820s, treasury vales were considered to be temporary debts and were seen as a means of covering cash flow problems believed to be transitory. The cause could be interruption of accustomed sources of revenue or the need to provide for some emergency service, such as pensioning off military officers or paying prize money voted to liberating armies by overly generous congresses. (Prize obligations indeed became the overriding factor in Bolivian state finances in the period 1825–28). Most states usually found a ready-made market for their treasury vales, provided they are issued in moderate amounts and are in denominations large enough that they do not penetrate retail transactions and cause damage to the circulating medium of the country. In Latin America after independence, treasury vales were of considerable convenience for commercial transactions and served the purpose of banking paper and as a medium for temporary investments. They were made negotiable for paying off state and clerical taxes and for buying state-owned properties. The main difficulty with short-term loan bonds was that the emergency outlasted the running times on the bonds and the states were pressed to pay off the principals before the emergency drain on revenues had passed.

In contrast, the purpose of long-term debt was to organize large portions of the population into a voluntary savings program.

Whether a state's creditor class should be composed of holders of short-term debt, with the attendant speculative and commercial uses, or of a larger cross section of the population whose savings habits are being cultivated by the state, depends among other things on the state's credibility. Orienting its debt structure toward commercial convenience is the prerogative of a politically established state. But where it is precisely the political foundations of the state that need to be established—where the state needs to create its authority in the face of competing loyalty demands by demonstrating its superior scope—it is necessary to structure the public debt in a way that makes the state responsible to the largest number of citizens possible. Funding the existing internal debt provides a means to do so. In the United States, Hamilton's Funding Act of 1790, more than any other single factor, shifted the balance of loyalties from parochial state governments to the federal government and allowed the Constitution to replace the Articles of Confederation legitimately. Under the act the federal government assumed the responsibility to fund not only the war debt of the Continental Congress but also the individual state debts that arose during the course of the revolutionary wars. Many of Hamilton's insights into funding as a way to capitalize politically on public debt by converting it into a national bond applied with even greater pertinence to the Latin American states, given their notoriously weak national foundations.

The funded debt paper and treasury debt paper in Latin America in the 1820s differed fundamentally in terms of marketability. Funded debt paper was salable on the market, but it was designed more to resemble savings bonds with the expectation that it would be held over the long term by the original holders or until such time that the state amortized the paper by purchase in the market out of sinking funds. In this sense the funding programs were attempts to *capitalize* the debt by turning it into these annuity-like savings bonds. In contrast, the temporary debt paper was marketed by making it negotiable in the custom houses or to purchase state property or eliminate state-held mortgages on property. The marketability of the temporary debt paper rested on its commercial value. The pressures to *commercialize* the public debt stemmed from the state of underdeveloped commercial credit systems in Latin America in the immediate postcolonial period. Due to the absence of banks the credit systems relied necessarily on short-term negotiable state debt paper along with credit funds in religious brotherhoods (*depósitos irregulares*) and letters of exchange of domestic and foreign merchant guilds. Bank notes and bank deposits were not yet part of the credit milieu. State debt paper became even more necessary, to take up the slack in the credit systems left by the elimination of clerical credit (censos) in the colonial period. Thus the pressure to commercialize the public debt by keeping it on a temporary, quasi-floating basis conflicted with the pressure to capitalize the public debt by funding it. The two factors that proved vital to the successful financing of the U.S. funding—a large and steadily increasing volume of federal import tax revenues and a relatively highly developed banking system—were unavailable to the Latin American states.[9]

Internal Debt Management after Independence

Toward the end of the colonial period the class of state creditors holding money claims on the state fiscs included the church, merchant lenders, confraternities, cities, holders of tax loan notes (*págares*) charged against future state revenues, holders of fisc notes resulting from transfers pursuant to the Spanish Consolidación de Vales Reales, holders of deposits on call, state employees with salary arrearage, and buyers of public offices that had not yet become vacant. These debts were defaulted because of the outbreak of the independence movement.

State debt was vastly expanded during the republican period. The new states assumed responsibility not only for the defaulted Spanish state debt extending back into the late colonial period but also the massive, floating internal debts that had been generated during the revolutionary period from 1810 to 1825. They fell heir to obligations incurred by both the Spanish forces and patriot forces, ranging from sequestered property to

forced loans, back salaries both civilian and military, and damage claims
of every conceivable variety.

The so-called Spanish Debt included individuals holding documented
claims against the old colonial authorities.[10] Initially the republican governments confined the Spanish Debt to the period preceding the outbreak
of the independence struggles, but gradually they became willing to extend the recognized debt to include the insurrectionary period up until the
time when Spanish governments actually fell. This second period was relatively short in the case of Argentina but protracted in the cases of Bolivia
and Peru. The Spanish government insisted on the extension of the Spanish Debt up to the actual end of Spanish rule as a condition to signing
treaties with the republics. The Spanish Debt was also widened by these
treaties to include Spanish functionaries' salary losses and even salary
taxes imposed by the Spanish.[11]

The Patriotic Debt consisted of indemnifications of those who had suffered persecutions and confiscations at the hands of the Spanish because
of their adherence to the patriotic cause. Most of the republican governments were ostensibly enthusiastic about consolidating this debt into a
new interest-bearing issue.[12]

Superficially, the politics of the Spanish Debt and Patriotic Debt creditor groups were different. The holders of the Spanish Debt, particularly
those of the period after the outbreak of the independence struggle, were
seen in republican circles as enemies of the new state, but the holders of
the Patriotic Debt were applauded. The difference between the two constituencies, however, is often exaggerated in liberalist historiography. In the
first place both groups were awarded the same consolidated debt paper,
the main difference being that the Spanish Debt holders received a slightly
lower interest rate. The consolidated paper (a preliminary step toward
funding) was an automatic upgrading of the unrecognized claims that
had existed previously. The negotiability of this consolidated paper for
acquisitive or speculative purposes was therefore less important in the first
instance to the holders; they now held paper that was genuine on its face
rather than paper held previously which was ad hoc. The consolidated
paper was assigned through public credit administrations to holders of
verified claims from the colonial and revolutionary periods. The gains to
be made by the states in making good on this paper were politically and
psychologically crucial. These circumstances put the holders of both the
Spanish and the Patriotic Debts in a mutually different position from that
of the speculative and acquisitive class of state creditors, which consisted

of (1) the holders of consolidated paper who had bought it cheaply from the original holders, Spanish or patriotic, for speculative purposes, and (2) the holders of new treasury vales that were either bought at auction, received from the state as a form of prize money for military service, or purchased from prize recipients by speculators. The best evidence of the ephemerality of any distinction made between the Spanish and the Patriotic Debt is the fact that the two were soon joined as republican governments undertook intermittently to consolidate the internal debt.[13]

Within the structure of the internal debt, émigré claims on the state occupied a discrete space but eventually came to be allocated to the holders of the Spanish and Patriotic Debts. As the level of fighting and turmoil increased, so did the portions of the populations who opted to flee to safer environments. Many of these émigré groups returned or had their interests represented by relatives or pressed by the Spanish state diplomatically. Inevitably conflicts arose between these émigré efforts to rescue their stake and the activities of key clienteles of the new states, military and commercial, which had emerged from the ruins of the old order. The internal debt acted as one battleground in the competition between the coalition of holders of the consolidated debt and these clienteles. The latter wanted to consolidate their position as state clienteles by holding new debt charged on state revenues while trying to force the émigré claims into the Spanish Debt where chances of collection were even less than in the Patriotic Debt. The émigrés also entered into conflict with new state clienteles who were attempting to buy their old *fincas* with consolidated debt paper they had bought cheaply from the original holders. In many cases, the new states had accumulated so much land—as a result of sequestering of loyalist properties and the taking of church lands—that they were anxious to unburden themselves and were willing to restore fincas to the returning émigrés or their agents. But more often, the state had already adjudicated these lands over to people with influence, particularly military leaders. In the final analysis, the voluntary creditors (people who bought the debt deliberately) had the edge over the involuntary creditors (the original holders of the Spanish and Patriotic Debts, including émigrés) when it came to negotiating their paper for state lands; and new loan issues had a definite advantage over consolidated issues in this market.[14] This edge is why émigré groups tended to become the leading advocates of funding the internal debt as an alternative to basing debt policy on floating new short-term loans. It was no coincidence that the architect of Bolivian funding, Juan Bernarbe de Madero, was himself a former member of the émigré group of Bolivians living in Buenos Aires who held a large volume of the internal debt.

Besides the whole complex matter of the internal debt, the new states' revenues were drained by the enormous burden of paying the maintenance, salaries, and prize monies claimed by the large and slow-to-demobilize military establishments that had been recruited to fight the Spanish forces. The outbreak of large-scale fighting between the new states in the 1820s and 1830s and within them (where *caudillo* armies took to the field) undermined the demilitarization impetus and increased army claims on state revenues.

The prospect of state bankruptcy gradually began to overshadow the early optimism that the transformation from mercantilistic colonies of Spain into liberal and secular, free-trading, capital-importing republics would open up vast horizons of economic activity and prosperity. None of the new wealth fully materialized. In most cases the state appropriation of church wealth proved to be not only politically difficult in the new states but also administratively difficult because church wealth was tied up in complicated entailments that were difficult to nationalize. The republican states laid claim to more of the tithe income than the colonial states did, but they received less of it because they were less efficient at collecting it. Colonial transfers to Spain were eliminated, but they amounted to much less than expected. Even more significantly, the colonies that had relied on transfers from other surplus colonies no longer could do so. The mining industry collapsed across the board in America as a result of the London crash and would not be recapitalized until the second half of the century. Direct taxation policies proved enormously difficult to implement. But the new states found it complicated to tap into the old sources of state revenue which had been massively dislocated due to the fighting and disruptions of the wars for independence from Spain. Not only that, new liberal doctrines in vogue dictated the deliberate elimination of the key tax areas of the colonial period—the tribute, the tithe, and the *alcabalas*—on the grounds that they were impediments to social and economic progress. Customs revenues from increased foreign trade did expand, but they proved ephemeral because of the damage that free trade inflicted on domestic industries and the consequent rise in protectionism.[15]

Fiscal deficits were expanded by the costs of developing new state functions in the areas of education, health, welfare, and culture that had previously been left to private charity and the church. Hospitals, asylums, theaters, schools, universities, and cooperatives all had to be funded and organized. This effort entailed costly attempts to centralize the state apparatus and to create large and complex administrative agencies. Alongside of the whole range of new state functions in the social area stood new ones in the monetary and fiscal policy areas: redistribution of the wealth through progressive tax systems, expanding savings and consolidating the internal debts through public credit systems, and laying the groundwork for the gradual transition from metallic currency to paper money.[16]

In the first half of the nineteenth century, efforts undertaken in all of the new states to manage the internal debt can be grouped into three broad categories: efforts to convert the internal debt into deposits in newly created banks; efforts to create priorities through a selective amortization policy; and efforts to fund the entire internal debt.

In the first category the idea was to use consolidated debt paper to capitalize commercial banks as the basis for an expansion of the credit systems. A good example is the Discount and Deposit Bank created in Venezuela in 1834 with a capital of 1 million pesos in 10,000 shares at 100 pesos each. Half of the capital was to be in metallic currency, the other 500,000 in consolidated public debt securities bearing 5 percent annual interest.[17] The bank could issue notes to depositors of metallic or the debt securities. Other Latin American states made tentative steps in this same direction—notably Argentina and Brazil—but they all eventually failed, mainly because the credit systems were still too grounded in commercial houses and the church; deposit banks did not become established parts of credit systems until the second half of the century.[18] Thus states had to sell the internal debt to commercial houses, foreign and domestic, which used it not as banks would for loan reserves but as a means of levering their business interests into state policy making.

A second major approach to the problem of managing the internal debt was characterized by a selective amortization policy that favored commercial creditors. An important Argentine decree of March 29, 1817, stipulated the use of internal debt paper in the customs to pay off state duties on land or sea imports. Holders of debt paper who were not active in the import business (the vast majority) were left out in the cold; they received consolidated paper which proved to be worthless.[19]

In the Argentine case the effort to pay internal debts until 1815 consisted largely of paying off the holders of forced loans. In 1815 it began to shift to a strategy of using letters of exchange in customs essentially to pay off merchants who had advanced credit to the government or to the army. This shift in the pattern was signaled by the creation of a *centro de pagos* in the customs administration and a disappearance of amortization payments from the treasury.[20]

In the third approach to the management of the internal debt, efforts were made to consolidate it into titles of public credit (billetes de credito publico) that did not have commercial (exchange) value but were politically significant in the sense of the potential for creating a public order. Internal debt paper that had commercial or transactional value tended to overshadow this more general, consolidated internal debt paper despite the greater importance of the latter in building up the accountability of the state to the citizenry at large. The consolidated paper entailed potentially a more fiduciary relationship between state and holders because of its long-term character: holding it in order to receive annuity payments over the long term implied reciprocal accountability that was not entailed in the relationship between the state and the holders of short-term commercialized debt paper. These observations applied particularly to those consolidations that were tied to valid funding enterprises.

In the first half of the nineteenth century the two major Latin American efforts in funding were undertaken in Argentina and Bolivia. These efforts were designed to achieve the political advantage that long-term funded debt paper held over short-term debt paper.

The Argentine funding operation originated in the Caja Nacional de Fondos de Sud America, instituted by President Juan Martín de Pueyrredón in 1819. Among his many far-reaching reforms, Pueyrredón had developed a global plan for the absorption of the heterogenous collection of debts to citizens compiled by the independence governments in the course of conducting the wars against Spanish and Portuguese forces. These debts took the form of forced loans, confiscations of property, promissory notes, and bonds of every class. The indemnification of these claims was essential in Pueyrredón's view if the central government, newly established by him at Buenos Aires, were to ever legitimize its authority. The Caja Nacional de Fondos de Sud America was the first institution of its kind—somewhere between a deposit bank and a funding institution—to be established on the continent. The essence of this approach was to convert all of the old debt into a new issue of public credit billetes bearing a fixed rate of interest. The Caja was capitalized at 3 million pesos. Old state debt paper could be amortized in the Caja by converting it into billetes. Eventually the Caja failed, and one reason for its failure was the absence of a sinking fund out of which the billetes could be gradually retired, thereby increasing their market value. As it was, the market value of the billetes declined steeply, and the costs of servicing the billetes outran the Caja's capital.[21]

The Argentine Caja appears to have been modeled more on the French funding of 1800 than on the earlier British funding under Pitt. In 1800 the French government set up the Bank of France and an amortization fund as twin institutions to be concerned exclusively with the amortization of the large floating debt left over from the Revolution and Napoleon's wars. They operated independently of the treasury. These institutions were successful after 1813 in amortizing the public debt, although they did not attempt to convert it into long-term debt along the lines of the British fundings or to employ a sinking fund.[22]

With the failure of the Caja de Fondos de Sud America, Argentine financial opinion shifted more toward the British model. It was said in Congress on November 28, 1822, that the old adage that " 'a state either liquidates the debt or the debt liquidates the state' has come to be a false one due to the appearance of another term—the debt liquidates itself." Public credit was not perfected until "the force of a capital fund destined to amortize each loan" was realized "as in Pitt's Ministry in 1786."[23] Farther along in the on-going funding debate another deputy in Congress observed that the "English were the first to use the techniques of consolidating the public debt—heterogenous debts of the state and funds earmarked to paying them off—into one mass, the purpose being to pay off the united debt after liquidating it" through a consolidated issue.[24] It was thus the English concept of perpetual debt and a sinking fund strategy that were being scrutinized.

In 1821 Argentina attempted to convert all of the outstanding public debt stretching back to the colonial period into long-term funded debt. By a law of October 30, 1821, an amortization fund was instituted and capitalized from state surcharges on notarized paper, imports, patents, cattle sales taxes, and real estate sales taxes at a legislated rate of 300,000 pesos per year. The fund was authorized to issue annuity paper up to 5 million pesos, 2 million in 4 percent annuities and 3 million in 6 percent annuities. Claims dating before May 25, 1810, independence day, were convertible into the 4 percent annuity paper. All of the later debts were convertible into the 6 percent paper. The annuity paper was to be guaranteed by state revenues and assets. Significantly, state-owned land was cited as collateral for foreign debt only. Under no conditions were state properties to be made salable for the annuity paper. This provision reflected the strong Argentine emphyteusis policy of preventing the concentration of large landholdings in few hands (latifundism) by establishing state leasing regimes on all land currently possessed by the state in the interior. (This feature was to carry over into Bolivian funding, creating a sharp confict with the powerful tendencies toward private land accumulation that had developed in the Bolivian hacienda system.) The funding was completed by subsequent issues of annuity paper—1.8 million in 1823 and 300,000 in 1824— and by the creation of in 1825 another Consolidation Fund, authorized to issue annuity paper in the amount of 15 million pesos in anticipation that, with the funds from a large loan pending in London, the annuity paper could be bought back by the state at a low market price (hence the largeness of the issue), thereby forcing up the market price and paving the way for new issues.[25]

The introduction of the Argentine funding coincided with the end of the era of customs domination of Argentine financial life. A central treasury was established as the depository for all customs revenues; *libranzas* or *giros* against the customs were made illegal. An administrative Department of Public Finance was established to administer all public rents. An annual state budget was mandated to be submitted by the executive to the Congress.[26]

The Bolivian funding experiment took the form of the public credit system established in 1826. It was modeled explicitly on the Argentine funding of 1821. The Argentine and Bolivian cases represent the two leading Latin American examples of efforts undertaken in the early independence period to convert the internal debt into long-term funded debt held for its savings value as opposed to short-term debt held for its commercial and transactional value. Approximations of these cases can be found in the Chilean consolidation in 1831, the Peruvian consolidations in 1826 and 1850, a subsequent Bolivian consolidation in 1846, and a Colombian consolidation in 1853.

The Spanish Debt-Disentailment Precedent: The Consolidación de Vales Reales

Consolidación de Vales Reales is the name for a project undertaken by the Spanish Crown in the late seventeenth century. It sought to redeem royal debt paper (*vales reales*) by making it negotiable for rural properties that were being put up for sale as a result of a vast disentailment program initiated simultaneously by the Crown. Although intended originally only for Spain, the Consolidación de Vales Reales was extended to the American empire in 1804.

The Consolidación de Vales Reales was highly relevant to the debt management policies that were pursued by the new Latin American states. The Latin American disentailments were in fact set in motion by the Consolidación. They continued during the independence period and created a ready market outlet for new state debt paper, much as they had for the vales reales in Spain. The redemption of the debt paper through sales of disentailed property undermined the foundations of the Latin American funding attempts in much the same way that the vales reales role in the Spanish disentailment market had undermined the Crown's own funding plans. The similarity was not coincidental. Both the Spanish and the Latin American disentailments derived from the same liberal ideology that at the time opposed funding on the grounds that a better use for state debt paper could be found by employing it in the rural land market in order to increase the volume of transactions in that market.

The Spanish funding experience provides a valuable reference point for any analysis of the relationship between Latin American state finances and the phenomenon of slow capital accumulation process in the rural sectors. The Spanish disentailments did not lead to increased economic efficiency and entrepreneurial regimes of rural ownership as expected by liberals, nor did the Latin American disentailments. In both cases, it can be shown that the channeling of nonfunded state debt paper into the rural land market was a factor in this outcome.

***

The great Bourbon experimenter, Charles III, inserted Spain in the Seven Years' War on the French side. The war marked the beginning of a large drain on the Spanish Treasury incident up to its involvement in the imperial struggles between France and Great Britain. The war also intensified a pattern of British hostility to the Spanish *flotas* at sea, with resulting interruptions in the flow of American silver wealth to the Spanish Treasury. In the American War of Independence, Spain sided with France and the North American colonies against Britain. Its finances went more deeply than ever into the red.

The introduction of vales reales in September 1780 was intended to meet the defense needs of the Spanish state occasioned by the war, to cover the hiatus in receipt of American wealth, and at the same time to foment the Spanish economy with a view to expanding the tax revenues

of the Crown. This initiative grew out of discussions held between Treasury officials and the Spanish-French-Dutch banking syndicate directed
by Francisco Carrabus. The syndicate's proposal was to deposit in the
Royal Treasury 9 million pesos in metallic currency or letters of credit in
exchange for royal notes (vales reales) in denominations of 600 pesos
equaling in face amount the 9 million pesos, plus commission, and yielding 4 percent interest yearly. This worked out to 16,500 in bonds of 600-
peso denominations, which was the issue authorized by a lengthy royal
cédula dated September 20, 1780.[27]

The vales reales were really terminable annuities, similar to the British
Exchequer Bills; theoretically they could have paved the way to funding
the royal debt, as the British Exchequer Bills actually did, had the Crown
been able to rely on powerful banks to cash out the vales in exchange for
annuity contracts with the Crown. The vales had the important feature of
being redeemable at the king's pleasure anytime within a twenty-year period from the date of issue. The vales would be renovated yearly at the
time of interest payment to the holder. The treasury would redeem a pro-
portional amount of the circulating vales each year, buying them at market
price, until the issue was entirely retired. A separate accounting system
was set up in the treasury to service the circulating vales, although no separate fund was yet established to provide for interest and amortization
costs.

In addition to serving as terminable annuities, the vales were transfer-
able by endorsement and could be used to pay royal taxes or any other
debt owed to the Royal Treasury. They were to be accepted as such in the
treasury, in the army, and in all fiscal agencies of the Crown across the
land. The vales were also intended to be used as effective money in commercial transactions. Any business person refusing to accept them as such
was liable to exile "without being able to ever return to carry on commerce
in the realm." The major difference between the vales and a fiduciary currency (beyond the fact that vales paid interest and were redeemable) was
that salaries and pensions could not be paid in them and day laborers, artisans, and shopkeepers were to accept them only if they so chose.

The costs of the American War of Independence and the campaign to
take Gibraltar had caused new issues of vales reales in 1781 and 1782 totaling 20,099,900 pesos. These new issues drove down the market price to
13–25 percent below par, but with the signing of peace it rose to 1–2.4
percent above par and stayed there for the next six years. This allowed

Charles III to use new issues of vales to finance public works and to create a state trading company for the Philippines. The market absorbed these issues totaling 10.5 million pesos at prices for 1–2 percent over par. Given their receptivity in the domestic market, the vales reales were regarded by the Crown as superior to raising foreign loans because the interest payments stayed in the country and they circulated in benefit of commerce. In fact much idle capital found an outlet in the vales reales. Until 1793, the Spanish money market had little trouble in absorbing the vales issues. But new issues made by Charles IV to finance the war against revolutionary France, totaling 114 million in 1794–95, strained the market. They sold at a 21 percent discount, although with peace they rose but never to par. The signing of a new alliance with France against England in 1796 and the outbreak of a new war against England forced a new issue of 53 million vales reales in 1799, which drove the market price down to 47 percent under par. In 1800 the vales were selling at a 75 percent discount by holders who feared that Napoleon's power was beginning to compromise the Spanish Crown. Legally, the Crown had to accept the vales at face value for tax payments, thus severely curtailing its fiscal revenue.[28]

A new issue of vales to finance the war against England and to make forced payments to Napoleon was out of the question. The vales already in circulation had to be systematically amortized and their market value raised in order to avoid royal bankruptcy. The response to this challenge took the form of the Consolidación de Vales Reales.

The appointment to the royal cabinet of Gaspar Melchor de Jovellanos (Justice) and Francisco de Saavedra (Treasury) had signaled the new effort to move the management of royal debt from a temporary, emergency basis onto a permanent, funded basis. As an example of this shift in concept, Charles IV, in his decree of 1794 authorizing a new vales issue, had appealed to emergency conditions by stating that he was obliged to wage war by the "monstrous revolution that devours France and that marches on to disturb the domestic and foreign tranquility of all the states [of Europe]." But his decree of February 26, 1798, emphasized the need to secure the domestic foundations of the Spanish state. By moving the royal debt from the temporary, floating basis onto a permanent, funded basis, the idea of reigns having their own separate loan structures would give way to the idea of the continuity of state liability. "The State being permanent, it should be subject permanently to the obligations it contracts in the name of the legislative authority which represents it, without permitting arbitrary exceptions or giving currency to the erroneous opinion, so prejudicial to the decorum and sovereign authority, that [the loans kings make have] no more force than during the time of their individual reign."[29]

This decree announced the establishment of a permanent Caja of Amortización, whose objective would be to consolidate all of the royal debts including the rapidly depreciating vales reales in circulation. Amortization of the vales reales up to this point had been conducted out of ad hoc funds that lacked independence from the treasury. The Caja represented a step toward the creation of a sinking fund; it was to be entirely separate from the treasury. Its capital for retiring the vales was to come from earmarked portions of the royal municipal and minting taxes (heavily increased over what was previously allotted from them to the earlier amortization funds) and allocation to the Caja of increases in the taxes on church wealth and property held in lay mortmain. The Caja's purpose was the prompt payment of interest due on the vales reales and "progressive retirement" of the principal and the whole range of the floating debt in the form of royal domestic and foreign loans. The Caja displayed the aspects of a genuine sinking fund in the sense that the money to pay the interest on circulating vales at the starting point would be taken from an aggregate pool of royal revenue, earmarking to each fiscal branch a set proportion of its income for this purpose. The assignations would continue intact until the entire extinction of the vales (or other loans). "And so the rate of amortization will increase as a function of the ever increasing difference between the sum of assignations received in the Caja de Amortización and that which it will pay in money toward the interest due" on the outstanding vales. It was announced that no future loans would be contracted without being covered by prior assignation funds in order to prevent losing ground on the projected increase in the rate of amortization. The Caja authorities were also given the power to convert outstanding debt to new debt at lower interest rates, in order to achieve more savings on interest payments and to speed up the amortization operations of the Caja's fund.

Saavedra was replaced by Miguel Caetano Soler at the same time that Mariano Luis de Urquiza was appointed as first secretary of the cabinet. Urquiza was an enemy of the papacy and of the conservative clergy in Spain. He stayed until December 1800, but Soler lasted until 1808 and oversaw the implementation of the Consolidación de Vales Reales project. His first step took the form of a series of royal decrees dated September 24 and 25, 1798, which he discussed at length with Urquiza and with Jovellanos.

These decrees set the stage for Charles IV to sell properties in Spain held under mortmain in order to raise money to meet the rising costs of war with Britain. The key was to convert the entailments into the public debt via the Caja de Amortización. It envisaged the creation of a new class of small rural proprietors to take the place of the landed class based on clerical and lay entailments while converting the latter into public creditors by transferring their holdings into interest-bearing notes issued by the Caja de Amortización. The object was to transfer property out of "dead hands" and into economically "active and tax-paying hands." In the key decree drafted by Soler, Charles IV announced that entailments represented public establishments under his sovereign authority. He decided that all of the real property (*bienes raices*, meaning land and all appurtenances to lands such as buildings, crops, or mineral rights, as distinguished from personal property) belonging to hospitals, hospicios, charity homes, retreats, religious confraternities, *memorias*, *obras pías*, and noble estates, should be sold at auction. The proceeds of these sales, as well as the proceeds from the liquidation of all mortgages and liens (censos) attached to these entailments, were to be placed in the Caja de Amortización where they would yield 3 percent yearly interest to the parties whose property was sold under the decree. The decree was careful to state that the intent was not confiscatory; the property rights were simply being transferred from entailed real property (where they acted as impediments to economic productivity) into the Caja where interest payments would be made more promptly and securely than through the entailment regimes, which were notoriously slow and uncertain. Additional decrees issued in the week of September 19–24 mandated transfer of the liquid assets of religious schools to the Caja de Amortización along with proceeds from the sale of their rural estates; a new tax on all hereditary property successions; transfer to the Caja of all liquid assets held by administrators of disentailed property; rights granted to all holders of primogenitures and *patronatos de legos* to transfer their pensions into the Caja de Amortización.[30]

Soler contemplated a downward conversion of the debt, using the savings in interest payments to create a fund to amortize it. The intent was to replace (*subrogar*) the 4 percent interest payments owed on outstanding vales with the 3 percent interest payments owed to the mortmain holders whose capital had been transferred to the Caja de Amortización. A further step toward strengthening the funding operation was taken in a decree of August 30, 1800, which erased the Caja de Amortización and created a Comisión Gubernativa de Consolidación de Vales Reales. This was separated from the treasury collection and payment of all funds related to the guarantee and amortization of the vales reales.[31]

Besides the step toward funding the debt, the other innovative feature of Soler's decrees was the intent to have the state take over and administer all of the welfare arrangements that were embedded in the operation of the entailment establishments. The objective was to shift these responsibilities from the domain of private and ecclesiastic charity onto a modern welfare state basis where the pattern of administration and payment of interest money to the people dependent on them could be made more efficient.

The attack on entailed real property in Spain was firmly rooted in the liberal ideology which had become current in the country after the 1740s. It reflected a strong influence of the French physiocrats. The subject of disentailments (*desamortización*) was prominent in the work of Francisco Carrasco, who advocated in 1765 that a state embargo be placed on all property under mortmain in order to limit its expansion. He argued that large estates held under mortmain rarely produced enough to support a single monastery, while under ownership by the cultivators they could produce enough to sustain whole towns. Under mortmain the rural workers worked the land without any hope of ever owning it themselves, and this fact inherently reduced their incentive. In the same year Campomanes agreed in his *Tratado de Regalía de Amortización* that the lands would be better worked by people who have longevity on them as owners or long-term tenants than they would by day workers or renters who could be expelled any time so long as the land they worked was entailed. More economic activity on the land would produce more revenues for the state, an extra dividend that Campomanes predicted would accrue from disentailment. The work of these earlier writers was pressed ahead by Jovellanos, whose imposing work favoring a free land market was published in 1794 and set the intellectual stage for Soler's decrees.[32]

There was ample precedent for Soler's decree for pushing the Crown's fiscal operations into the wide domain of entailed property, lay and ecclesiastic. Charles III had negotiated a papal concordat that gave the Crown the right to tax the large tracts of nontransferrable (mortmain) lands held by the church in Spain. Even the noble entailments contributed taxes. Charles IV had imposed a 15 percent tax on obras pías in September 1794 to increase the fund in the Caja de Amortización and also a 15 percent tax on all real property and property rights from that point on that were acquired under mortmain regimes, lay or clerical. The tax was computed on the appraised value of property, and, if the pension were in money, it was fixed at 3 percent of the amount annually. In his decrees of March 1795 all of the income from vacant church offices (*dignidades* and *beneficios*) belonging to the Patronato Real was applied to the Caja fund, and this decree was extended to all vacant church offices by later ones of that year.[33]

The attack on entailed property was vastly accelerated by the implementation of Soler's decree and a progressive widening of its scope. The early years of the new century saw a massive transformation of the real property wealth under mortmain into royal debt. This change effectively began the process of the dissolution of the old estate society based on the two pillars of the church and the nobility.

The established historiographic view is that disentailment contributed to the stagnation of the Spanish agricultural sector, diverted savings from more productive uses, and set the stage for the formation of a rural landholding class which was prone to accumulating large landholdings for speculative and social purposes rather than the establishment of more productive regimes.[34] That disentailment did not lead to the creation of a yeoman rural society of small landholders is commonly attributed to its domination by a bourgeois class more intent on mimicking the nobles' attachment to the land, prompted to do so by the availability of cheap vales reales to buy disentailed lands. The bourgeois propagated the belief that "the public debt could only be repaid by having the State conduct extraordinary sales of mortmain property. . . . Disentailment was part of a liberal bourgeois individualistic political program in which the financial concerns of the state on the verge of bankruptcy came into play." Armed with vales reales "the bourgeois bought disentailed land from nobles, flocked to auctions and put under cultivation the farmlands abandoned by the monasteries and the convents. . . . The main achievement of disentailment was the substitution of a capitalist structure on the land, with vestiges of feudalism, for [an outright] feudal structure. Latifundia replaced large family estates and Church property, feeding off communal property and driving municipalities to ruin. . . . Extensive areas of the country remained in the hands of a few hundred families; ploughmen were deprived of most of their communal rights; and emancipated serfs became day workers. A vast agricultural proletariat emerged with an ardent desire for land redistribution."[35]

This historiographic view of the Spanish disentailment and its relationship to royal finance has been challenged by the monumental research of Richard Herr.[36] He argues that disentailment in the Spanish countryside expanded the land market and contributed to an overall higher level of productivity in the agricultural economy. On balance it accelerated the process of commercialization of agriculture that was already under way because of demographic changes that produced higher levels of urban demand for food. He does concede, however, that Spanish agricultural production did not grow as much at it might have. But Herr's underlying thesis is that disentailment did not essentially extend the bourgeoisie and that it therefore cannot be held accountable for any resultant slack in the agricultural economy. In his view, the Spanish disentailment extended the old order by giving rural oligarchies more direct control over the land than they possessed under entailment regimes.

A lot of Herr's analysis rests on evidence that merchant capital did not bulk large in the purchases of the disentailed properties. He found that members of the church and the state dominated the ranks of the bigger buyers of disentailed properties. Their capital came from salary and emolument funds channeled to them through the operation of taxes, tariffs, and tithes and also, in the case of the church, rents and seigniorial dues— all mechanisms of "income redistribution" in the Spanish economy which rewarded services of a military, ecclesiastic, or administrative nature. The other major category of buyers included local and regional notables who drew income from marketing agrarian products and who used disentailment purchases to extend their estates or to assume direct ownership. The third category included those who spent less money and personally worked the land to produce products for local consumption. An entrepreneurially motivated bourgeois did not represent an identifiable category of buyers.[37]

It was not merchant capital but rather the redistributive capital in the hands of state and church members that fashioned disentailment as an avenue for the extension of the old feudalistic aristocratic regime and not as a tool for the triumph of capitalism over feudalism. The question arises whether this trend was reinforced by the role played by the vales reales in the disentailment market.

Herr's argument is that the vales reales were used predominantly by the larger buyers in his first two buyer categories as opposed to the smaller buyers who tended to be in the third category. Payments in vales reales indicated cheap prices and little bidding on the property, since a bidder could always forestall further bids in vales by offering hard currency. The competitive bidding was conducted mainly for purchase of smaller properties in metallic currency. It occurred mainly among the third class of buyers who were interested in production for local markets. The vales reales predominated in the essentially noncompetitive bidding for the larger properties that were oriented to production for more distant markets. Herr is not willing to say that the noncompetitive bidding process associated with the vales reales signaled a feudalistic buyer class. If anything, disentailment purchases fueled by vales reales encouraged the "more venturesome of the people associated with the agricultural market economy." Yet his comments do suggest a connection between the noncompetitive purchases and the practice of spreading purchases around as a method of avoiding disasters, natural and human, and thereby ensuring a steady flow of income from the land. In doing so, buyers were emulating the practices of the church and nobles of old; they were acting as rentiers not entrepreneurs.[38]

On balance, Herr wants to rebut the charges that disentailment produced a flaccid landowning class and diverted savings from more productive use in both industry and agriculture. He argues that the big buyers in the disentailment market were cautious people who would not have risked their money in a capitalistic venture. He further maintains that the vales reales used in disentailment purchases could not have been used to purchase capital goods anyway. Herr does not, however, directly confront the charge that the large role of the vales reales in the disentailment purchases might itself have been responsible for keeping merchant capital out of the market, to have, in effect, subsidized the nonentrepreneurs linked to the church and the state and local oligarchies at the expense of a more aggressive bourgeois. Herr's response to this charge is ambiguous. On the one hand he says that the role of vales reales in disentailment purchases diluted the productive impetus of those purchases. Thus he refers to the "investment" in the properties purchased with vales reales. By placing investment in quotation marks he is apparently indicating that it was not really productive investment that characterized the properties bought with vales reales. At the same time (in the same paragraph) he says that the large buyers in the disentailment market who were the "most likely sources for productive investment" were the same ones who were predominantly using the vales reales.[39]

Herr's nominal position on the role of the vales in disentailment is that the form of purchase of the lands was not a critical factor in determining their subsequent degree of productive use. Underproduction in the Spanish countryside resulted from structural factors involving the internal economy of production units, market conditions, availability of cheap labor, technological lag, and the persistence of an investor rather than an entrepreneurial mentality. On balance, the disentailment process speeded up production by giving owners more direct control over the land; the liberal concept of bringing economic freedom to the land market in order to raise the level of economic activity was valid, in Herr's view. The problem was that the concept did not penetrate the land market adequately. The reason for this, he argued, was that even when property was freed up, social structures proved to be "sticky" and resistant to change; customs and attitudes were too engrained to be changed by royal fiat. It was impossible for the king to obtain compliance of rural oligarchies with any decrees adverse to their interests. Disentailment succeeded to the extent it did because it was supported by the groups it was intended to weaken. Strategic adjustments made by local groups showed them how to use disentailment to extend their own control over land; how to "keep their property without entail." Local oligarchs, for example, learned how to use the device of *caciquismo* to frustrate royal enforcement of a completely free land market. "Social structures were closer to an immovable mass than royal decrees were to an irresistible force. The weakness on the Crown's side lay in the lack of linkage between the central government and local society. The king's authority might be absolute, insofar as no one could challenge it legally or effectively, at the center but the king lacked the machinery to enforce his wishes, for power at the local level rested with those who controlled municipal institutions and those were the local notabilities."[40]

Notwithstanding Herr's argument that the role of the vales reales in the disentailment process was essentially neutral, it is clear that this role undermined the Crown's funding initiative. The linking of the Spanish debt to the disentailment process involved a deep contradiction: if the vales reales could be retired as a result of being used to buy disentailed properties, they did not have to be amortized out of a sinking fund. The Spanish state thus took the "cheap" way to retiring its vales but the price it paid was loss of control over the disentailment process, which Herr precisely describes, and loss of the possibility of steering it into more economically and socially dynamic directions. The funding initiative, in effect, was swallowed up by the retirement of vales through disentailment sales as opposed to their being amortized out of the Caja de Amortización. As this happened, revenues earmarked to the Caja to pay interest on the vales did not go there and in fact its funds were subject to royal raids. A brazen example occurred in 1803–4 during an agricultural crisis when the Crown used Caja funds to buy foreign grain.[41]

The unenforceability of the royal fiat at the local level was certainly a

result of the strategic behaviors at that level so richly documented by
Herr. But it was also a result of the failure to establish a funding framework for royal debt policy. More exactly, it was the failure to fund the
vales that led to their autonomous role in the disentailment process, which
made that process itself more autonomous and therefore manipulable at
the local level. Whereas Herr emphasized the conservative rural dynamics
that prevented disentailment from creating a really free land market and
circumscribed the royal will behind disentailment, the emphasis can be
placed in a complementary way on the institutional flaws in the funding
enterprise. Thus the perspective of the governmental-institutional analyst
can be combined with that of the rural historian to give a fuller account
of the interaction between rural change and royal finances. The same is
true with regard to the relationship between Latin American state finances
and the rural development process in much of the nineteenth century.

In a last-ditch effort to save the funding initiative, and to bring the
vales back into an amortization process from their vast migration into the
rural Spanish disentailment market, the Crown turned to the American
empire. It hoped to rescue its vales reales at home from total absorption
into the disentailment process by funding the Caja from the proceeds of
royally mandated disentailment sales in the American empire. In the process it crippled the institutional and political ability of the new Latin
American states to try to fund their own debts after independence.

The Crown had by 1804 already begun to create taxes on entailed
property in America and to earmark larger portions of existing taxes, especially on the church, into the Fondo de Consolidación in Spain. Citing
the putative benefits to Spain of the 1798 decree—more productive activity on the land and more efficient administration of welfare functions of
entailed establishments—a decree of November 28 and December 26, 1804,
established procedures for the application of the 1798 decree in the American empire. These decrees mandated the sale of all of the real property
under church entailment as well as the liquidation of all church-held liens
and trust funds (censos) with the proceeds to be placed into local royal cajas for transfer to the Fondo in Madrid. The affected individuals and
groups who lost benefits from the disentailment would receive interest
payments (adjusted to the local market rate of the day) on the appraised
amount of property that had been transferred, with local crown revenues
being carefully earmarked to cover the interest costs. Since vales reales did
not circulate in the American empire, the proceeds from disentailment
sales were to be in metallic only, with bids having to be at least three-

quarters of the appraised value of the property; arrangements for install-
ment payments were allowed with more time allowed for larger purchases.
Juntas Superiores were set up in all of the Viceregal capitals of the American empire—Mexico City, Lima, Santa Fé, Buenos Aires. Subordinated
agencies called "juntas subalternas" were created in the capitals of the
Capitanías Generales—the Philippines, Guatemala, Chile, Venezuela—and
in the capitals of the Bishoprics and Audiencias. The subaltern juntas
concerned themselves with taking inventories of all property liens and trust
funds comprising church entailment in their districts. Since lay entailments
were much scarcer in the empire than in Spain—because a noble class did
not exist and all mayorazgos were carefully controlled by the Crown—the
decrees concentrated on church entailment exclusively as their object.[42]

Various decrees handed down by the Spanish Crown after 1535 prohibited the church from acquiring land in the American empire. This caused
the American church to accumulate its wealth in a different manner from
the church's accumulation in Spain. Rather than owning property, the
American church imposed on property owners financial obligations to the
church, either as recipients of loans or as payers of annuities charged on
property or payers of mortgages held by the church. The financial obligations charged on property by the church ranged from liens to loans. Thus
an elusive line existed in church finances in America between its role in
mortmain and its role in the colonial credit system. On the surface, the in-
terdiction against accumulation of land pushed church wealth into more
liquid forms (depósitos) that were actually pools of loan capital for commerce and agriculture to draw on.[43] Thus, in the early Mexican complaints against the Consolidación de Vales Reales in America, the allegation
is prominent that redemption of church funds would raise havoc in the
Mexican economy by crippling its credit supply.[44] It is clear that in Mexico, censos and chaplaincies represented forms of credit in the rural economy especially and that the overall role of the church as a lending institution was a critical one in the rural sector. On the other hand, it is also
clear that credit supplied to the commercial sector and the state by merchant guilds eclipsed the role of church credit in those areas.[45] In any
case, the assessment of the volume of church credit, as opposed to mortmain, requires a differentiation between liens that subtracted from productive economic activity and loans (préstamos) that fomented it. The use of
the generic term censos, common in the colonial period and afterward,
confounded this distinction.[46]

In Mexico, the Consolidación de Vales Reales indeed raised havoc with the credit system, created a highly differential impact on the level of economic activity, and had an important shaping influence on the public debt as it emerged from the colonial period. The Consolidación de Vales Reales figured importantly into the internal debt that the Mexican state inherited from the colonial period, and it necessarily exerted influence on the composition of the class of state creditors in the early independence period. Mexico, however, was unusual in this direct linkage between the Consolidación de Vales Reales and the public debt formation. Although the Consolidación de Vales Reales was implemented in the years 1804–9 in other sectors of the empire, most notably in Upper Peru (Bolivia),[47] the scope of its application was nowhere near the scope of Mexico, and the composition of the state creditor class did not contain significant components of holders of paper issued by the Cajas de Consolidación. The relevance of the Consolidación de Vales Reales for the debt policy of the new states resided in the fact that the disentailment process initiated under it was begun, and it lay there waiting to be carried forward under the banner of liberalism. In important respects, the debt policy of the new states can be seen as picking up the thread of the Consolidación de Vales Reales where it left off in 1809, that is, using the disentailment process as a way to avoid the legitimate funding of state debt paper.

The pressure on debt policy to redeem censos with depreciated debt paper was acute in the cases of Colombia, Chile, Peru, and Bolivia as they strove to consolidate their internal debts in the first half of the nineteenth century. In these countries censos were heavily embedded in rural property. Bolivia was at the forefront of this process because of the powerful anticlericalism of its first postindependence government. Unlike Spain, however, there were no large church latifundia and noble estates waiting to be auctioned off. But the new states found themselves in possession of large landholdings as a result of four processes: expropriation of church lands occurring in the late colonial period, especially the Jesuit expropriations; the steady transformation of the *encomiendas* into Crown trusts as the original *encomenderos* died off; state ownership of large segments of land under communal Indian ownership; and sequestering of rural properties during the fighting. In addition to the censos, the favorite targets of the state debt paper were precisely these state-owned properties. They were considered as lands under mortmain that would produce more under private ownership and free circulation, except in Argentina where a strong emphytuesis policy took hold.

2

Basis of the Debt-Disentailment Link in Bolivia: Rise and Fall of Church Credit in the Rural Sector

IN UPPER PERU, the mechanisms of ecclesiastical entailment took the form of censos on rural haciendas and fincas. These censos were heavily concentrated in the province of La Paz, a fact that was implicit in the evidence on the operation of the Consolidación de Vales Reales in Upper Peru. In the province of La Paz, the prospect of redeeming censos was particularly appealing to property holders, and it was easy to create a demand there for discounted state debt paper that could be used to redeem those censos cheaply.

Consolidación de Vales Reales in Upper Peru (Bolivia)

Evidence of the operation of the Consolidación de Vales Reales in Upper Peru can be gleaned in the fiscal accounts of the royal cajas operating in the area. The 15 percent tax on church mortmain property ordered by the Crown began to appear in 1805. The taxes on censos (*imposiciones a censo*) also appeared at the same time and showed a rapid increase, especially in the accounts of the La Paz caja in the period 1805–6, as did the new administrative costs associated with raising this new revenue for the Consolidación. The *novena real* also shows as a portion of the *diezmos* income earmarked for the Consolidación.[1]

Subaltern offices of the Consolidación were established according to the Crown decree in La Plata and in La Paz, the capitals of the two dioceses of Upper Peru. The Junta Superior of the Consolidación was established in the capital of the Viceroyalty of Rio de la Plata to which Upper

Peru belonged at the time. Other diocesan capitals of the Viceroyalty joined with La Plata and La Paz in sending Consolidación funds to Buenos Aires for transfer to Madrid. Potosi, although the hub of the mining industry in Upper Peru, was not a diocesan capital so no subaltern office of the Consolidación needed to be established there.

The junta superior in Buenos Aires acted as a subaltern office for the inventorying and sale of church wealth in the diocese of Buenos Aires. It collected little due to political instabilites, the British invasion of the port, and the relative thinness of church mortmain holdings in the area. The vast majority of Consolidación funds came from the interior of the viceroyalty especially from La Plata and La Paz in Upper Peru (see table 2.1).[2]

Susana Liberté saw in the much larger contribution of Consolidación funds remitted from La Paz, compared to the meager amounts that arrived from Asuncion, "another sign of the greater economic possiblilities that in the colonial period existed in the mining region in comparison to the pastoral region of the empire."[3] Although her data do not include the exact source of the Consolidación funds in Upper Peru, it is most likely that the Consolidación funds came not from the mining region in Upper Peru but from the agricultural provinces of La Plata and La Paz. This is because the disentailment targets (real property under clerical censos) were

Table 2.1. Remittances of Consolidación Funds in the
Plata Viceroyalty

Date	Origin	Peso amount
April 25, 1807	Cordoba	3,007
April 29, 1807	Cordoba	3,517
May 2, 1808	Cordoba	2,962
May 2, 1808	Ciudad de Paraguay	11,815
May 2, 1808	La Plata	8,015
August 4, 1808	La Paz, La Plata, Cordoba	78,010
September 19, 1808	La Plata	30,457
October 26, 1808	La Paz	5,184
October 26, 1808	La Paz	48,696
November 7, 1808	La Paz	1,901
June 6, 1809	La Paz	74,226
March 17, 1808	Cordoba	5,515
May 8, 1809	La Plata	20,900
Total		294,205

Source: Liberté, 316.

more concentrated outside of the mining belt and in areas that were under-going a dynamic rural intensification process that grouped censos around an emergent hacienda system. This hacienda system was adjacent to the "agrarian frontiers" of Upper Peru. The most powerful agrarian frontiers were in the provinces of La Paz and La Plata.

Rural Intensification and the Rise of Haciendas

Prior to independence Bolivia was a juridical entity known as the Audi-encia of Charcas. Executively, it was divided into four provinces or inten-dencies, Santa Cruz, La Paz, Potosi, and Plata, and each was subdivided into corregimientos and partidos. Ecclesiastically, it was divided into three dioceses: Plata (1552, elevated to metropolitan capital in 1611), La Paz (1605), and Santa Cruz (1605), each of which was divided into parish dis-tricts. Significantly, Potosi was subsumed into the diocese of Plata instead of being constituted as a diocese in its own right. This was done in order to keep Potosi from becoming a diocesan capital, thereby preserving its autonomy from ecclesiastic writ just as it had traditionally resisted the writ of the Audiencia. The hub of a vast, multispoked mining industry geared to the export of gold and silver to Spain, Potosi was organized and administered as a royal treasury district from Lima and then Buenos Aires. Potosi was the first and most powerful of the nine treasury districts that were eventually established in Upper Peru.

According to an 1831 census, Bolivia's counted population in the 1820s was 1,373,896 people, plus another half a million Indians who lived in the interior and had infrequent contact with missionaries. Half of the popula-tion were descendants of the Spanish settlers and one-half descendants of the aboriginal populations. The heaviest concentration of Indian popula-tions (especially if the nomadic populations of the interior are not counted) was in the provinces of Potosi and La Paz, where whites were far outnum-bered. White majorities existed in Santa Cruz and Cochabamba depart-ments. In the 1820s, over two-thirds of the population were rural, that is, not living in cities or towns. The 1831 census broke down the population by departments, into which the provinces were divided after independence (see table 2.2).[4]

In the second half of the 1500s and for most of the 1600s, the mining sector with its source at Potosi provided the economic pillar of the Span-ish empire in America. By virtue of its supply networks, it integrated a

Table 2.2. Bolivian Population Distribution in 1831

Department	City-dwelling	Rural	Total
Cochabamba	30,396	196,358	226,754
Atacama		3,836	3,836
Sucre (Plata)	19,235	93,355	112,590
Tarija	5,129	31,086	36,215
Santa Cruz	6,005	37,770	43,775
Beni		41,228	41,228
La Paz	42,849	305,293	348,142
Oruro	5,687	78,413	84,100
Potosi	16,711	175,404	192,115

Source: Delance, 187.

coherent and largely self-sufficient economic space upon which a political and administrative superstructure was imposed in the form of the Peruvian viceroyalty, the audiencias, and the treasury districts. This space was dominated by two dynamic poles. Potosi was the center of silver extraction and the dominant sector within the productive structure of the viceroyalty. Lima was the political and commercial center. Its merchant class exercised monopolistic power in the economic sphere because Lima was the exclusive port for all imported goods from Europe as well as all exports. By virtue of their massive population concentrations, Lima and Potosi provided large consumption markets and generated a demand that penetrated the whole expanse of the Peruvian economic space.[5]

This space was fleshed out by the operation of another economy, largely subsistent and oriented toward the circulation of indigenously produced goods in the internal market. This internal economy possessed its own means of maritime and land transport, its own system of markets, and its own regional division of labor and specialization of production. Its circulating products consisted of textiles, manufactures, and agricultural products, as well as animals.[6]

The subsistent sector and the export-import sector in fact comprised parts of the same regional productive structure; they were dynamically connected with each other and were engaged in resource trading. An enormous reallocation of resources from the import-export sector to the subsistence sector was occasioned by the decline of the mining sector and the resulting population movements.

Beginning in the mid-1600s silver production in Potosi and Oruro, and in other secondary mining centers, declined steadily. Until 1700 taxes on silver production entering the caja at Potosi averaged over 1 million pesos and accounted for 55 percent of its revenues. In the course of the 1700s, the average dropped to 300,000 pesos annually, accounting for less than 45 percent of the revenues. The story in the Oruro caja and in those of the boom districts of Carangas and Chuquitos was the same and even steeper in the case of the latter two. These falloffs in mining tax revenues directly paralleled the drop in mining production. Part of the cause was a drop in European demand for silver incident to periodic recessions, a drop graphically reflected in the bankruptcy of the Spanish flotilla system. In forty years from 1685 to 1726 only five armadas left Lima with Upper Peruvian silver. Internal, interacting causes also contributed to the decline in production: play-out of the silver lodes, exhaustion of mercury supplies, rising costs of refinement, increasing diseconomies of the labor-intensive system of production, and absence of local capital for investment in new technologies needed to recover the earlier levels of production.[7]

Largely because of the drop in mining tax revenues in Upper Peru, the Lima caja experienced a decline in surpluses remitted from the Upper Peruvian cajas, which had amounted to over 200 million pesos in the years from 1561 to 1700. Only some 20 million pesos were remitted from 1700 to 1770. Remittances to Lima were drained not only by the drop in mining taxes but also by the tendency of officials in Upper Peru to plough back other kinds of tax revenues into their districts and the need to shore up imperial defense in Chile and Rio de la Plata (Upper Peru was joined to the Rio viceroy in 1776). As this happened, Lima lost its role as the monopolistic import-export center of the viceroyalty and even as the political center. For its part, Potosi continued to be the most powerful caja in Upper Peru, making large remittances in tax revenues to Buenos Aires, but the decline in mining production was reflected in the rapid decline in the city's population from nearly a quarter of a million in the late 1600s to under 20,000 at the time of independence. Like Lima, Spanish ports saw less and less Upper Peruvian silver, receiving virtually none at all in the first half of the 1700s before Bourbon reforms improved the picture somewhat. The decline in silver production, combined with the increased administrative and defense costs of maintaining the American empire, were the reasons.[8]

The decline of the import-export economy, with its bipolar growth structure centered on Potosi and Lima, caused a massive flight of resources into the indigenous economy and its supporting social structures.

On the one hand, treasury officials began to show a distinct disinclination to draw on the tax revenues unrelated to the mining sector for the purposes of making remittances to Lima. Even as they expanded those other kinds of taxes, they retained the lion's share for payment of salaries, defense, missionary activities, public works, and capital grants in the form of obras pías to support church welfare activities. This rise in the local spending of tax revenues reflected the modification in the caja roles resulting from the decline of the mining industry. On the other hand, the decline of the mining industry, with its lower earnings from silver exports, reduced demand for the official imports through Lima, increased demand for contraband as well as for products produced regionally, and freed a large volume of labor, much of it forced Indian labor. This twin growth of internal demand and growth of labor supply produced a large extension of the subsistent economy within an overall dynamic ruralization process that penetrated the mining belts and fleshed out the areas lying outside of them.[9]

In the 1500s most of the land of the empire was held under feudal grants of jurisdiction given by the Crown to the conquerors. Indian populations living on the land included in the encomienda came under the jurisdiction of the encomendero. The Indians, in addition to rendering personal service, were obligated to apportion their labor between producing what they needed for subsistence (usually determined on a communal basis) and producing another quantity to be divided between the encomendero's portion and the Crown's portion (usually one-third, a *tercio*) in the form of tribute in kind.

In a process that was extraordinarily complex and widespread in Latin America, the encomiendas in Upper Peru were transformed into commercial haciendas. But the transformation was fundamentally a consequence of the decline in the mining industry and the resulting alteration of the tributary system. While the mining industry boomed, the state relied mainly on the Indians as a source of forced, cheap labor (the *mita*); the operation of the tribute tax through the encomiendas never figured importantly in the royal revenues. As the industry declined, the focus of exploitation of the Indians shifted to the tribute tax in order to make up for the declining tax revenues on silver production. But the encomiendas were not structured to generate the needed levels of tribute revenue. The problem was that the tribute was paid haphazardly and, by custom, in kind. The Crown looked for ways to improve tributary collection techniques and convert them to specie payments. The stage for implementing this policy was set by the elimination of the encomendero intermediaries between the Crown and the tributary Indians; as the original encomenderos gradually died off, the Crown assumed control over the encomienda Indians. Royal agents found it easier to count the Indians on the communal lands, who were not as intent on avoiding the dreaded mita. The other solution found was to encourage Indians to move off their communal lands into more intense forms of interaction with the Spanish, both as producers and consumers. Key roles were played by Crown agents, the *corregidores*, and the clan leaders, the *kurakas*, in brokering the Indians into becoming economic participants in the growing regional market economies as producers and consumers and into entering a rural labor market, regulated by the haciendas, where they could earn money wages and thereby generate more specie tribute.[10] The increased tributary role of the Indians paralleled almost exactly their decreased role as *mitayos*; the increase in the tributary income of the royal cajas in Upper Peru matched the decline in mining tax revenues. Tribute income reached almost 9 million pesos for Upper Peru at the end of the colonial period; mining tax revenues leveled off at less than 5 million.[11] Particularly noticeable in these statistics is the fact that the rural intensification process, of which the ascendant tributary system was a part, occurred largely outside of the Potosi-Oruro mining belt. The provinces of La Paz and Plata were at the forefront of this new, alternative system based on a ruralization dynamic that was displacing Potosi as the chief supplier of revenue in Upper Peru.

Even before the decline of mining, the Indians had begun moving off the communal lands because they were vulnerable to both the mita and tribute extraction. These migrants came to constitute a landless class of Indians called *forasteros* or *yanaconas*, as distinguished from the *originarios* or communal Indians sharing title to communal lands. Hacienda estates exerted a large attraction for the forastero population. Originally they were exempted by Crown decree from the mita and the tribute, but after 1734, as yanaconas, they were required to pay tribute. In practice, however, the *hacendado* paid wages plus the tribute dues on his yanacona labor force as a means of attracting them on a free market basis. What allowed the Crown to expand its tribute revenues geometrically in response to the mining decline, was the role of the hacienda in creating a new and dynamic class of tributary Indians—the *forasteros*.[12]

Haciendas made their appearance originally as the result of encomenderos and *vecinos* securing land grants from growing Spanish towns on which to set up production units based on cultivation or grazing, with specialized labor forces made up mostly of yanaconas to meet the new consumer demands of the towns. In this form, haciendas were integrated units within a developing regional market economy.[13] The hacienda structure is evident in some of the early production units set up to supply mining populations specifically. But on closer inspection, these units were more manorial than market oriented like haciendas; they functioned as labor reservoirs for the mines and as a means to gain the feudal stature that derived from controlling land and labor. They reverted to self-sufficiency when their markets periodically fell off.[14] The truer haciendas tended to grow up around the regional markets and towns and tended to be less oriented to the mining sector. Geographically they dispersed away from the mining belts into the fertile valleys, the agrarian frontier areas of Upper Peru. Since the Spanish were zealous in organizing communal villages to serve as mita pools, the haciendas tended to develop outside of the mita districts because of the heavy incidence there of communal land titles. The agrarian frontiers defined in these various terms were located essentially in the provinces of La Paz and Plata; Cochabamba was a particularly dynamic agrarian frontier area within Plata. Both sections were heavily populated by commercial haciendas embedded in regional market networks. Some investors diversified their capital outside of mining and into these haciendas. A rising new merchant class operating in both the mining and the regional market systems also invested heavily in them.

By the end of the colonial period a powerful hacendado class existed in La Paz, and one on which we have considerable empirical information through Herbert Klein's work. La Paz had served a double economic role as a self-contained market economy, with La Paz itself the hub of an intricate trading network, and as a provisioning area for the mines. Merchant wealth derived from both, but the rapid concentration of haciendas marked a strong tilt toward the former. The wealth from its merchant commerce went increasingly into the purchase of haciendas. Their geographic concentration was in the provinces of Larecaja, Chulimani, and Sicasica, all of which contained semitropical valleys lying along the eastern escarpment of the Andes. "Where the hacienda least penetrated," Klein noted, "was the most traditional and densely populated of all zones [Pacajes]. Here the *ayllu* [Indian communities] remained dominant and the relative inhospitality of the soil discouraged hacendados interested in creating new farm units."[15]

By the end of the 1700s there were 1,100 haciendas in the La Paz intendency and 719 hacendados, many of them living in the city of La Paz as absentee landowners. There were 491 Indian communities. The haciendas contained 82,661 yanacona Indians out of a total Indian population of 207,369. The most powerful members of this class, defined in terms of control over numbers of yanaconas, owned multiple, ecologically dispersed haciendas. This approach permitted them to meld the different factor inputs of the separate hacienda environments into one optimal production mix. Family memberships were thus yielding to a managerial cadre in the running of the system, which had important consequences with regard to the type of debt carried by the system. Church-controlled debt, the traditional bedrock of the familial hacienda system, was becoming obsolete.[16]

Church Wealth and Censos Penetration of the Rural Sector

The burgeoning hacienda system in Upper Peru was organized to a considerable degree by ecclesiastic capital in the form of censos, which largely defined the rural debt structure at the end of the colonial period. In the American empire the regular or missionary orders were the first agents of the Catholic church to arrive and to commence the evangelical function. They depended directly on the Pope. Later, as the secular clergy (dependent on the Spanish Crown) began to arrive and to establish ecclesiastic districts (dioceses), each with a hierarchy ascending from parish priests to a bishop, the regular orders adapted differently. Some of them, like the Jesuits, maintained their dependence on the Pope directly as opposed to the Crown and formed a virtual state within a state. Other orders submitted to the diocesan structure, which was dominated by secular clergy.[17]

But in any case the regular clergy were administratively divided from the diocesan or episcopal structure. They followed a special rule of life (*regula*) beyond priestly vows. The rules prescribed modes of confinement and, in some cases, a commitment to poverty. On the other hand, the secular clergy accepted that they lived in the world (*saeculum*) and they fit administratively into the hierarchy, with the Crown the recognized ultimate authority by virtue of the *patronato real*.[18] In the American empire there were forty-four dioceses or bishoprics broken down into parish districts (*curatos*) and six major orders operating large chains of monasteries and convents: Augustinians, Jesuits (until their expulsion by the Crown in 1767), Carmelites, Franciscans, Mercedarians, and Dominicans.[19]

The growth of the secular clergy in the later 1500s precipitated a power struggle with the regular orders, which had gained control of the rural Indian populations by virtue of arriving first. The Spanish Crown saw the regular clergy as a threat since they did not fit into the episcopal hierarchy which it controlled. A bitter power struggle between the regulars and the seculars occurred over control of the Indian parishes. It was highlighted in the mid-1500s by a dispute over diezmos policy—the church's warrant from the Crown to take as a tax one-tenth of agricultural production in certain lands. The regulars argued for exemption of Indians; the secular clergy wanted them to pay. The seculars had a larger stake in the diezmos, since diezmos formed an important part of the seculars' income but not of the regulars' income.[20]

Beginning with the Jesuit expulsion in 1767, the regular orders in the empire were systematically suppressed by the Crown. Before suppression started, Upper Peru had 1,432 secular clergy distributed among 358 parish districts. There were 40 monasteries holding about 320 regular clergy, to which the female orders, distributed in convents and *beaterios*, added 598 women. At the time of independence the monasteries in particular had undergone depopulation; the regular clergy still living in them were estimated to number 189. Of these, only thirty-nine lived in the mining districts of Potosi and Oruro. The cities located nearer to the agricultural frontiers, La Paz, Cochabamba, and Chuquisaca, held fifty, forty-nine, and thirty-five, respectively. Thus regular strength in numbers tended to be concentrated outside of the mining provinces and in the agrarian areas. With regard to regular women, before the suppression about sixty nuns lived in the convents at Potosi and none in Oruro. The convents at La Paz had 154 nuns, Cochabamba 100, and Chuquisaca 174. These numbers parallel the orientation of the male regular clergy away from the mining districts.[21]

Both the regular and secular clergy benefitted from the dissemination of pious works (obras pias). The common element was the reliance on invested capital to generate an income adequate to execute the philanthropic intention of the benefactor. Obras pias provided funds for founding hospitals, convents, and monasteries and funding chantries, dowries for poor girls, and burial funds. An obra pia endowment could take the form of a cash grant, a real property grant (land, mills, ingenios), or a lien placed on a piece of real property. The secular and regular clergy were the beneficiaries and the administrators of the obras pias. Chantries specifically created funds to say perpetual masses for family members, pay for a priest's maintenance, and endow posts in monasteries, convents, churches, and hospitals.[22]

The main difference between regular and secular clergy benefits from obras pías was that the latter were prevented from receiving them as outright land grants. The regular clergy had already amassed large land-holdings before Crown policies interdicting clerical property ownership took effect. A large portion of the income of the regular clergy was de-rived from the working and leasing out lands granted to it and attached to a monastery. Much of the regulars' welfare activities in urban areas (schools, poorhouses, and hospitals) were financed out of the income from rural properties.[23]

By contrast, the secular clergy relied on income from direct and indi-rect taxes. Indirect taxes consisted of the revenues collected from Indian communities by the state and shared with the church: diezmos, *sinódos*, and *primicias*. Direct taxes consisted of contributions in money, in kind, and in personal services that were extracted from parishioners—*bulas* in the case of Spanish, and for Indians and *mestizos* a whole range of charges for sacramental services (*arenceles*) and special contributions ex-pected from Indians who were given privileged roles in religious services (*alferados* and *mayordomazgos*). It also derived income from leasing ac-tivities but not at the level that the regular clergy did.[24]

The lending activities of regular and secular clergy generated perhaps the most dynamic stream of income for both, although the lending pat-terns were somewhat different. Censos was a generic term used to cover obligations charged against property, urban but more often rural, in bene-fit of the church. But censos could mean the interest realized on rural loans made by the church, or on the leasing out of property by the church, or on mortgages held by the church on rural property. Censos could also include the assignment to the church of a determinate yield from liens imposed on real property in the form of obras pías and *capel-lanías*.[25] This form of censos was imposed on property and given a capital value in money terms that would guarantee an annuity payment at 5 per-cent to the church or sometimes to heirs. Bauer has demonstrated the considerable value, in assessing the economic role of the church in the Latin American rural sector prior to independence, of making a distinc-tion between liens and loans. But he placed censos in the category of liens. This choice fails to recognize that the income from many liens was used by the church to make loans, and this diminishes the value of his dis-tinction.[26] It is convenient to think of the income from censos as *réditos hipotecarios*—pledged income charged against property. It includes liens as well as loans.

In Upper Peru regulars and seculars benefitted from censos income, but it is clear that the former benefitted more; seculars relied more on taxation income than censos income. It is also clear, however, that the taxation income derived by the secular clergy from the rural population amounted to considerably less than the censos income, possibly even less than their share of the censos income.[27] Within the censos income flow, given the greater portion of it controlled by the regulars, a further distinction has to be made between male orders and female orders. Upper Peru confirms the widespread pattern of female orders controlling more of the censos wealth than male orders did. Although there were only nine convents and forty monasteries in Upper Peru the convent capital amounted to 3.8 million pesos, exceeding monastery capital by 800,000 pesos.[28]

The pattern in Upper Peru, as in the whole Peruvian viceroyalty, was for the administrators of the convents and the monasteries to process requests for censos loan contracts at the usual 5 percent interest subject to a mortgage guarantee by the borrower. Applications for loans from the funds held in obras pías and chantries were made to the Juzgado de Capellanías y Obras Pías of the archdiocese at Chuquisaca. The secular clergy also kept track, but with varying degrees of autonomy, of the censos loans and obras pías created from funds collected from memberships of religious brotherhoods known as *cofradías*.[29]

The whole process of economic diversification away from mining and into the agricultural sector involved large amounts of investment capital, most of which was supplied in the form of clerical censos. The private mining sector relied for its credit mainly on merchant credit guilds (*azogueros*) and mining banks; these credit models are clearly in evidence in the reports by the azogueros drafted in the late 1820s.[30] Mining ventures were high-risk endeavors with little collateral in real property and needing steady sources of funding. The credit guilds and mining banks served their purposes better, even though their loans carried higher interest rates than the standard 5 percent of the censos. Further, church censos were offered to borrowers only when surplus funds were available, and then they were normally given only to low-risk, high-collateral projects. The overwhelming preference in censos contracts was therefore for rural landowners.[31] Even in Potosi, when convent censos were placed in the mining sector, it was not to private miners but the mint, the treasury, and the mining bank itself; there was only one instance of a censo being placed in a private refinery.[32]

The spread of censos into the Upper Peruvian rural sector during the seventeenth and eighteenth centuries reflected the pattern of extremely high rural debt levels that existed throughout Latin America by the late colonial period. In this pattern, hacienda debt was defined mostly by censos structures.[33] The province of Cuzco, bordering on Upper Peru and resembling it economically and demographically, is data-rich in regard to the distribution and functions of censos in the hacienda system.[34]

It is also true that convent censos in Potosi were in a high rate of default due to the depression of the mining economy and its supporting systems. By contrast, the convent incomes including censos incomes were higher and more dynamic in Cochabamba, in an agricultural setting. The censos network emanating from the Santa Clara Convent in Cochabamba was the most widespread one in Upper Peru; it accounted for 200,000 pesos in investment capital, while the Mercedarians' censos capital was 46,000 pesos and the Dominicans' 35,000, most of it placed on haciendas, houses, and mills.[35] The censos spread in Cochabamba is richly documented in the inventory done in the period immediately following independence. The inventory is also well developed for La Paz.[36] Klein's work on the hacendado class in La Paz clearly shows that the church was unimportant as an owner of haciendas but very important as the supplier of large volumes of mortgage money and as the beneficiary of capellanías and obras pías created by the hacendados.

Significantly, there is no censos inventory of Potosi extant in the Bolivian archives. The reasons for this omission probably vary, but the absence only tends to confirm that censos were more widespread in the economies of La Paz and Cochabamba than they were in Potosi's. The significance of this circumstance will emerge as we proceed with the analysis of the use to which state debt paper was put in Bolivia in the 1820s. We will see that the patterns were different in Potosi compared to Cochabamba and La Paz: the real pressure for using state debt paper to redeem censos and to acquire haciendas emanated from La Paz and Cochabamba. In contrast the funding paper tended to be concentrated in Potosi, where mining interests were strong.

Censos were systematically eliminated in Bolivia before they were in Peru, but in the late colonial period the censos structures were in all probability analogous. If this is true, Morner's data on Cuzco can serve as a proxy for censos behavior in Upper Peru in the colonial period. His data clearly show that censos were dynamically involved in the hacienda system's functioning as credit mechanisms in the *compraventa* market; they were far from the drag factor customarily assumed, and in fact they facilitated the early articulation of the hacienda system not only as the suppliers of investment capital but as credit vehicles that facilitated the buying and selling of haciendas. By assuming the censos obligations on a hacienda, a purchaser was required to put up that much less money as a down payment for the purchase. Censos transferals were regularly built into sales contracts as credit devices in this sense. Morner's data include categories of censos credit employed in a data set of 105 compraventa transactions taking place between 1825 and 1869 in Cuzco. This market was presumably a continuation of the compraventa market in haciendas that existed in the colonial period; the main difference seems to be that clergy were more active as buyers and sellers in the colonial period because they were exempted from land sales tax.[37]

By the time of independence the whole network of censos was beginning to get in the way of the continued growth of the hacienda system. Censos may have served to preserve the family unity of rural properties by encumbering them, but at the same time they blocked efforts to commercialize hacienda properties and siphoned off investment funds. In addition, the previous role of censos in providing credit and facilitating a compraventa market was becoming obsolete because of increasing opportunities to make use of state debt paper in the compraventa market; using censos as a credit device was inferior to using state debt paper because the latter allowed more equity (a future source of bank credit) to be achieved in the purchased property. Finally, church credit was drying up at the source; the church was clearly beginning to lose its wealth in Upper Peru and to decline as a lending institution. Regular and secular income had fallen drastically in Upper Peru, beginning in 1769 with the expropriations of Jesuit property. Diezmos income fell off due to increasing fraud in the collection system; haciendas themselves seemed to be responsible.[38] The credit system of Upper Peru, like the credit systems of all of the Latin American states, was poised for secularization by the time of independence. During the course of the nineteenth century, rural debt was indeed transferred from the church to the commercial banks. The disentailing of censos through state debt paper, and the substitution of censos as credit devices in the compraventa market by state debt paper that was usable to purchase state-owned haciendas and haciendas encumbered by censos that the state had appropriated from the church, became the first steps in this transformation. Nonfunded state debt paper was vaulted to the forefront by its utility in substituting censos. The use of funded debt paper as a vehicle for public savings (a long-term investment in the state) was eclipsed as a result.

Liberation and Disentailment: Confiscation of Church Wealth by the Sucre Government

The French invasion of the Spanish peninsula in 1808 and Napoleon's usurpation of the Spanish throne triggered independence movements all over the American empire in the name of "preserving" loyalty to Ferdinand. In Upper Peru, the audiencia judges alleged Napoleon's influence over the viceroy in Buenos Aires in order to justify their calls for the separation of Upper Peru from the Plata viceroyalty. The audiencia judges subsequently received letters from the Portuguese princess, Carlota, proposing her regency over Upper Peru, as well as the whole area of the Plata viceroyalty, during the period of Napoleon's captivity of Ferdinand (her brother). It was known to the judges that in Buenos Aires, Pueyrredón and some followers looked favorably on Carlota's proposal. Countering the alleged Braganza projects of political expansionism provided the second ostensible purpose for staging the revolt of the Upper Peruvian Audiencia against the viceroy. In reality, the action of the audiencia in staging the revolt in 1809 was motivated by the designs of separatist creoles (descendants of Spanish settlers born in America) to turn Upper Peru into an independent state.[39]

The Plata viceroy put down the audiencia rebellion but was unable to follow through with the pacification of Upper Peru because of a revolutionary movement that broke out in Buenos Aires in May 1810. In the meantime the Upper Peruvian rebellion had spread from the seat of the audiencia in Chuquisaca to the city of La Paz. The Viceroy of Peru, Fernando Abascal, decided to step into the revolutionary breach. He was determined to restore viceregal authority not only in Upper Peru but to invade the Plata also and restore viceregal rule in Buenos Aires. Peruvian armies in fact invaded Upper Peru in 1809, severely punished the La Paz revolutionaries, and reincorporated the area to the Viceroyalty of Peru pending the hoped-for restoration of viceregal authority in Buenos Aires. Abascal's invasion of the Plata region ran into stiff opposition from local patriot forces, however, and was turned back.

Armies were subsequently dispatched by the revolutionary government in Buenos Aires to invade Upper Peru, wrest control of the area from the Peruvian viceroyalty, and annex it to the emergent Argentine state. These armies were ultimately successful only in alienating the Upper Peruvians and producing as much hatred toward Buenos Aires, if not more, as had existed toward Lima. Although the guerrilla forces appearing in Upper Peru were originally allied to the Buenos Aires armies against the Peruvians, they soon tended to turn against them and to strike out on their own against both "foreign" invaders. In the course of the resistance against both the Peruvian and Argentine armies in Upper Peru, which continued sporadically from 1809 to 1824, Upper Peruvian guerrilla forces fomented a regional, patriotic sentiment. These guerrilla armies controlled their own enclaves, many of which resembled miniature nations with their own patriotic ethos and quasi-political structures. These *republiquetas*, as they were called, were ephemeral and of questionable political significance, but they did embody a tradition of patriotic struggle. They added another layer to that tradition of Upper Peruvian separatism which started in the early activities of the encomenderos and continued to develop under the auspices of the audiencia.[40]

In January 1825, a Colombian army, numbering almost 10,000 men under the command of Antonio José de Sucre, liberated Upper Peru from Spanish control. A deep conflict existed between Sucre and his chief, Simon Bolivar, over whether a separate state should be created in Upper Peru. Sucre's decision to do that set in motion a process that converted Upper Peru into Bolivia. His actions were ultimately approved by Bolivar, who forced neighboring Peru to recognize the new state. Bolivar visited Sucre in Bolivia from August 1825 to January 1826, during which time he drafted innumerable codes for progressive reformation of the society and economy of the new state. Bolivar also sketched out a constitution for Bolivia which he sent subsequently from Peru in its final form. It was adopted by the Bolivians in August 1826. Bolivar left Sucre in charge of Bolivia pending adoption of the constitution. Colombia agreed to leave 2,000 of its troops in Bolivia for security purposes.

In August 1826, Sucre was elected to the lifetime presidency created by Bolivar's constitution. He remained as president until April 1828, when he was injured in a mutiny staged by a Colombian cavalry unit in Chuquisaca. Shortly afterward he was forced to leave Bolivia as a result of an invasion by Peruvian forces. Peruvian nationalists had overthrown Bolivar's government in Peru and were intent on eliminating Sucre's in Bolivia also.

Sucre was assisted in his efforts to introduce large-scale reforms by the work of various legislative agencies that existed during his period in Bolivia: the General Assembly (July–August 1825), the assembly's Permanent Delegation (September 1825–August 1826), and the Constitutive Assembly (May–September, 1826). All of Sucre's reforms involved the substitution of state institutions for ecclesiastical ones. The financing of the new institutions came from confiscated church wealth, including the income from church censos that had been appropriated by the state. The essential problem for Sucre was that the censos could not at the same time be used to capitalize his welfare institutions and be made objects of redemption through his debt policy. What were the origins of the public institutions created by Sucre, and how well situated were they to withstand the redemption of their censos capital by state debt paper?

*   *   *

Education in Upper Peru was the prerogative of the wealthy at the upper social levels and the domain of religious charity at the lower levels. The concept of public education came late to Upper Peru and took on a fragile form only when, as a result of Bourbon reforms, some primary schools in municipalities were opened. Until that time the church sponsored most primary education. Monasteries, parish churches, and chapels doubled as schools where priests and nuns taught letters and catechism to Indian and mestizo children. Orphanages and poorhouses run by the church and supported by private charity and obras pías also served as elementary schools of sorts. Beateríos functioned as asylums for lower-class, usually mestizo women; they were supported by private charity and administered by the church and served also as orphanages, handiwork training centers, religious communities, and primary schools. Primary education was afforded to children on a tutorial basis, taking advantage of a learned priest, in the homes of those who could afford it—landowners, merchants, and state officials. In the middle echelons of education the tutorial pattern persisted for the wealthy but not for others. There were no secondary schools as such. There were a handful of high schools (*colegios*) and seminaries, where pre-university education was offered to a chosen few. La Paz and Santa Cruz had several seminaries. In Chuquisaca the Jesuits had started several others and also had founded in the University of San Francisco and the Caroline Academy, a graduate law school, both of which drew students not only from Upper Peru but also Argentina, Chile, Lower Peru, and even Colombia. The scions of wealthy creoles dominated the student populations at these two schools.[41]

Education was perceived as the emblem of social prestige at the top and as an act of charity at the bottom. Social welfare figured in with education at the charity level. Both were organized by the guiding hand of the church, supported by private donors. Thus the orphanages, manual training centers, poorhouses, and beaterios did double duty as welfare and educational agencies.[42] Unorganized welfare in the forms of alms-giving was widespread in the cities of Upper Peru. Monasteries, cathedrals, and parishes were primary locations for handouts of clothing and food. Plaintive beggars pleading "por Dios" (for the sake of God) were ubiquitous in the cities; they represented a class known as the *pordioseros*. Often deep symbiotic relationships developed between the givers, prompted by Christian piety, and the receivers. Other times, shiftless young men preyed on passersby, shaking them down while brandishing a cross.[43]

That education and welfare should become policy areas of the state, and not of church-mediated charity or free-lance activity, was new in Bolivia. But such was a major objective of both Sucre and Bolivar.

Bolivar felt strongly that the salvation of Latin American societies lay in the establishment of vigorous public educational systems to create more equality—and hence a capability for citizenship—among the population. Purging these systems of a sterile scholasticism and Catholic lore was at the top of Bolivar's educational agenda. Sucre was equally zealous about the need to establish public education in Bolivia. Even before Bolivar had arrived in Upper Peru he had received letters from Sucre citing this imperative. Sucre had pressed Bolivian leaders to apply the funds in capellanías to public education. His address to the General Assembly included an exhortation on this matter. The money was there, he argued, in capellanías and in the assets of the suppressed convents if only action from the assembly was forthcoming. In Cochabamba in November 1825, while Bolivar was at Chuquisaca, Sucre busied himself with the conversion of the convent of Recoleta into a school building, packaging obras pías and earmarking the funds from some of the suppressed convents to the new school. "If the Liberator agrees to what I have done," he wrote to Bolivar's secretary, "then a great part of my desires for this country will be realized."[44]

The December decrees of Bolivar envisaged the standardizing of the whole religious and secular educational system and bringing it under state control. The state schools to be established in Chuquisaca were to be the prototypes for state schools in the other departments. The seminary at Chuquisaca was to become the General Seminary of the Republic until the shift over to state schools was completed. Its curriculum was to be organized by the state to cover only the ecclesiastical "sciences": church history, writing, canons, and theology. A school of arts and sciences was to be housed in the seminary temporarily with its curriculum also to be drafted by the state and embracing Latin and Spanish, rhetoric, mathematics and architecture, medicine, agriculture and botany, modern philosophy, natural and civil law, and international law with emphasis on the study of the Constitution of Bolivia and its laws.[45] Bolivar's decrees also established the office of National Director of Education in the Republic, charged with developing a national plan laying out the curriculum and organizational codes for all public schools. That design was initiated by Bolivar's old friend and mentor, Simon Rodriguez, who had surfaced in Peru to renew his friendship with the Liberator. Rodriguez, by virtue of his idiosyncratic behavior, botched the job and caused Sucre considerable anxiety and embarrassment. He left Bolivia and the National Directorship of Education fell vacant, with Sucre exercising policy decisions on an ad hoc basis. In December 1826 he was arranging to bring a professor from Buenos Aires to begin an experimental school in Chuquisaca on the Lancester model, then widely in vogue in all of Latin America.[46]

In this area of reform as well as other areas, Facundo Infante supplied much of the drive. Infante, Sucre's right arm, was a Spanish military officer, born in 1786 in Badajoz, Spain. He developed a prominent military record in the armed struggle against the French occupation and subsequently in the liberal movement that developed among some Spanish officers against Ferdinand's absolutism after the king returned to the throne in 1812. In 1819 Infante was forced to leave Spain because of his political opinions. He traveled in Europe, then, in the wake of the Holy Alliances' intervention in 1822 that restored Ferdinand to absolutism in Spain, sailed for America to join the Spanish army in Peru which was commanded by officers of the liberal persuasion and enemies of Ferdinand's absolutism like Infante. He was en route by land from Brazil when news reached him of Sucre's victory at Ayacucho over the Spanish army. He continued into Upper Peru, where Sucre ordered him arrested along with other Spanish officers in the area. Infante fled and went to Cuzco, where he was able to get an audience with Bolivar who was at that time himself en route to Upper Peru to link up with Sucre. Bolivar determined to make use of Infante's services in the development of the Bolivian state, a curious decision given that Infante was Spanish. Once in Bolivia, Bolivar instructed Sucre to make Infante a minister in the state. Sucre obliged although he was aware that Bolivians were disenchanted with Infante because he was Spanish. Infante's haughty character and didactic discourse did little to ingratiate him among them. His relationship with Madero seems to have been abrasive. He was, however, completely loyal to Sucre although their relationship was businesslike.[47]

In the first part of 1826, between legislative sessions, Sucre went headlong into the creation of public schools and welfare institutions. Bolivar had left behind him in December a spate of decrees ranging across the social and economic continuum. "The most essential" for Sucre were those relating to public education. The months of February and March found him and Infante in Potosi. His first decree announced that "the principles of the Government are opposed to any kind of inequalities based on birth among citizens." Parishes classified as Indian and white were abolished in favor of classification by neighborhood. The hospital at Belem was converted to a school of arts and sciences, with provision for thirty full scholarship students, ten of them to be pure Indians and twenty war orphans. On March 3, 1826, he decreed the founding of a male orphanage in a former convent, to serve also as a primary school. A female orphanage was decreed on March 4, also in a suppressed convent, to take the place of an asylum for the poor formerly run there by the church. By a March 5 decree, primary schools were set up for each canton in the Potosi Department. On March 7 a decree established a home for mendicants.[48]

The Potosi schools used as their models the primary schools that had already been established by Sucre in Chuquisaca. The Potosi welfare establishments were likewise modeled on their counterparts in Chuquisaca. Similar combinations of public establishments appeared under state directives in Cochabamba and La Paz. Santa Cruz lagged somewhat behind and by midyear was the only department capital lacking a school of arts and sciences.

The implementation of the welfare and educational establishments in Bolivia, initiated as it was by Bolivar's decrees and Sucre's own industriousness, reflected also the style and outlook of Infante. He was a product of the Spanish liberal movement, which saw the charitable activities of the church as encouraging indolence among the population. A militant confinement movement developed in Spain in the second half of the eighteenth century, under liberal prompting. Infante brought the Spanish confinement movement into Bolivia through Bolivar's and Sucre's decrees. The phrase "It is the duty of the Government to collect all beggars," reflecting the confinement mentality, undoubtedly showed Infante's touch on the Potosi decree setting up the house for mendicants.

A hostel for beggars was established in Chuquisaca in a convent under the directorship of the superintendent of hospitals. The prefect was charged with certifying beggars for the institution and with prosecution of all pordioseros in the streets. One was established in La Paz and Cochabamba to complement those at Potosi and Chuquisaca. On May 14, Infante promulgated a seventy-article code to govern the daily regimes in these hostels and to place them under the jurisdiction of welfare boards to be set up in all of the departmental capitals.[49]

Bolivar's decrees had not contemplated starting a confinement movement of these proportions in Bolivia. Sucre was more involved with the schools. Infante was the spirit behind the confinement movement, its rhetoric, and the elaborate codes drafted to govern the daily regimes of the poorhouses. It was the schools that Sucre gave priority to when the time came for protection of the welfare institutions against his own debt policy.

On the educational side, Infante's style was less militant. He followed Sucre's instructions, adding sometimes nuances of his own which jarred with the diplomatic style of Sucre. But even when he tried to be diplomatic, the effect was gratuitous, as in his communication to the church relative to Sucre's intention to convert a former monastery to a colegio:

> President Sucre would like to convert the convent of St. Augustine into a school. Therefore all religious objects remaining in the convent should be removed. It is not the desire of the Government to mandate anything which is openly opposed to the foundations of our saintly religion. If you find nothing wrong with the convent serving as a school, you may please order instructions that all effigies and other objects of the cult be removed, the Government reserving to itself the right to arrange the interior decorum of the building in such a way that it loses to the extent possible any semblance of its [religious] function.[50]

Infante and *Condor*, the official newspaper of the administration, carried on a running polemic with the church over the issue of the social reforms. Infante failed to see how the church could oppose the principle of public education. Although the state did not recognize any legislators other than the representatives of the people, complaints of the church concerning hardships caused by funding public education would be studied and consulted on with the legislature. But he felt the church should agree that "public education is more agreeable than anything in the eyes of God and ought to be so for his Apostles, since good education forms better priests who are able to conserve [through] the solid principles of the religion of Jesus Christ the spiritual consolation which man needs in society, and in whose education superstition and the ideas of false philosophy are dissolved."[51]

Condor expressed what "enlightened" thinking on the subject of education should be:

In the relations by which we are joined together in society only the advantages of education give an improved gloss to the imprints of nature, making them more estimable. Education might be called the barometer of social virtue and it is alone in proportioning an equilibrium among the different classes which compose society. It is that which, by opening its doors to equal competition, offers the same reception to rich and poor, to white and Indians, to men and women. It is the only means by which men who do not possess the qualities of genius can hope to put themselves on the same level as those in whom Nature has placed her gifts with more favor. . . . [Education is] the reformer of Nature.[52]

The whole network of state establishments in the welfare and educational areas, launched with such noble intentions, was for the most part to be financed out of confiscated church assets in accordance with Bolivar's decree of December 11, 1825.[53] The new state institutions were funded from confiscated church assets, including a significant range of censos whose income was vested over to the new institutions. The remaining range of censos existed in a twilight zone, facing possible vesting over to welfare and education but finding sanctuary in the fact that it was often difficult to sort out the ecclesiastic from the lay components.

The effort launched by Bolivar and continued by Sucre to bring internal finances of the church under state control provided the larger framework of church reform within which the educational and welfare initiatives were implemented. Although widespread support existed in the legislative bodies for turning the welfare and educational functions of the church over to the state and for suppressing the regular orders, the question of making state inroads into the church's diocesan structure, and into the financial and administrative arrangements of the secular as opposed to regular orders, created political conflict.

The stance of Sucre's administration toward the church was defined largely by the patronato that he inherited from Spanish royal government. The patronato was a grant to the Spanish Crown, from the pope, of authority over the operations of the church in America. It included rights of appointment of bishops, oversight responsibilities for the activities of the

regular orders, rights to levy the church as needed to cover extraordinary
government costs, rights to a certain portion of the tithe or agricultural
tax (called diezmos in Bolivia) collected by the church, and rights to draw
up ecclesiastical boundaries to coincide with political boundaries of the
empire. All of these rights vis-à-vis the church had been variously exercised in Upper Peru by the viceroys in Lima as well as by the Audiencia
of Charcas, with a minimum of interference; the internal financial and
administrative systems of the church in Bolivia remained essentially autonomous and self-contained. Thus the state did not actually participate in
the collection of the diezmos but normally applied to the church's treasury
(*clavería*) for its quota under the patronato. Occasionally it would use its
rights to future diezmos collections as collateral for a loan from the church.

During his first months in Chuquisaca, Sucre had established quite
agreeable relations with Matías Terrazas, the archbishop of Upper Peru.
Terrazas had hoped that independence could be fended off in Upper Peru.
He exhorted the renegade loyalist Pedro Olañeta to mend his relations
with the Spanish general Jerónimo Valdez and to combine forces against
Bolivar.[54] But Sucre's great victory at Ayacucho, and the arrival of Sucre
in Upper Peru with his army and the collapse of Olañeta, had left Terrazas
with no alternative except to try to exert influence politically and diplomatically in the interest of reconciling independence with the vested interests the church had acquired during the colonial period. His first letter
to Sucre, dated February 25, 1825, was obsequious and stood in hypocrit-
ical contrast to his letter to Valdez six weeks earlier.[55]

His first conversations with Sucre were cordial enough, and Sucre waxed
enthusiastic about the land. But Sucre told him that the state must facilitate the development of the human and economic resources of Upper
Peru. Terrazas wrote to Sucre after one of these conversations that he was
"very happy that you find my country agreeable. It is of course susceptible
to much progress. But it is a palpable truth, that which you say about the
need for a decided protection of the Government if it is to be achieved.
This it will have because I do not doubt for a minute that the reins of
Government will be placed in the skillful and beneficent hands of Your
Excellency."[56]

Terrazas accepted Sucre's claim to the patronato. He assisted Sucre in
making more than eighty appointments to vacant posts in the church hierarchy in Bolivia by submitting slates of candidates for each one, empha-
sizing, somewhat hypocritically, their revolutionary credentials. There was
some opposition from the La Paz ecclesiastic *cabildo* to Sucre's appoint-

ment of a capitular head. It refused to recognize the vesting of appointive powers in the Sucre administration. But basically the right of the Sucre administration to exercise this aspect of the patronato power was not widely contested inside or outside the church. The Permanent Deputation seconded Sucre's rights of appointment to religious posts as a legitimate part of his rights under the patronato.[57]

The extension of patronato rights into the regulation of parish activities did cause more friction because of vested interests in exploitative customs. Of particular concern was the practice of many parishes (a consequence of declining diezmos income) of covering costs by charging fees to parishioners, mostly Indians, for religious holidays, fiestas, and masses. Minister Infante informed church authorities that any priests proved to have charged such fees would be required to pay a 500-peso fine to the person bringing the complaint to the attention of the government. Infante maintained that the abuses of credulous Indians by unscrupulous priests extended beyond simply the charging of fees to a broad pattern of fraud and extortion, involving violation of both canon and civil law that inspired Indian complaints to the government that "have the character of desperation." He acknowledged, however, the church's immunity from criminal prosecution. He went so far as to encourage the Congress to pass laws stipulating fines for the whole range of parish abuses of Indians. The purpose of the administration, Infante stated, was not to provoke the priests—although it was aware that many of them were offended by the effort to call them to account—but rather to "look after the dignity of the Church as its patron, and [after] the rights of the Indians."[58]

It was the regular orders of the church that felt the full brunt of Sucre's reforms in the early phase. The regular orders lacked the political influence of the seculars in Bolivia, so the wealth that was thought to be controlled by them could be safely confiscated and applied to reform programs.

The regular orders operated a network of monasteries and convents in Upper Peru, each of which in its heyday was the basis of a large of socioeconomic system. The regular orders gained ownership and control over large amounts of urban and rural property, rented out and worked under their auspices. The Franciscan friars in Upper Peru at the time of independence ran ten monasteries, the Recoletas thirty-two, the Mercedarians seven, the Dominicans seven, and the Augustianians eight. In addition to satellite economies and social structures attaching to these monasteries, the regular clergy operated or controlled considerable amounts of wealth, including mortgages held against houses, mines, and farms, as well as ownership and rental of income-producing properties. The regular orders, in addition to operating out of their monastery bases, set up and oversaw numerous convents that also became socioeconomic units of major importance, more heavily capitalized than even the monasteries were. The Augustine convent at Potosi (Santa Monica) owned numerous houses and haciendas as income-producing property and held mortgages and made loans to the mint, the treasury, and the customs service. The convent of Santa Teresa even overshadowed that of Santa Monica. The Santa Clara convent at Cochabamba was the largest and wealthiest of all. It held mortgages on sixty-eight rural and urban properties and had provided large loans to the government.[59]

By the time Sucre arrived in Upper Peru, all of the monasteries and, to a lesser extent, the convents were in a state of decline and depopulation, the result of harassment by Crown authorities starting with the expulsion of the Jesuits in 1767. In Upper Peru the viceroy, La Serna, had commenced a policy of suppressing monasteries. Bolivar's decrees continued this process. The Permanent Delegation of the Assembly encouraged Sucre to expand the scope of his suppression policy to include the monasteries in Cochabamba. It approved Sucre's timetable for suppression and its draft laid the basis for Sucre's decree of March 29, 1826, which turned the religious objects of suppressed monasteries over to the secular church for distribution to the parishes and nationalized all remaining assets and property holdings of these monasteries. Of the thirty monasteries extant in 1825, by virtue of this decree only two were left in Chuquisaca, two in Potosi, three in La Paz, one in Santa Cruz, one in Oruro, and one in Mizque, twelve all told.[60]

Sucre assured Terrazas that the regular orders, after suppression of all of the larger monasteries, would be placed in smaller communities under the direct authority of the secular authorities. Terrazas willingly consented to the suppression of the regulars.[61]

The general expectation was that the assets locked up by the regular orders could be turned to better account by the state through, for example, its initiatives in the public education field. The Constitutive Assembly continued the momentum by legislating the suppression of most of the remaining monasteries and the secularization of friars and nuns. By the end of 1826, twenty-five monasteries and communities had been suppressed, some of them pursuant to Sucre's decree of March 29 and the rest by a congressional law of November 11, 1826.[62]

Much of the impetus for the suppression policy lay in Bolivar's decree of December 11, 1825, which stipulated that assets of all suppressed monasteries and convents would be applied to the state reforms in the educational area. Yet that decree also mentioned forms of wealth-holding that were not peculiar to the regular orders but were practiced also by the secular hierarchy, namely, the whole range of obras pías and trust funds of the confraternities. The decree assigned the conversion of all obras pías funds of whatever category, save those under a strict family trust arrangement, to the endowments of the public establishments and to the welfare boards that were to be set up for each department. Article 10 said that deposit of these assets would be separate from all other state revenues and in no case would any use be made of them other than capitalizing the schools and poorhouses.[63]

Terrazas began to take vigorous exception to the December 11 decree and to look for political support. If the state confiscated the capellanías, obras pías, and *sacristías* today, would it take the censos and the diezmos tomorrow? And the confiscation would not stop there; the very principles of private property and free choice were being placed at risk by this policy.

Terrazas opened his campaign in a letter to Infante dated January 31, 1826. He questioned parts of Bolivar's December 11 decree and argued that only capellanías of the *derecho devuelto* kind, lacking a specified or known *capellan*, should be subject to state confiscation. Even in these cases some of their income should be reserved to pay for masses and to fulfill the intentions of the founder to the extent possible. Most definitely, Terrazas continued, capellanías with legally named clerical beneficiaries often served as the title for their ordination and should be exempted from the decree. For otherwise "many clerics would be left incongruous" and the state in the obligation to maintain them. Terrazas tried to turn the republican rhetoric against the disentailment policy. "In an independent Republic based on the association of free men," he wrote, "nothing should be so sacred as the security of individuals, of property, of the right to dispose of these howsoever one intends so long as [that intent includes] . . . honest purposes which do not prejudice the public welfare. From this it follows as a necessary corollary that just as private citizens can leave their property to another private person with an even greater right they can leave it to God, to his Church, and to its Ministers."[64]

Terrazas argued that the threat of expropriation of any future capellanías having beneficiaries other than state institutions of public education would cause them to cease and the state would be denied income from them when they would have become derecho devuelto. He included with capellanías the cofradias, sacristías, and obras pías in his plea for exemption from the December 11 decree. He predicted much litigation would be brought by heirs for misappropriation of these trusts.

The administration had begun to use *Condor* to anticipate the church's resistance to the channeling of its trust funds into public education. Charges of hypocrisy were hurled at priests who had said they supported public education while maintaining that their own capellanías should not bear the burden of paying for it when plenty of lay trusts could be confiscated instead. A group of priests in La Paz who signed a public statement to this effect came in for direct attack from *Condor*. In a Voltairian vein, a *Condor* editorial stated in the April 6, 1826, issue:

> Greek priests poisoned Socrates for questioning the plurality of the Gods. Why? Because the priests enjoyed taxes and contributions from cult worship, and they did not want that men erect in their hearts an altar to the Author of Nature where he would be worshipped with a pure and simple faith without the need for importers and tricksters. . . . Their only object was to live off the stupid credulity of the masses. . . . When will reason and philosophy be seated on top of the structures which ignorance, vested interest and superstition have raised?[65]

Beyond the issues raised by the state's appropriation of obras pías, there was the matter of asserting state control over the censos taking the form of property income earmarked to pay off loans and mortgages. This could be done, and in fact was done, in considerable volume on an ad hoc basis, along with obras pías. However, the matter of bringing the diezmos under state control required the incorporation of the church clavería into the state treasury.

These diezmos were the American counterpart of the European tithe. Under a Papal bull of 1501, the Spanish Crown was granted diezmos rights to help it support the operations of the church in its American empire. In Upper Peru, the church by custom had auctioned off contracts to collect the diezmos to the highest bidder. "Tax farmers" who purchased these contracts paid in advance to the Archdiocese Treasury and then collected the diezmos for themselves. Only the agricultural production of whites and mestizos was subject to the diezmos tax since the Indians paid tribute.

The concern of the church over state inroads into its diezmos system was aroused by one of Bolivar's decrees, which had separated two Peruvian provinces of Puno from the religious jurisdiction of the La Paz bishopric,

and shifted two cantons to the La Paz jurisdiction from the Archdiocese of
La Plata. These changes reduced the diezmos income of the church considerably. Sucre, while the political separation of Upper Peru from Peru was
still fluid, proceeded on August 8, 1825, to vest the diezmos formerly collected in Puno by the La Paz bishopric in a school of arts and sciences in
Puno. By a decree of December 31, 1825, Sucre vested the diezmos formerly collected in Sicasica by the Chuquisaca archdiocese in a school of arts
and sciences in La Paz. Terrazas pointed out to Sucre the decline of the
church's diezmos income that would result from these dismemberments of
the two Puno cantons. He objected vigorously to the change and called
Sucre's attention to the historic decline in diezmos income of the church
from the wars for independence.[66]

Terrazas had tried to head off Sucre in the area of diezmos by arguing
in March 1825 that the state had a legitimate right to a quota of the diezmos pool but that it should be drawn from the claveria. The issue came up
over Sucre's intention to use diezmos to pay the overhead costs of the departmental government in Cochabamba. Terrazas told Infante that the
church of Chuquisaca could not be maintained except as a "poor parish"
without the income from the diezmos. The religious cabildo of La Paz
similarly protested the rechanneling of its diezmos income into public education, a protest carrying some political significance since one of its
signers was also a member of the Permanent Deputation.[67]

The skirmishes over diezmos became deeper and more complex in
1826. In the first place, diezmos were usually tied to an intricate distribution system by the church, in which only a certain portion was reserved in
the clavería for the state. Application of diezmos to education ran into the
problem of sorting out state claims from other claims to the diezmos,
some by ecclesiastical bodies and some by lay groups. But the fundamental need was to centralize the diezmos system in the Finance Ministry and
get it out of the clavería. A step was taken in this direction by Sucre's Bolivian minister of finance and architect of Bolivia's funding experiment,
Juan Bernarbe y Madero, in a decree of May 15, 1826. This set out a code
for public auctions of diezmos contracts, to be held by state officials with
claveria officials as observers. Diezmos were to be placed in the same
category as other property assets of the state. Madero said that this decree
made it clear that diezmos "belong to the state" as did the right to auction
them off, and the treasury adopted the practice of issuing letters of credit
against future diezmos revenues to meet current obligations of the state.[68]

These state inroads required first bringing the diezmos system under executive control, a step accomplished by a bill introduced by Sucre and a congressional commission; it incorporated the whole diezmos system along with the clavería bureaucracy into the office of the National Treasury. The law in this session of Congress stipulated the direct deposit of all diezmos in the state treasury, effective January 1827. Sucre's decree of December 1826 converted clavería employees into state employees and organized all of the cathedral finances, in addition to the diezmos, through the state treasury. An April decree did the same for the La Paz cathedral finances. These consolidated Madero's May 1826 decree, which had already placed diezmos auctions under state supervision. Considerable friction arose between clavería officials and their support lay personnel (civilian notaries) and administration bureaucrats in consequence of these decrees and laws.[69]

Given the historic abuses in the diezmos system as it was run by the clavería, the political support for this move was available, although not without some reservations. Certain deputies vigorously opposed the bill, arguing that the diezmos originated in church law and that only church authorities could rightfully collect them. Charges of laxity meant simply that the remedy lay in strict adherence by the clavería to its codes and that absorbing the claveria into the state treasury would make it dependent on the various contingencies of state finances, which would weaken the cult—"something not permissible without incurring a note of atheism." Terrazas supported this line, arguing that any irregularities in the collection of diezmos were a result of the war.[70]

Terrazas was up against a persuasive advocate of Sucre in the Constituent Assembly in the person of Casimiro Olañeta. Olañeta's voice was a powerful, nationalistic one. He had not fled the war, he said, in order to use his influence with his uncle Pedro Olañeta to get him to break with the Peruvian Viceroy, surrender his forces to Sucre, and thereby shorten the war. Accused of being a collaborator and an enemy of independence caused Olañeta to issue an apology in which he argued that it was due to him that Olañeta had in fact split with the Peruvian Viceroy, thereby giving Bolivar and Sucre the opportunity to attack a divided Spanish army. Sucre was convinced of Olañeta's patriotic credentials. Olañeta made contact with Sucre soon after Sucre's arrival with his army in Upper Peru. Olañeta acted as a close political advisor of both Sucre and Bolivar. He eloquently pleaded the cause of Sucre's reforms in the General Assembly and in the Constituent Assembly until mid-1827, when he turned against both Sucre and Bolivar.[71]

In his support for state reforms, Olañeta gave a voice to a state-building sentiment that was widespread among the delegates and in fact provided the Sucre administration with unwavering support for its reform initiatives throughout the key year of 1826 and for funding the internal debt.

> States sometimes find themselves in a situation where they can take, without any risk, great steps toward their prosperity. Our State happily finds itself in this situation and it is high time to cut out obstacles at their roots and to make disappear this monster called the clavería, this independent society embedded in the heart of the State. Diezmos can be collected more efficiently by the Government, and with the same hand, those who serve the cult can be paid, as well as those who serve society.[72]

Aside from the vesting of diezmos assets that was accomplished as part of the incorporation of the clavería accounts, the vestable assets under Bolivar's December 11 decree required department-by-department inventories. Pending the establishment of the welfare boards, Sucre's first task in early 1826 was to launch these inventories of the incomes of convents monasteries, and parishes, including the whole range of obras pías both regular and secular. The parish "spread sheets," dutifully provided by Terrazas, provided a vivid and pathetic sociological picture of life at the parish level in rural Bolivia. The Cochabamba inventory, submitted by its delegate to the Permanent Delegation, listed all convent income from agricultural production and rented lands, capellanías established in favor of poor children, obras pías established in favor of orphanage children, obras pías established in favor of monasteries, obras pías established to clothe twelve poor people, and obras pías established in favor of Indians. The Cochabamba inventory included also excise tax revenues of the departmental treasury as well as mortgages held in the treasury dating back to the colonial period. The endowments of all public establishments were improvised from inventories similar to this one, supplemented by community lands, excise tax revenues, taxes on wheat and flour crossing departmental boundaries, and interest payments received on mortgages held by departmental treasuries. In the case of the poorhouses, the convent lands were to be worked by inmates as part of the financing package. Where public orphanages replaced church orphanages or hospitals, their income was turned over. Ongoing departmental revenue from administrative and legal fees was earmarked for primary schools.[73]

In many instances the property under a religious benefice or lien was understood to be leased to the public establishments. The particular public establishment did not technically own the underlying property but was legally entitled to a share of its annual income covered by the capellanía, obra pía, or mortgage payments held by the church or departmental governments. Bolivar's decree of December 11 made this point clear by stating that, in connection with a particular obra pía fixed on the income of a hacienda's lands, that the hacienda itself became part of the capital of public education, under the portfolio management of the Welfare Board.

The attitudes toward censos changed considerably as a result of this process. People were psychologically resistant to buying out censos held by the church. But matters were different now that many censos were held by the new, secularized welfare institutions which lacked much legitimacy.

Toward the end of 1826 the process of vesting the obras pías over to education and welfare had been largely completed. But the vesting of a remaining range of censos and of the diezmos slowed down, and a definite reticence began to appear in executive pronouncements on this subject.

The diezmos controversy did not end with the approval by the Congress of the bill incorporating the clavería into the state treasury. The channeling of diezmos into public education was bound to conflict with the diversity of claims on them. Was only the state's share to be diverted? Were any of the other shares also vestable? Which ones? The Congress clearly began to get ahead of the executive in this area. A law that it passed vesting diezmos in Tarija over to public education evoked from Infante the comment that it "suffered from inexactitude given the diversity of diezmos claims and would be certain to cause litigation." It was not clear in that law, Infante said, whether the state was speaking for its own share or whether the shares claimed by various parishes were also claimed by the law. That point had to be made clear so that there would be no appearance of a confiscatory intent on the part of the government.[74]

This problem in vesting the diezmos applied also to the vesting of censos with lay components: what was the state's share and what was private property? The evident slowing down in the vesting of censos thus overlapped the slowing down in the vesting of diezmos contracts, but there was a crucial difference: censos were forms of entailment on property that citizens were anxious to redeem. Vesting *them* over to welfare and education contradicted the decision to make censos redemption the basis for making a market in state debt paper associated with a loan that Sucre determined to float domestically. Leaving a range of censos in the twilight zone of possible vesting over to welfare and education made them even more attractive to property owners against whom these censos were held to seek their redemption through the use of cheap state debt paper. Eventually even censos that had been vested were themselves made redeemable with state debt. The noble intentions of the Sucre administration in the areas of educational and welfare reform thus got turned upside down at the same time that the even vaster progressive reform of society associated with the effort to launch funded state debt paper was sabotaged.

Opposition Politics and Support for the Funding Question

The reform undertakings of the Sucre administration were played out on a landscape of strategic behaviors devised during the dislocation of the old order.

During the long period of deterioration of Spanish rule in Upper Peru, an inevitable question was posed: who stayed, who left, and why? Those who left did so in three major waves of emigration in 1809, 1813, and 1815. Among those who stayed there were, politically speaking, two components. One was the whole republiqueta population, but by 1824, when Sucre and the Colombians arrived, it was exhausted, dispersed, and virtually leaderless. The other was those willing to profess loyalty to Spanish rule but not so much loyalty that they were not able to adapt to an independence regime if and when the Spanish were overthrown. Matías Terrazas, archbishop of Upper Peru, gave a good example of this strategy by hoping for a Spanish victory in Upper Peru but being ready to make peace with the Colombians if they won. Casimiro Olañeta provided another example of the strategy by hoping that the Spanish would be overthrown in order that he, as a person who stayed and "tried" to convince the Spanish that it was a losing cause, could play a key political role in the transition to a new regime. Both Terrazas and Olañeta were major voices in the legislative assemblies that Sucre established in Upper Peru.

In a well-known conceptualization, Albert Hirschman has identified three parameters in the behavior of host populations of deteriorating states and economic organizations: voice, loyalty, and exit. Voice is the option of articulating dissatisfactions in the hope that the reasons for the deterioration will be corrected; it is an input strategy. Loyalty is persevering and staying deliberately in the face of deterioration, partly because of the fear that by leaving the deterioration will be accelerated. Deliberately staying under deteriorating conditions often gives a higher level of effective voice to the stayers. The point of exit in the face of a rising deterioration of the state, absent a loyalist factor, arrives early in the process of deterioration. Another key point is reached when loyalists begin to use the threat of exit as a means of achieving effective voice. A critical breaking point occurs when loyalists leave. A boycott is a borderline strategy between voice and exit, a kind of hybrid. The boycott version of exit (temporary exit) is used as a lever to achieve a change in the state performance. "The threat of exit as an instrument of voice is replaced here by its mirror image, the promise of reentry. [Boycotters] will reenter not just at the level of service when they left but at the point when they originally began to have qualms." Émigrés can pursue a boycott strategy upon return as their method of achieving the desired level of state service.[75]

Applying these ideas to Bolivian independence politics, we can identify two essential strategies. One was the loyalty-voice strategy epitomized by Olañeta and Terrazas and the political following that developed around them, particularly around Olañeta. Organized in the legislative assembly established during Sucre's period of rule, it expressed the feelings of Bolivian nationalism. The exit-boycott strategy was represented by the émigré population that returned in waves from Buenos Aires after liberation. It was organized essentially in Potosi, the staging area for the original emigrations, and the main reentry point. Its users systematically attempted to discredit the Sucre government.

Superficially, there was a conflict between these two constituencies and they traded accusatory polemics. One complaint made by the émigré community was that the Sucre government favored the loyalist collaborators in its appointments while discriminating against the true patriots who fled the country rather than support the Spanish.[76] However, beneath the surface they shared common oppositional interests vis-à-vis the Sucre administration which found expression in the debt funding project:

1. The Sucre government was made up largely of foreigners, causing the émigrés to boycott it and the voice-loyalists to complain privately about Colombian hegemony and to press for more input.
2. The émigré groups based at Potosi became involved with the demands of the mining community there for state capitalization of the industry and the creation of a powerful mining bank. The mining bank project had strong support in the nationalist circles in the legislature. The Sucre government was oriented to a liberal laissez-faire philosophy and did not respond to these statist demands. Furthermore, as a result of the depression of the mining industry, most of the loanable capital in the country was in the hands of the La Paz commercial-hacendado

class. In desperate need to raise funds to pay prize money to his own soldiers, Sucre was forced to look to La Paz, not to Potosí, for those funds.

3. On debt funding, the creation of a public credit administration was a means of increasing legislative independence and as a counter to the foreign influence which dominated the executive branch. The funding administration was seen by the voice-loyalists as a kind of parallel government with its own infrastrucure and a wide popular base. The émigré groups supported the Chuquisaca-based funding in order to recover the large portion of the internal debt they held and to try, by means of establishing a countervailing funded debt policy, to defeat the growing identification between the Sucre government's loan policy and the La Paz business community.

A "coalition" of voice-loyalists (controlling the legislature) and exit-boycotters (based in Potosí) was forged on these three issues. It was also poised against the La Paz–Cochabamba axis which was happy with economic liberalism, laissez-faire, and a floating debt policy that was focused on the redemption of censos, elimination of large state land holdings, and sale of haciendas to private owners.

3

Debt Policy Conflict: Madero's Funded Debt versus Sucre's Floating Debt

BOLIVIA DID NOT HAVE a large foreign debt. Its debt was shaped by the contradictory political and economic pressures created by the state's simultaneous efforts to make good on financial commitments to native sons prejudiced by a long war for independence and to a restive Colombian garrison. The first commitment took the form of funding the internal debt; the second took the form of floating a domestic loan in order to raise prize money. The conflict that arose between these two debt policies opened a large breach within the Sucre administration, soured its relations with the legislative branch, and undermined the state's commitment to welfare reform.

Funding Law and the Loan Float

Throughout 1825 Sucre and Bolivar administered Upper Peru through their general staffs. But on the advice of the Permanent Deputation, Sucre decided to create separate civilian staff structures for treasury (*hacienda*) and interior (*gobierno*). Infante took provisional charge of both of the new portfolios. While at Potosi in early 1826, Sucre met Juan Bernabe de Madero and recruited him for the treasury position. Madero was a Bolivian, born at Potosi. He was considerably senior to Sucre and Infante. In 1826, he was in his early fifties; Sucre was thirty-two and Infante was forty. At an early age, Madero had emigrated with his parents from Potosi to Buenos Aires. He was sent to Europe for study and travel and in his twenties returned to Buenos Aires, where he became engaged in the import-export business. He was recruited following the overthrow of the viceroy in 1810 to the position of commissar of the revolutionary army, serving in that capacity during one of Buenos Aires's ill-fated invasions of Alto Peru in 1813. He returned to Buenos Aires, where he spent the next ten years, until his return to Potosi, in various Argentine administrations. A British visitor to Bolivia who met Madero while he was serving as Sucre's minister of treasury noted his "decided partiality for the institutions of the Argentine Republic and attributed to him "the desire to introduce the financial reforms of that state into Bolivia."[1]

The concepts of public credit that Madero brought with him to Bolivia and put into practice as minister of treasury were drawn basically from the funding experiments that he had a hand in formulating in the Pueyrredón and Rivadavia administrations in Buenos Aires.[2] His main objective was to create a system of public credit in Bolivia based on the funding of the internal debt, using for his model Rivadavia's funding legislation of 1822 with its emphasis on the creation of a sinking fund and on emphyteusis.

Sucre was glad to recruit Madero at Potosi, not because he specifically endorsed his ideas about funding but because he felt that his Argentine connections might prove useful to Bolivia in offsetting Peruvian annexationist pressures. More important, Sucre was under some pressure to recruit more Bolivians into his administration, and Madero became the first Bolivian to serve in his cabinet. The only other ones would be Madero's successor, Miguel María Aguirre, and José María Perez de Urdininea, who became minister of war late in 1827. Although Sucre had considered initially creating a secretariat of foreign affairs and appointing Olañeta as minister while replacing Infante in interior with a Bolivian, neither of these moves materialized; Infante remained minister of interior to the end while retaining control over foreign affairs. But Madero was appointed minister of the treasury on March 28, 1826, in a government that was largely run by foreigners. Table 3.1 shows the situation at the prefectural level.

Fourteen of the twenty-six stints in the prefectureships were done by Bolivians and eleven by foreigners. Bolivians logged seventy-four months and foreigners eighty-two. But foreigners served a longer average time in office. More importantly, in the departments where economic power lay, La Paz and Potosi especially, foreigners logged many more hours than Bolivians. Bolivians dominated the Chuquisaca prefectureships because of the high political visibility of their position. But the stints there were among the most brief. (See table 3.2.)

Table 3.1. Prefect Appointments in the Sucre Administration, 1825–28

	Potosí	Chuquisaca	Santa Cruz	Cochabamba	Oruro	La Paz	Term in months	Civilian	Military	Bolivian-naturalized	Bolivian-born	Spanish	English	Argentine	Colombian
José Lanza	0	0	0	0	0	1	1	0	1	0	1	0	0	0	0
Andres Santa Cruz	0	1	0	0	0	0	6	0	1	0	1	0	0	0	0
Andres Santa Cruz	0	0	0	0	0	1	2	0	1	0	1	0	0	0	0
Gregorio Fernandez	0	0	0	0	0	1	24	0	1	1	0	0	0	1	0
Carlos Ortega	0	0	0	0	1	0	2	0	1	0	0	0	0	0	1
Rufino Martinez	0	0	0	0	1	0	1	0	1	9	9	9	9	9	9
José Guerrero	0	0	0	0	1	0	1	0	1	0	0	0	0	0	1
Miguel Sargánaga	0	0	0	0	1	0	12	0	1	9	1	0	0	0	0
Miguel Molina	0	0	0	0	1	0	1	0	1	0	0	0	0	0	1
William Miller	1	0	0	0	0	0	6	0	1	0	0	0	1	0	0
José Urdininea	1	0	0	0	0	0	4	0	1	0	1	0	0	0	0
José Urdininea	0	1	0	0	0	0	6	0	1	0	1	0	0	0	0
Casimiro Olañeta	1	0	0	0	0	0	1	1	0	0	0	0	0	0	0
León Galindo	1	0	0	0	0	0	21	0	1	1	0	0	0	0	1

Francisco Lopez	1	0	0	0	0	0	4	0	1	0	1	0	0	0
Carlos Ortega	0	1	0	0	0	0	3	0	1	0	0	0	0	1
Casimiro Olañeta	0	1	0	0	0	0	3	1	0	1	0	0	0	0
Luis Urdaneta	0	1	0	0	0	0	1	0	1	0	0	0	0	1
Mariano Calvo	0	1	0	0	0	0	2	1	0	0	0	0	0	0
Manuel Tardio	0	1	0	0	0	0	7	0	1	0	0	0	0	0
Gavino Ibañez	0	1	0	0	0	0	6	0	1	0	1	0	0	0
José Lanza	0	1	0	0	0	0	4	0	1	0	0	0	0	0
Antonio Sanchez	0	0	1	0	0	0	1	0	1	0	0	1	0	0
José Plaza	0	0	0	1	0	0	15	0	1	0	0	1	0	0
Francisco Lopez	0	0	0	1	0	0	16	0	1	0	0	0	0	0
Agustín Geraldino	0	0	0	1	0	0	6	0	1	0	0	0	0	1
Totals	5	9	1	3	5	3	156	3	23	2	14	1	3	7

Sources: Compiled from prefectural data in Lofstrom, *Presidencia*, 99–111, supplemented by *Condor* no. 111, January 11, 1828, 1; O'Leary Memorias, 9:403–10; A. Arguedas, *Historia General de Bolivia*, 10–11; MH, t. 5, no. 3. The following additions were made to Lofstrom's data: Sargánaga: Bolivian by virtue of the name (cf. Arguedas); Guerrero: Colombian by virtue of receipt of vales (cf. *Condor*); Luis Urdaneta: Colombian by virtue of correspondence with Bolivar (cf. O'Leary); Gavino Ibañez: six-month term by virtue of signatures on vale (cf. MH).

Key: 1 = yes; 2 = no; 9 = unknown.

Table 3.2. Months Logged by Bolivians and Foreigners in
Departmental Prefects, 1825–28

```
        36
             *  Chuquisaca
        30
Months
logged by  24
Bolivians
        18                                    *  Cochabamba

        12   *  Oruro
                                                *  La Paz  .
         6
             *  Santa Cruz                        *  Potosi

         0       6        12       18       24       30       36

                    Months logged by foreigners
```

Source: Plotted from table 3-1. Total Bolivian prefectural months, 74; total foreign prefectural months, 82.

All of the foreign prefects were officers serving in the Liberating Army, mainly Argentines and Colombians. Gregory Fernandez, an Argentine, controlled the La Paz prefecture from mid-1825. Leon Galindo, a Colombian (New Granada), controlled Potosi from mid-1826. There were no Peruvian officers appointed or Chileans. The latter is not surprising since there were few Chilean officers still serving under Bolivar. Peruvian officers, however, were plentiful in the ranks of the Liberating Army in Bolivia. But Peruvian prefects in Bolivia were unacceptable politically to Sucre, given his sensitivity to the Peruvian annexationist designs on Bolivia. Moreover, the Peruvian nationalist administrations, after the revolution against Bolivar, would not have permitted their nationals to serve in Bolivia in any official capacity and in fact punished those who did. It is true that a prominent Bolivian military figure, Andres Santa Cruz, held Peruvian citizenship and was for a while the prefect of La Paz. But Bolivar had insisted on this appointment, and Sucre had no choice.[3]

By the time Madero took office, it was already evident that the decline in tax revenue, caused by Bolivar's lifting of the various colonial taxes on the economy, was going to make it hard for the administration to cover current expenditures. The technical difficulties encountered in implementing direct taxation contributed to the inadequacy of revenues. The budget for current expenditures in 1826 called for an outlay of 2,139,763 pesos, whose distribution is given in table 3.3.

Madero and Sucre were convinced that the new procedures for direct taxation prepared by the Congress's Commission on Finance were still inadequate to make up the revenue shortfall. Even under the most optimistic estimates, a shortfall of one-half million pesos was predicted. Madero returned the direct taxation bill to the Congress, asking for postponement of its implementation until collection features and quotas could be more exactly and realistically stated. In the meantime, authorization was requested to reinstate the indirect taxes as they stood in 1825 in order for the administration to cover its current expenditures for 1826. There still remained the problem of public debt. The external debt consisted of 250,000 pesos owed to Peru, and the 1 million peso gratification decreed to the Liberating Army. The internal debt consisted of the colonial debts accumulated by the Spanish state and compensations owed to independence fighters and the supporters of the guerrilla armies. There was also the matter of money owed to the state in the form of unpaid diezmos and censos obligations. Bolivar had seen fit to promulgate two decrees that reduced amounts on liens owed to the state in cases where the underlying property had been damaged during the war. These decrees were the first ones to recognize the financial obligation of the new state to the native population, including the returning émigrés, who had suffered war damages. Included in a third decree were individuals who had paid for a public office but never occupied it because of the war. Their financial claims were recognized. By virtue of a decree of December 11, 1825, these catego-

Table 3.3. Bolivian Budget Allocations for 1826

Congress	50,000
Executive	72,000
Supreme Court	34,000
Revenue Office	8,000
Foreign relations	52,000
Military	1,314,000
Department governments	323,805
Welfare and education	185,958
Cathedrals	100,000
Total	2,139,763

Source: CO, vol. 2, 1827–29, 10–38.

ries of public debt were in the process of being consolidated and documented by Madero.[4]

With regard to the payment of the Peruvian debt and the Liberation Army gratification, the Permanent Deputation had authorized Bolivar to raise a foreign loan for that purpose, to be guaranteed by the sale of the publicly owned mines. While Sucre and Infante focused their attention on the possibilities of floating this loan, Madero invested his effort in the creation of a Public Credit Administration to issue interest-bearing billetes not as a means of increasing the administration's cash flow but rather to fund the internal debt.

A decree of the Permanent Delegation on December 15, 1825, had left it to the future determination of the Congress whether the recognition of the colonial debts of the Spanish administration was incumbent on subsequent Bolivian administrations. Madero instituted procedures for documenting the internal debt which seemed to Sucre to give equal status to debts of the Spanish state and debts arising from the operations of guerrilla armies in Alto Peru. In parallel fashion Madero developed his plan for public credit, involving the issue of 3 million in interest-bearing billetes into which the global internal debt was to be converted. This approach was the same employed by the Caja Nacional established in Argentina. That Madero was paying close attention to the Argentine funding experience is suggested by the trip he took to Buenos Aires in September 1826 just prior to the submission of his plan to the Bolivian Congress. It is a reasonable speculation also that Madero encouraged the émigré Bolivian community in Buenos Aires to apply for the Bolivian billetes as indemnification for property losses they had suffered in Alto Peru during the war.[5]

Unlike Argentina, the Bolivian Administration could not count on large port customs to finance its funding program. Moreover state debt paper had only been slightly, and unhappily, experienced in Bolivia. Notes had been issued in 1815 and again in 1820 by the Spanish authorities to finance the war. Each time, the market value of the notes dropped quickly to the smallest fraction of their face value, and eventually they became totally worthless. *Condor* nevertheless applauded Madero's ideas and looked forward to the the establishment of public credit as "something good for the administration and good for the citizens." Yet it was apparent that *Condor* was thinking of the commercial value of state debt paper and not the social and political value of a funding system. It noted in its May 18, 1826, issue that the institution of public credit could correct "the custom [in Bolivia] of doing everything with money in hand. . . . [This is] one of the great evils facing the prosperity of the country, its commerce and its investments [*especulaciones*]. Without money in hand everything is suspect and people who are suspicious in the extreme are not in general people of good will." *Condor* thus did not distinguish between funded state debt and floating state debt. That state debt paper serving in place of "money in hand" was "something good for the government and good for the people" was a highly debatable proposition in the Bolivian context, as events would prove.[6]

Sucre was lukewarm about the prospects of Madero's funding program. He and Infante expected that the market value of Madero's billetes would drop rapidly because of the long term of the return. In addition, Sucre was impressed by the fact that the 10 million worth of bank notes that the Argentine administration had recently circulated to finance the war against Brazil were already worthless and still circulating only in Buenos Aires and in the army. Sucre therefore was not sanguine about the overall prospects of the Bolivian billetes. In fact he had opposed the whole establishment of the public credit program in Bolivia but deferred to Madero's financial expertise. Mainly, his financial expectations were pegged to the loan from which would come the funds to pay off the gratification to the Liberating Army, a debt for which Sucre felt himself personally accountable. His main concern regarding Madero's billetes was that they not spoil the domestic market for the treasury vales should the loan have to be floated domestically as he preferred.[7]

Like Bolivar, Sucre was unenthusiastic about resorting to a loan in order to pay the debt to the army, but by August 20, 1826, he was convinced that there was no other alternative. "Although the Congress wants it paid," he wrote Bolivar, "it still has not said from where and I do not know how to raise it except by loan." By September 1826 he expected that the Congress would give him the authorization to raise the loan by floating loan vales with a 2 million face value. Sucre suggested also to Bolivar that in addition to paying the gratifications to the Liberating Army, the proceeds from the loan float could be used to finance the sending of a military expedition from Bolivia to participate in the assault on Havana which the Liberator was contemplating. That Sucre clearly put the prizing of foreign military officers and even the financing of a distant military campaign ahead of reimbursing the holders of the internal debt revealed how distant his thinking on state debt was from the funding concept.[8]

Even though Madero's funding bill had already been introduced in the Congress, under pressure from Infante the bill authorizing the raising of a

1 million peso loan in the form of interest-bearing vales came up first for congressional debate on October 23, 1827. The deputies knew well that Sucre was pushing hard. The loan bill lacked much support in the Congress. Olañeta was a barometer of political sentiment. He objected to the amount of the loan and seemed to side with Madero, who objected that any consideration of the loan bill was "extemporaneous" since the law authorizing his funding program had not passed yet. But Sucre and Infante clearly preferred passage of the loan bill beforehand. Molina supported the bill as presented by the Congressional Commission. The bill was passed three weeks later. It contained a mere five one-sentence articles authorizing the executive to raise a 2 million peso loan at 6 percent annual interest with a floor of 60 percent of face value placed under selling price at which the loan vales were marketed. Article 3 stipulated a sinking fund (capital amorzante) capitalized at the rate of 1 percent annually of the total face value amount of loan vales issued. Article 4 stated that "all of the property, fixed and eventual" of the state would serve as collateral (presentará como hipotecas) for the loan. This was stronger than the term "guarantee" originally employed and was changed by the commission in the expectation that it would make the loan vales more attractive to foreign creditors. The predominant expectation in the Congress, in fact, was that the loan would be floated abroad, in view of the fact that Madero's billetes were expected to dominate the domestic credit market. The last article stipulated that all proceeds from the marketing of the loan vales would be used to pay off the external debt owed to Peru and to the Liberating Army. Clearly the role of Congress in this law was minimal and perfunctory in comparison to its role in the funding law.[9]

On December 1, 1826, Madero's funding bill was voted into law without any material changes, although there was considerable discussion of the state's ability to amortize the notes and meet the interest payments on them (a 3 million issue was contemplated) in view of revenue shortfall the administration was already experiencing. Two leading deputies, Olañeta and Carpio, who had questioned the loan bill enthusiastically supported the funding law. Madero was ill and unable to attend the debate. But his supporters argued that the funding bill was self-justifying. The 3 million corresponded to the amount of the public debt that Madero had documented; it was not pulled out of thin air. Further, the billetes put into circulation would be regulated by the amount of debt which the state validated through the Public Credit Administration. The funding law created a "concourse of creditors which it believed most qualified (dignos)" to receive state recognition. "Madero presented a quantity [in billetes] with which to guarantee these debts, a quantity that will increase as a ratio of the amount of increase in the public credit." These ideas were so self-evident that Madero did not need to explain them.[10]

Manuel María Aguirre was on the Congress's Commission on Public Credit and a close collaborator of Madero's. He was silent during the debate on the loan but waxed eloquent over the funding law. He pointed out the societal advantages of funding the internal debt, placing particular emphasis on affording relief to families orphaned by the war. He said that "these amounts put into circulation will expand the fortunes of private citizens which underpin all areas of industry and will finally multiply the volume of all taxes." His was a theme close to Madero's idea that through a funding system the wealth of the state became interactive with the wealth of the citizens. The administration's "true wealth is the sum of that of the citizens," he had said in one of his first decrees concerned with eliminating rigged auctions for the sale of public property. "The only intentions of the administration," he said in that decree, "are to foment the fortune of all of the citizens" by encouraging them to accumulate capital instead of frittering away their money on frivolous consumption. Madero seems to have been particularly hopeful that the laboring class (*jornaleros*), instead of living from day to day, would learn to save by buying the billetes and thereby improve the motivational structure of the society from below. If the problem at the base was dissolute behavior, the problem at the top was conspicuous consumption of luxury goods, including recreational haciendas. By channeling their money into billetes, wealthier Bolivians would be encouraged to shun speculative investments and ostentation and instead slowly accumulate their capital in the form of annuity payments from the states.[11]

In the bill passed by the Congress, the ceiling on the billetes was placed at 3 million pesos. The billetes were to be in denominations of 100 and 1,000 pesos and would bear a 6 percent annuity to be paid three times a year. The billetes were "guaranteed by all of the revenue, direct and indirect, which the Republic of Bolivia possesses now and may possess in the future; by all of its active credit lines and by all of the movable and immovable property of the Republic under special pledge [*hipoteca*]." The emphasis here was on state assets serving to *guarantee* the billetes, not on mortgaging them to the note holder much less allowing the use of the billetes to purchase state property. If this were not the case, the verb *hipotecar* would have been used instead of *garantizar*. This provision reflected

the Argentine example which carefully prohibited the use of public credit
billetes to purchase state properties. The bill also established a sinking
fund to be capitalized at 30,000 pesos in the first year which would start
the process of retiring the billetes. The fund's capital would be invested.
The bill established amortization offices in all of the departments to manage the sinking fund and disburse annuity payments on circulating billetes. These offices were to be "under the immediate protection of the
Congress and administered with entire independence of all other authority." Departmental treasuries were required to deposit monthly with the
amortization offices interest and amortization capital from their revenues
from direct taxation and from proceeds from the sale of mines and real
estate belonging to the state. It was illegal for the treasuries to divert
funds earmarked for deposit in the amortization offices to any other purpose. In the expectation that 3 million worth of billetes would be put into
circulation in 1827, the treasuries were required to deposit with the amortization offices 210,000 pesos to cover annuity obligations and 30,000 in
twelve monthly deposits into the sinking fund. The funding law included
forty-two elaborate articles compared to the five one-sentence articles of
the loan law.[12]

Having passed Sucre's loan bill and, shortly afterward, Madero's public
credit program, the Congress turned to the use of Madero's billetes to ab-
sorb the internal debt. All of the debts accruing against the Spanish state
up until 1809, as well as all of the debt and damage claims arising from
the operation of the guerrilla armies in Alto Peru, were to be consolidated
and converted into the billetes of the Public Credit Administration. Debts
contracted by the Spanish state after the revolt of the Audiencia in 1809
and the onset of the independence movement in Upper Peru were decided
by the Congress to be nonbinding. Holders of debts against the Spanish
state from the pre-1809 period would receive a face value amount of the
billetes which would yield to them, at the fixed 6 percent interest, 3 percent annually of the total amount of their claims. A wide range of creditors of the guerrilla armies was identified and slated to receive amounts of
billetes that would yield to them annual interest payments equivalent to 4
percent of their claims. Also, debts owed to the Spanish administration,
mainly in the form of back taxes, were made payable in Madero's billetes.
Employees of the Spanish state who had been forced to emigrate because
of favoritism to the independence cause were to be paid in billetes at a
face value equivalent to five years of lost salary. Clearly the returning
émigré population was making its presence felt politically. Madero was re-

ceptive. He submitted to the Congress a twenty-two-article draft law that broke down the émigré population into exact categories to which compensation in billetes was due.[13] It paid particular attention to indemnification of those émigrés who had returned to Bolivia but were unable to find jobs in the government. The bill dwelled at length on the indemnification rights of the widows of émigrés and their children. Article 2 of the bill virtually confined the legitimate émigrés to the Buenos Aires community. Madero's draft bill, which read like a social anatomy of the émigré population, was formulated into the law of January 11, 1827, represented the close identification of émigré cause with the funding law. It was a political breakthrough except that the law deleted the strong slant in Madero's bill toward the Buenos Aires community.

Significantly, Article 3 of a law of December 15 specifically excluded all censos belonging either to the church or to the welfare institutions from being redeemed through the billetes. The only exceptions were those cases in which the Public Credit Administration agreed in advance. In the main, amortization of the billetes was expected to occur through payments out of the sinking fund.[14]

The administration's budgetary outlook in 1826 was constrained mainly by the current expenditures to maintain the military establishment (701,419 pesos). These costs had constituted the largest drain on the departmental treasuries. In the Department of Santa Cruz, garrison costs were larger than the revenues of the department's treasury, while in Cochabamba and Chuquisaca they were over 70 percent of revenue. Garrison costs in La Paz and Potosí, with their larger revenue bases, amounted still to 40 percent of income. It was 40 percent also in Oruro, where garrison costs were about the same as in Santa Cruz but which had double the revenue. These military outlays would rise even higher in 1827, to over 1 million pesos including equipment and armament, because of the expansion of Bolivian units. Some relief came with the departure of the first Colombian units, yet the costs involved in these evacuations outweighed the saving in salaries and maintenance costs. It cost 70,000 pesos to get Voltigeros ready to be evacuated. In addition, and even more critically, the increased urgency imposed on the evacuation schedules by the anti-Colombian revolution in Peru increased the pressure from Sucre's compatriots for their share of the 1 million peso gratification.[15]

Sucre's frame of reference throughout 1827 was heavily influenced by the need he perceived to evacuate all of the Colombian units from Bolivia before the mutiny spread from Peru. It became for Sucre essentially a matter of squeezing money out of the domestic credit market to cover the costs of evacuation and paying off enough of the gratification owed the soldiers to satisfy them. Madero's billetes threatened to orient the debt market in the opposite direction. His billetes would need decades of gradual amortization before they began to become scarce enough for their market value to start to rise. Even if Sucre had ever considered using Madero's billetes to pay off the troop gratification, the troops would not be around long enough to collect interest payments or to wait for the market value of the billetes to increase. If he were going to try to pay them in state debt paper, that paper would have to have a relatively high immediate market value so military recipients could sell and leave. The real question facing Sucre was how to push his vales in the domestic market on the basis of an accelerated amortization program that would yield a high initial market price—exactly the reverse of Madero's funding concept.

If Sucre could have raised his loan abroad, this problem would have been avoided, yet the foreign option was out of the picture by February 1827. He had become convinced by March that the loan should take the form of vales circulated domestically, an alternative that "results in less or not at all encumbering," in comparison to a foreign loan. By this time he also knew that the revolution in Peru ruled out any chances of a Bolivian loan being floated in that country, whereas up to this point he had hoped to get Santa Cruz's help in convincing the Peruvian Congress to make the loan. Sucre's decree of February 1, 1827, announced the opening of bidding on subscriptions to a 2 million loan for a period of one hundred days, after which foreign subscriptions would be sought. The interest rate would be 6 percent, and all of the "fixed and eventual" property of the republic was offered, per the congressional law authorizing the loan, as collateral (hipoteca).[16] The domestic bidding was weak, and Sucre never used the foreign option.

While Madero stayed at Chuquisaca issuing his billetes through the Public Credit offices, Sucre in the company of Infante embarked on a three-month inspection tour of the departments. While in La Paz in early March 1827, and unknown to Madero, they determined to start the process of raising the loan through a domestic float. This decision was reached while the issuance of Madero's billetes had just barely begun. In fact the billetes had not yet reached La Paz because of slowness in the organization of the Public Credit Office there. This chronology is important in view of Infante's later allegation that it was the failure of Madero's billetes that prompted the decision to float the loan vales domestically. It is reasonable to speculate that Infante and Sucre heard advice in La Paz from local capitalists that the market for the loan vales would be more active if they were made negotiable for redemption of censos fixed against private property. In fact, as we know, censos were heavily concentrated in the La Paz Department. It is also reasonable to speculate that the advice Sucre and Infante heard in La Paz included pessimistic forecasts for Madero's funding billetes, precisely because they were not negotiable for purchase of either real property or for redemption of censos. And it would be better to steer the vales clear of the whole apparatus of the Public Credit Administration if the preliminary signs concerning its reception in La Paz were any guide. The La Paz branch of the Public Credit Administration was being very slowly and shakily organized, partly, at least, because of the ill health of the president of the office, a matter called to the attention of Madero by Infante and the prefect. Interestingly, Madero reminded both of them that the Public Credit apparatus was under the authority of the Congress and that the executive lacked any cognizance in its affairs. Finally, to continue this line of speculation, the fact that Infante could cite within days the positive reception of the loan program incorporating the La Paz "advice" suggests that the waters had been tested in advance.[17]

On March 12, 1827, at La Paz, Infante advised the prefect that it was necessary to raise a domestic loan to pay off the Peruvian debt and the gratification owed to the auxiliary troops. His plan involved a sweeping amortization scheme that abandoned the sinking fund concept. In the La Paz Department, creditors were to lend the administration 300,000 pesos in exchange for vales with a 500,000 face value and 6 percent annual interest. The purchasers of the vales "can with them buy any class of national goods [*cualquier clase de bienes nacionales*] and redeem every class of censos . . . [held] against their property." Infante explicitly included the censos held by the welfare establishments and the church.[18]

The rationale of the vales float was expounded further in a circular from Infante to the various departmental administrations. It rehearsed the terms of the congressional law authorizing Sucre to raise the loan either domestically or abroad. Sucre, the circular said, in deciding that a foreign loan would be too encumbering, "had meditated on all of the various alternatives which exist inside the Republic that could proportion the acquisition of a sum [of money] sufficient to satisfy the most urgent debts and has found one which results in the benefit of the property owners in Bolivia." The one Sucre "found" was the distribution in all of the depart-

ments of a vales with a face value of 1 million pesos, a real value of
600,000 pesos, and a 6 percent annual yield, which would give to the vales
holders the right to redeem censos against their properties "as if the vales
were real money." The circular continued by stating that "the property
owners of the Republic have their goods so laden with censos that His
Excellency [Sucre] does not doubt that they will take advantage of this
occasion [especially in view of loan conditions which are] highly favorable
to property owners."

Article 3 of these conditions stated that the "vales holders can with them
buy any class of national property including those of welfare institutions
and redeem any kind of censos on property belonging to welfare institutions or convents, chaplaincies, monasteries or cathedrals."

Article 4 placed the vales program outside of the Public Credit administration by specifying that the vales could be sold or negotiated only
"with the intervention of the Prefect of the Department." He would deal
only with actual vales holders and decide whether to pay them interest or
to take the vales for purchase of public properties or redemption of censos
on property.

Article 5 dealt with the cases in which the property purchase belonged
to welfare institutions or where the censos redeemed by vales had formed
part of the endowment of those institutions, convents, monasteries, or
cathedrals. It stated only that the administration would "recognize the
principals" involved and pay equivalent amounts to the affected institutions, or would in the cases of censos pass them over to other property still
owned by the administration.[19]

Significantly, the circular did not mention explicitly state fincas and
haciendas. The dominant emphasis was on censos being redeemable by
the vales. The decision to widen the market for vales to include the state
haciendas was apparently reached later by Sucre and Infante, perhaps
with a view to Cochabamba, where the hacienda holdings were larger
than in La Paz and could be expected to outweigh censos redemption in
terms of marketing the vales. Interestingly, Sucre and Infante stopped in
Cochabamba after their visit in La Paz on their "inspection tour."

The subject of placing state haciendas on the auction block had already
been raised in connection with a congressional search for means to finance
the Mining Bank at Potosi. The inclusion of state haciendas in the Sucre
market plan for vales placed it at cross purposes with the congressional
plan for the bank.

Derivative Conflict: The Mining Bank Debate

The difference between Sucre's vales and Madero's billetes was nominally the question of the desirability of the short-term negotiability of state debt paper. But between the vales and the billetes were underlying differences in social and economic philosophy, including what is today known as the privatization issue, as well as political differences. These larger differences were highlighted by an ongoing debate in the Congress concerning a projected sell-off of state haciendas to capitalize the Mining Bank.

Despite an early interest Sucre had taken in reorganizing the bank, the matter became increasingly theoretical to him. As he focused on selling off the mines or using them for collateral for his loan, he lost interest in asserting an active state role in fomenting the mining industry itself. Yet in the opinion of many Bolivians, the fomenting of the mining industry was the key to Bolivia's economic future. The General Assembly had cited the fomenting of the mining industry and capitalization of the Mining Bank in its bill of particulars. The mining community at Oruro had developed a project for capitalizing the bank at 50,000 pesos, a project Bolivar had initially encouraged.[20]

Support for developing the industry was strong in the Constituent Congress, where a bill to have the administration raise capital for the Mining Bank was introduced in August 1826. According to this bill, the capital was supposed to come out of proceeds from the sales of haciendas that the government owned and leased out or against which it held liens in the form, for example, of an obra pía which it had nationalized. The debate about the bank was simultaneously about the justification for a sell-off of these state assets. It anticipated, implicitly, the difference between the funding program (whose billetes would yield annuities paid out of a permanent fund and would not be negotiable for state property or for redemption of censos) and Sucre's concept of contracting a floating loan (whose vales were negotiable for state property and censos). Was it better to place state assets under private ownership in order to gain the advantages of free land market or to keep them under state ownership in order to regulate land distribution? Would the money raised by the sale of these state haciendas and vested in the Mining Bank be more profitable than the the rental value of these lands leased out by the state?[21]

A considerable amount of support for the sell-off of state haciendas came from the "circulationist" theory of political economy. As one delegate put it, "All securities or assets put into circulation improve their interest yields in proportion to their velocity. . . . The haciendas . . . placed in the bank will produce more value. . . . The bank could raise much more money from the loaning out of the proceeds from their sale than the money raised from leasing them out."[22]

Some delegates contended that renters of state haciendas or state administrators allowed the haciendas to decay, while outright owners would have more of a stake in their development and upkeep. In contrast to his statist position on the diezmos issue, Olañeta was at the forefront of this privatization argument. He cited the example of the Jesuit missions (expropriated by the Crown after the expulsion in 1767). Those that were auctioned off to private owners flourished. Those kept under state administration "have not been heard from since." Outright sale of the haciendas was preferable to leasing them out, both for the private sector and for the state. Private buyers would have the chance to become landowners, the state would gain from good auction prices, and the properties themselves would be free from being held in the "dead hands" of the state. One delegate, Molina, summed up the arguments in favor. He noted that "ignorance of the laws of circulation of specie, and its advantages, has been the cause of hoarding silver, building walls three feet thick around homes, and the general misery of life in Bolivia" and continued: "The value of the haciendas will have a different basis arising from their sale. The buyer will care for them more as well as produce more. The state will profit from higher competitive prices for them. The state benefits the private sector by creating a circulatory fund of capital to foment industry and capitalize the Mining Bank. Banks conserve public and private wealth and provide a basis for foreign credit . . . sale of the [state haciendas] benefits the private and the public interest."[23]

Yet there were objections to these arguments. Implicitly, these counterarguments supported the spirit of Madero's funding concept of the state debt, insofar as it did not permit state debt paper to be used to purchase state assets, rather than the Sucre-Infante concept of state debt paper, which did. These new arguments raised a fundamental question: was Bolivian society better served by a process whereby land came under the control of the wealthy few able to offer the most in public auctions? Would not the continuation of state ownership of the lands, even with its attendant inefficiencies, have the virtue of preventing accumulation of the land in a way that would only serve to widen the distance between classes and, derivatively, make it more difficult to create an egalitarian society of savers in the sense of Madero's funding system's objectives? It was argued that since only a few "capitalists" in fact would be able to bid in the auctions, "all of the haciendas would end up in their hands at their prices." Further, mixing private acquisitive interest into the picture, through the auction of state haciendas, would inevitably risk corruption of the public interest despite any safeguards that might be placed on the auctions. These arguments considered the maintenance of state equity in the haciendas to be more valuable socially than increasing the capital of a Mining Bank was economically. Even economically, the concept of bank-led growth in the mining industry was viewed skeptically, and considerable information on failed European banks was introduced.[24]

Continued state control over haciendas was critical also to the conduct of policy in the educational and welfare areas. Much of the endowment portfolios of the public educational and welfare establishments set up by Sucre were based on income from the haciendas owned by the state or from the censos liens held by the state against haciendas. Privatization of the state haciendas through sale or through the redemption of state-held censos threatened the progress that had already been made in the welfare and educational fields. The prospect of a privatization of haciendas was of a piece with the prospect of redemption of censos raised by Sucre's loan vales. Both evoked apprehension for those interested in the viability of the state institutions in education and welfare and in keeping this whole area on the state agenda. Thus, in respect to the pending bill for the privatization of state haciendas in the Department of La Paz, the Welfare Board, charged with the management of the endowments of the welfare and educational establishments in its department, raised serious objections. It did not see the merit of allowing the haciendas to fall under "capitalist ownership" if it meant that they ceased to be part of the endowments of the welfare institutes, which it necessarily did. The sale of these haciendas risked decapitalizing the public institutes that had been wrested into place with so much effort and rhetoric by the Sucre administration. These arguments applied by extension to the Sucre-Infante plan to sell off state-held censos by permitting their redemption for the loan vales.[25]

Those opposing the sale argued that weight should be given to the objections of the La Paz Welfare Board and that more information on the linkage of the haciendas to welfare endowments be secured before any reforms in the status of the haciendas were permitted.[26]

Other delegates were not worried. They believed that there was a public interest in the preservation of the educational and welfare establishments,

and as such they would be "safe and secure" despite the sale of haciendas
figuring in their endowments. But specifics were not supplied. The main
point was that haciendas would produce "more value" to be placed in the
bank than in the endowment portfolios of the state institutions. The value
of the state haciendas would be merely "positioned differently" as a result
of arising from their sale. Fears of concentration of the land in the hands
of the wealthy few were groundless, since most buyers could not afford to
buy more than one piece of land. The arguments of the Welfare Board of
La Paz (which anticipated arguments that came later from Madero's Public Credit boards in the matter of censos redemptions) were parochial and
based on "opposition to capitalists." It would be "demeaning to credit
its arguments and to have to consult with that Board about principles of
political economy."[27]

Making state haciendas purchasable through vales created a double
bind from the perspective of the Mining Bank debate. First, it threatened
to "steal" proceeds of hacienda sales from the bank. Second, it conflicted
with the prominent social philosophy in the debate, which held that sale
of state haciendas was wrong.

It might be supposed that the Sucre administration would take a leading role in discouraging the sale of those state haciendas that figured into
the endowments of the state institutes that Sucre himself had so meticu-
lously created. Yet Infante's comments on the subject revealed a strong
bias toward privatization that appears disingenuous in view of events.

> The government will apply all of its public force to protect the repub-
> lic, the [Mining] Bank and all of the public welfare and educational es-
> tablishments. The La Paz Welfare Board's opposition to the sale should
> not be credited. If there were no buyers, the haciendas simply would
> not be sold. If it fears that the haciendas would be bought up by just a
> few monopolists, it is not just that the rich be prevented from expanding
> their capital. Haciendas are better off in private hands. Even if the state
> could meet its costs and foment the public establishments, it should give
> them [the haciendas] away. The capitalization of the bank will avoid
> contraband in silver and the customs revenues will increase to the Na-
> tional Treasury. . . . Public auctions [of state haciendas] will be scrupu-
> lously held, if the Congress authorizes the executive to go ahead with
> the sale.[28]

In fact, the proceeds from the sale of the haciendas would never reach
the Mining Bank but would rather be absorbed by Sucre's loan vales.
And, Sucre's archipelago of public institutions would be left in the lurch.

Marketing the Treasury Vales: The June 12 Decrees

As might be expected, Madero was not enthusiastic about the whole idea of floating the loan domestically. He was clearly falling out of favor inside the Sucre administration at the time the loan decisions were being made. On the same day that Infante wrote his loan instructions to the prefect of La Paz, he wrote a note to Madero chastising him for laxity in developing uniform accounting codes for the departmental treasuries and for failing to make available to the public the figures on income and expenditures during the period of the Sucre administration. Madero was clearly affronted but made a correct reply to Infante. In fact, he was not even advised beforehand about the pilot loan Infante had set up in La Paz, and he was able to react to the Infante's circular only after it had been sent out to all of the departments. Two years later, Infante would make out an elaborate case that Madero's billetes were failing due to the ineptitude of Madero himself, who had overestimated demand and had failed to market them effectively. Infante contended that after he and Sucre returned to Chuquisaca in May 1827 from their "inspection tour," they discovered that Madero had overissued the billetes and that many people whose claims for indemnification were illegitimate had already received billetes. Since the "damage was already done," Sucre made the decision to protect the market value of the vales by making them negotiable for state haciendas (these were included in the June 12 decree, discussed below) and redemption of censos. But we know that this decision was reached in early March before it could have been clear that the "damage was done." Rather Sucre and Infante wanted their loan vales to stay clear of a market that was expected to be sluggish for Madero's billetes.[29]

In the meantime, Madero drafted a letter to Infante concerning "the loan which His Excellency the President is trying to raise." He objected to the terms of the loan not being published as a decree but taking the form of a circular to the departmental prefects. He objected to the loan being handled through prefects instead of through the Public Credit Administration where it belonged. He objected to inconsistencies between the loan conditions stipulated in the circular and the original decree authorizing the loan and specified in this connection the absence of provision of a sinking fund to amortize the loan vales. Madero included gratuitously in his note to Infante a copy of the congressional law "in order that he [Infante] present it to Sucre for whatever resolution he sees fit to make."[30]

Although his letter did not articulate this particular issue, Madero was obviously concerned that the vales would eclipse his billetes. To a reader familiar with Madero's philosophy, his technical criticisms of the vales were proxies for his larger concern that allowing vales to be used to purchase state haciendas would subsidize the consumptive interests of the privileged landowning class instead of furthering the legitimate purpose of state debt policy—"fomenting the fortunes of all of the citizens." Madero believed (like Rivadavia in Argentina) that the creation of savings capital in the hands of the many, rather than the accumulation of land in the hands of the few, was a more sound and egalitarian concept of wealth. He saw the funding system as a means to this end. Making state debt paper negotiable for state haciendas or for the redemption of censos undermined the funding philosophy that was predicated on the amortization of state debt paper through the slow constant stream of annuity payments from a permanent sinking fund.

Madero voiced his concerns over the loan float to Sucre, offered to resign, and sent him a lengthy note on April 12 which unfortunately does not exist; its contents can be reconstructed from Sucre's response to it, which is in the Bolivian archives. Madero's letter detailed his objections to the loan and expressed the fear that the handling of the loan outside of the Public Credit Administration would indicate the administration's loss of faith in that institution. It said also that the market value of the billetes was bound to suffer as a result of the appearance of the vales. It reiterated Madero's concerns over the absence of a sinking fund provision in the loan project. "This is as essential in this matter as the payment of interest," he had said in his earlier note to Infante and undoubtedly said much the same to Sucre. He evidently expanded his concerns over the conversion of vales into censos redemptions by citing the situation of the state welfare and educational establishments which had to rely on censos for their income. How would they be paid for their lost endowments? Would the departmental treasuries be able to finance them? Sucre's letter of response is the best text available concerning his concept of state debt policy. It is significant because of its candor and the fact that it was addressed to a Bolivian. It is still unpublished and has had an elusive history. It was a letter that Sucre probably would liked to have had back.[31]

Sucre obliquely linked Madero's offer to resign to émigré boycott politics. Sucre said that normally he would oppose Madero's resignation, but he then cited "superficial disturbances which enemies of the government have created in Potosi." By this reference he clearly meant efforts of émigrés returning from Buenos Aires to attack Sucre by generating opposition among the population to his direct taxes and to his administration's domination by foreigners. If Madero was sensitive to these politics, Sucre did not want to embarrass him by refusing his resignation: "If you give credence to the popular discontent [in Potosi], I don't want to compromise you."

Sucre began his letter by noting to Madero that the conflict between him (Madero) and Infante should not be made public. "But also," he said,

it is certain that [the Administration] has to pay its debts and in this conflict has to recur to some expedient. Whatever this expedient should be depends on the circumstances and mine are not suited for calculations which much await a late result. My quality of being a foreigner places me in the position of having to leave the soonest possible. In the meantime I should satisfy the obligations I have toward my comrades to see to it that they get paid [their prize money]. Bolivia decreed to the Liberating Army 1,000,000 pesos without having them. And my comrades believe that it is me, and not the Congress of the Republic, the one who has the obligation to pay and the worst of all is that this error involves my standing with them. Decreeing this prize without having the funds to cover it was the most perfect invention for demoralizing the army. Now, the only remedy is to pay them. This is now my objective. You go ahead thinking how you can help me achieve it in the shortest time.

Sucre left open the question of Madero's resignation, saying that with the country still peaceful, he "would try to abbreviate the time within which to return to my country, where some disturbances [the Venezuelan insurrection against the national administration at Bogota] require that good Colombians rally around their country to confront the factious elements. If you want to wait, we can finish together our work, and quickly."

In the second part of his letter, which he wrote after Madero's letter had arrived, Sucre dealt somewhat cryptically with Madero's concern about the fate of state educational and welfare institutions whose endowments became transformed into loan vales that ceased to bear interest once turned into the treasury. He said only that it was true that "since the redemption of censos occurs in the treasury the vales remain amortized there. The method of achieving the amortization of the amount which the treasury recognizes [in the converted endowments] I will explain to you when I see you—but you understand [in the meantime] that the treasuries do not have to disburse even one peso of their ordinary revenues for anything. When I explain myself you will see my reasons; if they are false I will be convinced." It was never really explained and the whole network of welfare establishments established at the cost of great effort by Sucre would be placed in a kind of limbo as a result.

Sucre delved in detail into the whole matter of the relationship between the vales and the billetes and the question of how far he was willing to place the vales under the authority of the Public Credit Administration. His theme was that the vales possessed a larger inherent value than the billetes because they were issued by the executive branch to people of choice for specific purposes and with a legal limit placed on their discount price. By contrast, the billetes, he implied, were of less inherent value because they were not executively managed but widely and loosely disseminated by the Congress through the Public Credit Administration. In Sucre's biased formulation the billetes were a kind of vague, floating debt while the vales were like guided missiles.

> I understand from what I have observed in people that they will place a higher value on vales issued through the departmental treasuries than if they are issued through the Public Credit Administration. But if you feel that this will disrupt things [*esto altere el orden*] then the vales will be deposited in the Public Credit Administration, so that from there they can be issued to interested persons, although they will lose their value in this circumstance. The loan vales do not go into circulation but one time, which is when the buyers sell them to property owners who want to redeem censos with them. Since the redemption occurs in the treasury, the vales remain amortized there. . . .

> Since the executive does not have a role in the Public Credit billetes, it was necessary to have resort to this loan, authorized by the Congress. In addition, the loan vales can be given by the executive to investors at the fixed price of 60 percent of face value, whereas the Public Credit billetes have no fixed price. . . . By making assignments in vales to military creditors for amounts equivalent to what is owed them, in order that they start to negotiate the vales when they receive them, we are all able to get out of a lot of debt. And they have not lost [as they would if they were paid in billetes] because the vales have been put into circulation at an effective price of 60 percent of face value.

The features of the loan program as designed by Infante and approved by Sucre were formalized into the controversial decrees of June 12, 1827. Madero initially refused flatly to sign them but then agreed to after he was given the opportunity to do some redrafting. The first decree simply stated the terms of the loan vales—1 million face value, 60 percent real value, and 6 percent annual interest—and housed the project in the departmental treasuries. Madero had lost the battle to bring the loan under the auspices of his Public Credit Administration. According to the second decree, vales could be used to buy properties (including haciendas) belonging to the state or the welfare institutions, or to redeem leases on private property belonging to the welfare institutions, to convents, to capellanías, to monasteries, or to cathedrals. The billetes were allowed to participate with the vales in these transactions, and the decree to this extent accommodated Madero's concerns and aimed at increasing the value of the notes along with the vales.

Madero could not but have helped feeling ambivalent about this method of "amortizing" his billetes; he probably had already given up on the sinking fund. The decrees stated that the state-owned haciendas, including those entailed in censos that were vested over to educational and welfare establishments, could be bought at public auctions with half loan vales and half billetes or with loan vales exclusively. In these cases the principal of the vested censos would be recognized by the treasuries and paid out to those affected state institutions triannually by the treasuries. The treasuries would recognize principals in the converted endowment amounting only up to 2 percent or 3 percent of the total appraised value of the underlying property. Thus, for example, if a welfare establishment got income from annual payments on a censo it held against a hacienda that was auctioned off for state debt paper, the treasury of the department would be obligated to pay it annually 2 percent or 3 percent of the auction price. Loan vales returning to the treasuries through purchases of properties or redemption of censos would not return to circulation, while billetes would not return to circulation without the express consent of the administration. No mention was even made of any sinking fund in the June 12 decrees. "Amortization" of state vales and billetes was to occur exclusively through the negotiation of that paper for purchase of state haciendas and redemption of censos held against private property and estates.[32]

The June 12 decrees effectively were a death warrant for the Bolivian funding law.

Hacienda Sales for Debt Paper

Sucre had intended originally to distribute the vales directly to military officers as payment of the gratification owed to them. He was mainly concerned with the payment of Colombian officers—Fernandez, Galindo, Geraldino, Leal, Alarcon, and Molina were to be the first recipients—but he also intended to distribute some vales to the former guerrilla leaders in Upper Peru in order to solidify their allegiance to the cause of the Liberating Army and to accomplish other political proposes which he did not identify to Bolivar. But gradually these political purposes gave way to the distribution of the vales exclusively to pay off Colombian military forces in order that they could be evacuated. He was aware of some popular pressure for the departure of the Colombian garrisons, although he felt that the property owners wanted them to stay. But by September 1827, Sucre was fed up with Peruvian "calumnies" against his administration, and said that "up to now it has been these [Colombian] forces which have kept me here but shortly nothing will make me forbear longer."[33]

By September, Sucre had elicited wide agreement in the Colombian army to accept the vales as payment of their gratification. Sucre's intention was that the soldiers sell the vales to Bolivians who would use them to buy state haciendas and to redeem censos on their property. The vales were sent out from the Ministry of Treasury in denominations of 100 and 1,000 pesos to the departmental treasuries, while drafts on the vales were given out to military personnel through the Ministry of the Interior. By the end of 1827, vales amounting to 890,000 pesos face value were distributed among the departmental treasuries. Of these, 551,000 had been assigned to military personnel, with by far the largest share being assigned in La Paz, which was the staging area for the departure of Colombian units—Pichincha, Voltigeros, the Grenadiers, and Husars. In La Paz the vales were assigned to individual officers as well as in blocs to troop units. In the other departments, vales were assigned to individual officers, many of whom—Geraldino was a prominent example—had married Bolivians and planned to stay. Table 3.4 shows the vales spread.

The uses postulated for the vales under the June 12 decrees were not being immediately exploited as vigorously as Sucre and Infante had hoped. Military officers reported to Sucre the difficulties they were encountering in selling their vales to civilians. Sucre and Infante, therefore, encouraged the process by inviting "the greatest adherents of the State" to commence buying state haciendas with billetes and vales, to set an example for civilians. To facilitate this enterprise, peso gifts which had been conferred by the Congress on military participants in the independence movement [haberes militares] were made equivalent to loan vales for the purposes of the June 12 decree. These decisions created an immediate conflict with the

Table 3.4. Loan Vales Assigned on Account of the 1 Million Pesos Decreed
to the Liberating Army (face value amounts)

La Paz	
To General Figueredo	25,000
To Pichincha Batallón	100,000
To Second Squadron of Grenadiers and Third Squadron of Husars	100,000
To Coronel Braun, to Husars Lieutenant José Ponces, and to Ensign Juan Pablo Correa	22,500
To Surgeon Antonio Merique	9,100
To various officers of the Ayacucho Batallón	12,100
To various officers of Husars	8,500
To various officers of Pichincha Batallón	25,833
To Ficico Ratera	2,500
To Sub Lieutenant Espinosa	500
To Major Gomes	500
Total	306,533
Cochabamba	
To Coronel Geraldino	8,300
To General Heres	25,000
To Lieutenant Coronel Castanon	7,500
To Coronel Guerrero	8,300
To Coronel Galindo	8,300
Total	57,400
Chuquisaca	
To General Castillo	25,000
To General Necochea	33,833
To Coronel O'Connor	8,300
To Lieutenant Coronel Alarcon	7,500
To Captain Miguel Salgar	5,000
To Lieutenant Arevalo	3,300
Total	82,933

Source: *Condor*, January 12, 1828.

congressional resolution that arose from the debate over the Mining Bank. It had instructed the executive to apply all proceeds from the sale of state haciendas to the state welfare and educational institutions whose endowments were affected and also to capitalization of the Mining Bank.[34]

The Sucre administration was already on record in supporting requests from military personnel that they be given state haciendas for their haberes. Specifically, it interpreted the phrase "national goods" (*bienes nacionales*), employed in the December 30, 1826, congressional law conferring them on independence fighters, to include these haciendas. Madero had placed a far more restrictive interpretation on this phrase in the law and confined it to property which was purely public—the mines and some lands—but excluded property that formed a part of the "social capital"—obras pías, capellanías, and real estate whose income was vested over to the state institutions in welfare and education. Since most state-owned haciendas had censos on them held by welfare, under Madero's interpretation they could not be purchased by independence fighters with their haberes or with vales or billetes. Infante placed no such strictures on the sale of state-owned haciendas, and of course the June 12 decree also made the whole range of censos held by the state institution, as well as obras pías and capellanías, fair game for liquidation with state debt paper. Thus Infante instructed the La Paz prefect to identify all of the vales concessionaires under the December 30 law and to allocate to them haciendas whose appraised value was equivalent to the amount of their prize money. Later, Infante approved the petition of the widow of an independence fighter to purchase a state-owned hacienda, using state haberes, billetes, and vales at face value. This approval was given even before the June 12 decree was in effect.[35]

Lieutenant Colonel Pedro Alarcon, Sucre's aide, was one of the administrations's "greatest adherents" who was "invited" to buy state property using vales and billetes. Clearly, the cheaper Alarcon could get the paper, which he could use at face value for half of the purchase price, the more lucrative for him the deal would be. In fact Alarcon, who originally intended to leave for Colombia, changed his mind and accepted the "invitation." He had already endorsed 1,900 of the 7,500 loan vales leaving him with a total of 6,000. He then purchased 400 vales at 60 percent face value. He also purchased 6,000 worth of billetes, probably at 15 percent face value. This gave him the legal amounts of half vales and half billetes to purchase a state hacienda. His cash outlay was therefore 1,140 pesos (60 percent of the 400 loan vales and 15 percent of the 6,000 in billetes). With the 12,000 in vales and billetes he proceeded to buy in a "public" auction a state-owned hacienda appraised at 12,000 pesos, considerably lower than the appraisal made four years earlier of 90,000 pesos. Alarcon's "bid" won, and he acquired the hacienda and provided an excellent example of the "advantages" that would accrue to those willing to acquire state debt paper.[36]

Another instance of a hacienda purchase by "adherents" of the administration—this time by General Fernandez—threw some light on the difficulties raised by the policy of making billetes and vales and haberes convertible into ownership of state-owned haciendas. By virtue of the congressional law of July 31, 1826, state-owned haciendas had been authorized for sale at public auction with the proceeds to go into capital of the Mining Bank and state institute endowments. The hacienda of Palca had been bought before the June 12 decree took effect, and the purchase contract was in pesos. Yet Fernandez, apparently initially with the support of Sucre, was making an effort to renegotiate the contract in vales and billetes. A similar case had occurred in La Paz, where the prefect had supported the rights of the Mining Bank to receive in pesos the proceeds from the sale of state-owned haciendas. Obviously, the bank preferred to receive money rather than state debt paper. Infante took the position in this case, and subsequently in the Fernandez case, that haciendas earmarked for sale in order to capitalize the Mining Bank and in fact sold before June 12 did not come under the jurisdiction of the decree of that date. Decrees could not take effect retroactively, he said. Sales of state-owned haciendas occurring after June 12, however, did come under the new provisions. "In sum," he said, "haciendas sold before the publication of the 12th of June have to be paid in real money which is what was stipulated [in the Congressional law] and the proceeds employed in the Mining Banks according to the resolution of Congress. And those which are sold afterwards sell for billetes and vales and the proceeds employed in the objectives expressed in the decree of June 12." He added, "All of this is so obvious that it appears there is no necessity to enter into explanations." But could the executive by virtue of its own decree preempt a congressional law and still maintain any semblance of constitutionality? In Infante's analysis, there was no problem in doing this, so long as it did not do it retroactively. Yet this conclusion was far from obvious, and the administration's reported favoritism toward Fernandez did not help matters, a fact Infante himself acknowledged.[37]

Censos Redemptions and State Welfare Dislocation

Sucre appointed Manuel Aguirre to replace Madero. He was the congressional deputy most conversant with state finances and was an active collaborator of Madero's. Like Madero, Aguirre was apprehensive about allowing state debt paper to be used in the redemption censos on property that served a social function, or represented a kind of social capital, whether it functioned through the welfare institutes, the family, or the church. Aguirre used a specialized form of censos called *capellanías de sangre* (family capellanías) as a pretext to question Infante about the validity of the clause in the June 12 decree that permitted vales and billetes to be used to redeem censos.

Unlike obras pías where in a will the church was made the beneficiary of future income from a private estate, in the case of the capellanías de sangre the beneficiary was a relative of the person writing the will with the church acting as a guardian of the trust. Capellanías could revert to the church on the death of the beneficiary (in which case they were no longer "de sangre") or they could be passed on through generations. Allowing capellanías, especially capellanías de sangre, to be liquidated by state debt paper under the June 12 decree posed a problem for Aguirre since they were clearly not included in the "fixed and eventual property of the state" specified as collateral for the vales in the congressional law. Moreover under Article 154 of the Constitution, capellanías de sangre were identified as "free properties" not alienable to the state and declared to be for the benefit of their actual possessors and conducive to the continuity of family structures. The inclusion of capellanías de sangre in Article 6 of the June decree therefore presented "difficulties." Aguirre used this occasion— raising questions about the status of capellanías de sangre—to express his larger concern to Infante over the deterioration of the endowments of the public welfare institutions that might occur as a result of allowing state debt paper to substitute for them. He selected the case of Geraldino's purchase of haciendas formerly yielding income to welfare institutions to illustrate his concern.[38]

Like Alarcon, Geraldino was a Colombian, but he had married a Bolivian and had become a citizen. He had received from Sucre 8,300 in loan vales. He transferred them to Cochabamba, where, while he was prefect of the department, he combined his vales with 4,080 in military haberes he had received and 12,266 billetes he had purchased in order to buy state-owned haciendas for 24,000. But 1,700 pesos from the production of the haciendas in 1826 had been vested to the welfare institutions and to a monastery. Aguirre found discrepancies in the provisions in the June 12 decree concerning endowments that were bought with debt paper. He cited Article 5 of the decree which required treasuries to pay to welfare boards an amount equivalent to the yield channeled to welfare in 1826 from haciendas which were subsequently sold for government vales or billetes. Yet Article 7 stated that only principals yielding annually 2 or 3 percent of the auction price of the haciendas would be recognized in the treasuries. In the case of Geraldino's haciendas it had produced 1,150 pesos for welfare in 1826 which, per Article 5, should be the amount paid by the treasury to the welfare boards. But Article 7 stipulated a much lower amount under the criteria of 2 and 3 percent of the auction price. If the larger amount were recognized, the interest payments due on the amount of billetes involved in the purchase (since these formed only half of the purchase price and neither vales nor haberes drew interest after returning to treasury) were inadequate to cover it. The only alternative Aguirre could see was to opt for the lower amount, thereby devaluing the endowment of the state institution, or to allow the Treasury to apply to the gap in welfare income created by Geraldino's purchase the interest from other billetes it had received.[39]

The impact of state debt paper on the educational and welfare structure of Bolivia grew in the later part of 1827 and in the first months of 1828. Clearly the expectation that Sucre would not stay in Bolivia beyond August, if that long, encouraged individuals to take advantage of the June 12 decree, while the administration was still in place, to wipe out censos against their property.

The records of state debt paper transactions in Chuquisaca demonstrate the consequences of the June 12 decree. The caption reads "Accounting of individuals who have made their payments in this administration in billetes of public credit for their debts contracted before 1825." There followed a list of thirty-five individuals who applied billetes to an intricate variety of debt, including diezmos taxes and sales taxes, tribute taxes and clerical taxes, with the median debt being 550 pesos. The total was 35,198 pesos of canceled debt. This much was apparently recorded before the June 12 decrees. After that date, the phrase "and to buy properties and to redeem censos principals" was added to the document's caption. There followed a listing of billetes used for the new purposes of buying properties and redeeming censos. (Alarcon headed the list with 6,000 billetes applied to his hacienda purchase.) Following this section is a list of individuals using vales and haberes to buy mortgages on haciendas and fincas that were vested over to a welfare institution. (Alarcon headed this list with 6,000 vales applied to his hacienda purchases.) The median amount transacted in the post–June 12 period is 2,050 pesos. The document records the change in the pattern of transactions in state debt paper before and after the June 12 decree: larger amounts, more acquisition of real property, fewer purchases, and massive inroads into the capital of welfare institutions. Two-thirds of the documented pre-1825 debt of 93,799 with all of the moral and social entailments in that, went unpaid due to the diversion of billetes into censos and property.[40]

The pattern was different in the Department of Cochabamba, where a bonanza developed in the purchase of haciendas with state debt paper. It constituted the main vehicle of invasion of welfare endowments. State debt paper worth 214,080 was employed in the direct purchase of state-owned haciendas, every one of them having some portion of its income vested over to welfare institutes. The amount of 28,916 in state debt paper was used to wipe out censos, again all of which formed parts of the endowments of welfare institutions. Billetes worth 123,914 figured into these purchases, with the balance made up by vales and haberes.[41]

In Potosi the scope of transactions involving state debt paper was smaller, amounting to 102,197 pesos in debt paper applied to the liquidation of pre-1825 debts (30,500), censos (51,078), and haciendas (33,925). These figures show that the amount of welfare institution capital that was transformed into debt paper was 86,406 pesos.[42]

In the Department of La Paz the purchase of haciendas was limited because most of the haciendas were privately owned and a lot of land was held communally by Indians. On the other hand, state debt paper was used massively to redeem censos held against existing haciendas, including obras pías and capellanías held by welfare institutions.

Thus by February, 51,516 worth of censos income supporting welfare was transformed into billetes and 54,197 worth of pre-1825 debt was canceled by billetes. Sixty-five thousand vales were transacted in La Paz. Lacking precise figures, if we assume that half were applied to censos and the other half to state and welfare property purchases, we conclude that 84,116 worth of censos supporting welfare were wiped out by vales and billetes by February 1828.[43] The Colegio de Ciencias alone had 32,000 of its censos capital transformed into billetes and the Asilo de Huérfanos 20,000. If we extrapolate these ratios to November 1828 in order to compare them to Cochabamba and Potosi, we can arrive at an estimate of 156,772 censos redeemed and 139,632 in property purchased from the state and welfare institutions. (See table 3.5.)

Sucre became actively concerned in the La Paz case about the erosion of the capital base of the educational and welfare institutions. The treasury reported that 1,545 was due to two institutions—the College of Sciences and the Orphans Asylum—in lost endowment and wondered where this money was to come from. The answer from Infante was not long in arriv-

Table 3.5. Transactions in Debt Paper by Department, 1827–28

Department	Billetes	Vales	Haberes	Pre-1825 debt	Censos redemption	Property purchased
Chuquisaca	53061	6100	11716	35198	39669	31251
Potosi	58857	30500	13970	37056	51078	33925
Cochabamba	123914 (est)	41297	70799	28914	28916	214080
La Paz	103400	65000	32178 (est)	54197	83116 (est)	45028 (est)
La Paz*	219275	138125	68378	109367	156772	139632

Sources:
Chuquisaca: Tesoro Publico, January 7, 1828, MH, t. 10, no. 10.
              Tesoro Publico, January, 1828, MH, t. 10, no. 2.
              Tesoro Publico, January, 1828, MH, t. 10, no. 2.
              Tesoro Publico, February 15, 1828, MH, t. 10, no. 10.
Potosi: Tesoro Publico, November 1828, MH, t. 10, no.
Cochabamba: Prefect, November 28, 1828, MH, t. 9, no. 9.
La Paz: Ministry of Hacienda, March 13, 1828, MH, t. 9, no. 5. Ministry of Hacienda,
              February 7, 1828, MH, t. 12, no. 2. Tesoro Publico, April 11, 1828, MH, t. 10,
              no. 11. Haberes are estimates, based on the average of the other departments
              and factored into the censos and property redemption estimates.
La Paz*:   Average rates of the period from June 1827 to February 1828 extrapolated to
              November 1828.

ing. Sucre had decided that 30,000 in billetes received in the treasury should be transferred to the colleges and 20,000 to the asylum. From the Public Credit Boards, then, these institutions could receive the interest due on their billetes—3,000 pesos annually at the 6 percent rate—which would almost double their original endowment loss, and the treasury would be kept free of direct financing responsibilities for them. Sucre's objective, Infante said, was to give "protection to the public institutions without prejudice to the Treasury." But just how the Public Credit Board was supposed to pay out these 3,000 pesos in interest to the institutions in question without receiving them first from the Treasury was not explained in Infante's note. If the interest payments were not met, the onus would fall on the Public Credit Board and not on the treasury. This was one meaning of the phrase "without prejudice to the Treasury." Another intent behind the phrase was that the treasury be freed from the direct claims by the state institutions on its revenues and be able to use the Public Credit Board as a buffer if needed.[44]

Although Sucre agonized about the decapitalizing of the educational and welfare institutions, his formula for financing the endowment losses of these institutions was not reassuring because it did not obligate the trea-

sury. Even before the June 12 decree was issued or the prospect was even
in sight that these endowments might be converted into debt paper, it was
clear that Sucre did not intend that the financing of these institutions
should become the responsibility of the departmental treasuries. Thus Infante, in a note sent in early 1827, praised the efforts of a particular prefect on behalf of the state institutions in his jurisdiction but reminded him
that his support for them "should not be achieved by throwing away
[*echando menos*] the funds of the Public Treasury which have charged
against them obligations of imperative exigency, while the welfare institutions permit some leeway [*admiten alguna duda*] and they have moreover
their incomes assigned and whose collection should be the concern of the
administrator [of the institution]." The question became, however, whether
the avoidance of departmental treasury responsibility for the financing of
the institutions was still a tenable policy after the incomes previously assigned to the institutions and collectible by their administrators had become converted into state debt paper.

Inescapably the treasuries became the collectors of the interest income
assigned to these institutions, if Article 7 of the June decree were to be
taken seriously. This was even more the case in instances where the endowments of these institutions were purchased by vales which could not be
transferred to these institutions for collection at the Public Credit Boards.
Article 7 required in this case, as Aguirre pointed out in early December
1827, "The vales which have entered the treasury for the purchase of
property or other motives, do not bear interest; thus according to Article 7
of the June 12 decree the treasury pays to the institution to which the sold
property was assigned, the amount which was being paid to it." Under Sucre's formula, instead of the treasury paying itself the amounts of endowment loss caused by censos redemption, this amount could be covered by
channeling more billetes to the institutions. Aguirre indeed had suggested
this option in the case of the endowment devaluation caused by the Geraldino haciendas purchase. But Aguirre's earlier position revealed his reservations about moving the responsibility for financing the welfare institutions from the Public Credit Boards to the departmental treasuries.[45]

Loan Pressure on the Public Credit Administration

According to the administration's numbers printed in *Condor* in January
1828, interest payments on the vales and billetes in circulation were cur-

rent. These payments were scheduled three times a year, January, May, and September. In the first payment in May 1827, 15,508 pesos were paid out in interest on 775,402 billetes in circulation at that time. In September, 40,026 pesos were paid out on the 2,101,318 billetes in circulation. In January 1828, 48,112 pesos were paid out on 2,405,642 billetes. Further, Infante stated, the administration had amortized 100,000 of the billetes through liquidation of censos and property purchases. "We cannot understand," he said, "that in any other country more is being done [to maintain public credit]; I include not just newly established institutions, but even those that have been consolidated by time."[46]

According to *Condor's* figures, the administration was meeting the obligation of the Public Credit law to pay out 6 percent interest on the face value of billetes in circulation in three installments of 2 percent each. But the law also required payment every month into the sinking fund at the rate of one-twelfth of the face value of billetes in circulation. *Condor* admitted to letting the sinking fund feature go by default, arguing that the revenues cited in the legislation were inadequate. It was tacitly assumed that retirement of the billetes through purchase of state-owned haciendas and redemption of censos eliminated the need for amortization by payments out of the sinking fund. This is what Infante meant when he later referred to a "twist" given to public credit by the June decree that was "very distant from the mind of its creator [Madero]."

The defaulted payments into the sinking fund amounted to 13,379 pesos in January 1828—not a bad record, if in fact the interest payments themselves were made as reported. If they were, it was at the cost of growing strain on the treasuries and ambiguous signals coming from the administration concerning the priority of these payments. The strain was reflected in Aguirre's circular citing the "extraordinary" increase in costs to the administration created by public credit but there was no ambiguity in the commitment to meet them: "The same public credit requires the faithful payment of interest." Austerity measures including a withholding of one-third of the salaries of all public officials were laid out in his circular. The ambiguity, rather, was reflected in the implications of laxity in the original issue of the notes.[47]

Although Aguirre was an advocate of the Public Credit Administration, he was under pressure from Infante to exercise surveillance over its activities and, in particular, to impose strict accounting procedures. Sucre and Infante were concerned that too many billetes were issued by Madero in the first place and that in the second place the boards were lax in assigning the billetes, with the result that they ended up in the wrong hands. Loose procedures in the issue of the billetes in fact were clearly indicated in the Department of La Paz. In the Department of Cochabamba, Aguirre indicated to Geraldino that all of the billetes be recalled in order to check the validity of the original assignment. Geraldino himself had to caution him that the implementation of these instructions was improbable and would give rise to intrigues that could only damage the credibility of the credit program. Now, in addition, Geraldino noted that many of the billetes that were improperly assigned had been quickly sold to third parties, while the one who obtained the billetes in good faith probably still had them. Thus the only billetes which could be reasonably recalled from the original assignees were precisely the ones that were properly assigned in the first place. But Infante kept up the pressure on Aguirre to trim the amounts of billetes issued on which the administration would have to meet interest payments.[48]

Geraldino expressed concern about whether the 7,000 pesos interest payments falling due in January on the billetes in circulation could be met out of departmental revenues—except if salary payments to the miliary garrison and civil list were postponed. He expected some relief would come from speeding up the collection of the Indian tribute but ruled out any help coming from raising a local loan from property owners. He assured Aguirre that he had the law concerning public credit "in full view and that [his] efforts would be directed only toward giving it the most exact compliance." It is not certain that the January payments were made on time, as Infante claimed. But the fact that the military salaries were allowed to slide by April is indirect evidence that the January interest payments were in fact made.[49]

A more definite case of delay in payment occurred in the Department of Potosi. There the president of the Credit Board had canceled the payment of interest on circulating billetes on the day before it fell due. But the amount of arrearage allowed to develop could not have been large, based on figures supplied by the prefect in November 1828. These indicated a payment of 34,790 pesos interest payments on billetes for the whole of 1827 and through the September payment of 1828. The amount of interest payment accumulating through the January third of 1828 can be calculated at 29,580 pesos. In all probability the 34,790 interest outlay reported by the prefecture was applied fully against the interest falling due through January 1828 and the balance applied in the May third of that year, when an arrearage would have begun to develop. The September payment might have gone, in Potosi, largely by default, since by that time the Sucre administration had been overthrown by the Peruvian invasion and the Public Credit program was in shambles. To this extent, then, Infante's claim that interest payments were current through the January third of 1828 are not contradicted by the Potosi figures, with the exception of the prefect's intervention in the September payment.[50]

With respect to the loan vales, the main concern for Sucre was to maintain a high enough market value for the vales so that Colombian military personnel receiving them as payment of the gratification decreed by Congress would be able to sell them at a reasonable amount of their face value. Sucre was aware in September that the soldiers were having trouble selling the vales and many wanted to return them to the state. In order to create a market for the vales, Sucre and Infante decided to "invite the friends of the Administration," by which they meant Colombian military officers, to use vales to buy state property and show civilians the advantages that could be obtained under the June 12 decree. To facilitate this demonstration, military haberes were made equivalent to vales for the purpose of the purchases of state property under the June 12 decree. In addition, it was decided that rather than waiting for military personnel to sell vales to civilians, it could be done directly in the prefects' offices in all of the departments. These sales were expected to yield money which could then be applied to the cost of evacuating Colombian troops. On November 2, 1827, Sucre issued the order allowing departmental prefects to sell vales directly to civilians at 60 percent of face value, because this is the "spirit" of the congressional law authorizing the bond float originally. It was more than the spirit of the law since the 60 percent figure was quoted precisely. But in his response to an inquiry from the La Paz prefect if the vales could be sold at a lower price, Aguirre responded that "if there is nobody who will buy the vales at 60 percent which the congressional law designated, be sure to push [*sacar todo partido posible*] the sale in the understanding [*inteligencia*] that the [sale price] should never be less than 50 percent. . . . The difference that results between 50 percent and 60 percent designated in the decree of Congress will be used to cover military [maintenance] costs." Aguirre conveyed Sucre's creative interpretation of the Congressional law this way:

> His Excellency, in the conflict of not finding ordinary revenues to cover the costs needed by the troops in order to leave, and with the objective in mind that the Republic should not be encumbered with the costs in-

cident to their prolonged stay here; and believing also that if the Congress designated the 60 percent as the base of the loan, it was in the expectation of it being floated abroad, since it would have stipulated without doubt a much lower real value in a domestic float, in view of the immense advantages that result for the all from this loan; is inclined to agree with your proposal so long as the Congress is notified for its approval. But he [Sucre] authorizes you by this instruction to proceed in this transaction with great speed, and only in the terms indicated.[51]

4

National Significance of the Funding Failure

THE MUTINY OF Colombian garrison units in Lima in late January 1827 provided Peruvian nationalists with the opportunity to begin dismantling Bolivar's influence in the country. The annexation of Bolivia ranked high on the Peruvian nationalist agenda. Sucre's administration in Bolivia was pictured in the nationalist press variously as a satrapy of Bolivar's and as a tool of Colombian hegemony. Bolivian statehood was portrayed as an artificial arrangement devised by Sucre and Bolivar to weaken Peru by separating from it these historically Peruvian upland provinces. Anything that served to undermine Sucre's support in Bolivia served as grist for this mill.[1]

Fenix Indictment of State Debt Policy under Sucre

A highly polemical article attacking the Sucre administration in Bolivia appeared in the Peruvian newspaper *El Fenix* in October 1827. It sought to exploit Madero's resignation by stating that "the Public Treasury, despite its published accounts of incomes and outlays, is a labyrinth whose thread only Sucre has. The orders and decrees are placed directly by him, the presence of the Minister [Madero] being purely immaterial." Decrees and orders went out over Madero's signature which he had never signed, and, "faced with an intolerable and indecorous situation, Madero was forced to resign his post." *Condor* had replied to these allegations saying that the "only" decree Madero had refused to sign was one of the June 12 decrees "which had long before originated in the Ministry of Interior. Convinced of the advantages of floating the loan domestically he edited the draft [*reformó la redacción*] and signed it." On the question of only Sucre

holding the key to treasury affairs, *Condor* exclaimed, in an apparent al-
lusion to Madero's involvement of the treasury in the launching of the
Public Credit Administration, "Poor Bolivia if Sucre did not take the
thread up which already had gotten lost in a labyrinth of projects which
had made a chaos of the treasury."[2]

The handling of Madero's resignation in a subsequent *Fenix* article
placed it in the context of a much larger indictment of the Sucre administration's handling of public credit in Bolivia; it was harder to dismiss as
plain polemics.[3] Like its predecessor, this article sought to promote dis-
affection inside the Colombian army in Bolivia and to capitalize specifically on a mutiny that occurred in a Colombian battalion (Voltígeros) in
La Paz in December 1827. It alleged that the 1 million pesos decreed by
the Bolivian Congress to the Liberating Army had been funneled to Colombia for distribution among Bolivar's friends who had "never set foot in
Alto Peru." (Peruvian nationalists always used the term *Alto Peru* instead
of Bolivia.) Duplicate gratifications were given to Sucre's friends—Molina,
Galindo, Geraldino, and Alarcon—and even to "the Spaniard Infante . . .
who had helped liberate Alto Peru about as much as his countrymen La
Serna [the Peruvian viceroy] and Valdez [a notorious Spanish general who
fought against Bolivar's and Sucre's forces in Peru and Upper Peru] had."
That these funds should not reach the hands of those deserving them in
the Auxiliary Army was no surprise, since the assets of the country "had
been handled with no less scandal and bad faith" as a result of Sucre and
Infante's "despotic" distortions of the purposes of the public credit program as Madero had originally conceived them.

The *Fenix* article had some information on the Mining Bank in Bolivia
but none concerning the conflict between the June 12 decree and the congressional law allocating proceeds from auctions of government haciendas
in favor of the Mining Bank. Rather, *Fenix* stated that 300,000 pesos had
been earmarked to capitalize the Mining Bank as a pretext for taking
that amount out of public funds and expatriating it to Colombia while
leaving the "imaginary" Mining Bank in a state of complete poverty. The
same result occurred in the church assets and censos income that had
been earmarked for the state educational and welfare institutions—it
"marched" to Colombia and served as a cache for Bolivar to be distributed among his followers.

With regard specifically to the Public Credit Administration, *Fenix*
stated that it had been established by the Congress on a basis "which
made it, as is natural, absolutely independent of the Executive [and, in

contradiction to the earlier allegation in the October article] remained so long as the honorable Señor Madero served in the Ministry of Treasury." But once Madero was out, the Public Credit program received such "blows" from Sucre and Infante that the billetes lost 87 percent of their real value. "But from this decline and common ruin," continued *Fenix*, "resulted the aggrandizement of the royal ruling family, which, buying the billetes at such a low price, amortized them for their face value in the purchasing of the best haciendas of the state." Alarcon's purchase was cited as an example of the combination of a rigged auction and appraisal.

The sinking fund feature, the article continued, so important in Madero's original plan for amortizing the notes, went by default under Sucre's handling. Significant arrearage was allowed to develop by January 1828 in the payment of interest due on the billetes in circulation. Additionally, Infante was guilty of gross intervention in the activities of the Credit Boards. This particular charge was made:

> With the second trimester payment due on September 10, on September 8 instructions from the Ministry of Interior were circulated ordering that the prefects and not the treasury administrators be the ones to turn over to the Credit Boards a sum of money which was very much less than the amount designated by law and did not cover the interest due on the notes. The Credit Boards protested the intervention given to the prefects, and the miserable amounts transferred as a serious infraction of the law which constituted them [the Credit Boards] as completely independent. Then the Minister of Government, His Excellency the Spaniard Infante, sent them through the principal Credit Board in Chuquisaca a note disparaging their protests and characterizing them as anarchic when they had not asked for anything except the compliance with the law. They [the Credit Boards] submitted. There was no way to resist a government which spoke to them with such despotism, acrimony, and threats. The billetes subsequently lost their value and public confidence, the heart of establishment of this kind, was completely withdrawn.

The *Fenix* attack is highly polemical, hyperbolic, and uncorroborated in many instances. For example, there was no evidence supplied that any of the pesos decreed to the Liberating Army were funneled to Colombia so that Bolivar could distribute them to supporters who had never even been in Bolivia. The nearest thing to the application of these funds to Bolivar's purposes was Sucre's suggestion that the gratification money raised by the loan might be used to finance the sending of a Bolivian expeditionary force to participate in the invasion of Cuba. Bolivar, the record showed, never sent to Sucre his own recommendations for recipients of the Bolivian gratification money, and Sucre discouraged him from doing so.[4]

The major thread that ran through the second *Fenix* article is that Sucre and Infante had deliberately sacrificed the Public Credit Administration; that they had a vested interest in the poor performance of the billetes and were not above placing obstacles in their way. These charges are by no means proven by *Fenix*, and the case can equally be made that Sucre and Infante genuinely hoped that the June 12 decree would help revive the market value of the billetes by coupling them to the loan vales. Sucre, even initially, was willing to let the vales be administered through the Public Credit Administration, against his better judgment and in an attempt to accommodate Madero's reservations about the June 12 decree. Moreover, Infante's contention that the interest payments on the billetes were kept current through the January third of 1828 is mainly correct; if there was arrearage, it was slight. It is certain that Aguirre was squarely behind the Public Credit Administration but probably more so than Infante was.

The *Fenix* article placed considerable weight on the allegation that Infante ordered prefects to take over the payment of funds to the Public Credit Offices in the September third of 1827 and ordered a large underpayment. It is true that, in the case of Potosi, interest payments for the September third were postponed at the last minute, even while the treasury had come into possession of 20,000 pesos from an early tribute collection—much more than enough to meet the interest due. That some communication from Infante was involved in this postponement is not completely beyond the realm of speculation. It has to be remembered that he and Sucre at this time were squeezing out all funds possible that might be applied to the military evacuation costs, and the windfall pesos in the Potosi Treasury must have been tempting. It should be remembered that exactly at this time the prefect was being encouraged to sell loan vales at less than the legal price if necessary to generate evacuation funds.

Yet all of this evidence is circumstantial. There is no direct evidence in the Bolivian archives of the existence of any circular from Infante on September 8 ordering prefectural intervention in the Credit Board payments. This is not to say that such a communication was never sent; it might have been and then misfiled or subsequently removed. The fact that the Ministry of Interior could be sending direct communications to the Public Credit Boards at all was irregular on the face of it, since those boards, as

Fenix correctly stated, were legally independent of the executive. Yet the fact that such communications were being sent is proved by reference to them in one communication from the Credit Board. It provided graphic evidence of attempts by the Public Credit Administration to defend the integrity of the funded state debt against the importunities of a cash-hungry executive.

The issue involved in this exchange between Infante and the Central Credit Board located at Chuquisaca concerned the question of whether persons who had declared their claims against the Spanish government in the pre-1825 period were entitled to receive interest on billetes they had received in indemnification of their claims from January 1, 1828. The congressional laws of December 15 and 17 and January 11 were premised on the date of January 1 as the commencement of the consolidation of the internal Spanish government debt for the purposes of indemnification by billetes. Persons receiving billetes were entitled to interest payments effective January 1. President Callejo of the Chuquisaca Board informed Infante that the board had in August advised all the departmental boards to honor interest payments effective January 1 on billetes issued after May third of that year. In doing so, the board, Callejo said, had studied carefully the congressional legislation and found it to be unequivocal in the matter of late claims being entitled to interest accrual effective January 1. The determining factor was the point from which the Congress recognized the debt globally, and the date of declaration of claims was "accidental." Article 40 and Article 41, he pointed out, required prefectures to place on deposit in the Credit Board offices funds adequate to cover legal interest due on the notes.

The Ministry of Interior sent a note, Number 12, to Callejo's board disavowing its action in this matter and ordering nonpayment of back interest. Callejo stated that it was the board's unanimous judgment that billetes issued after May third were entitled to interest payments retroactive to January 1 and reaffirmed the board's action:

> The same considerations [behind its original decision] have weighed in the motivation of the board upon reading your communication of September 1, Number 12. And with a tranquil conscience [the board] has been able to do no less than to ratify what it already decided and circulated on August 14. It happily accepts the responsibility for its actions [*gustosa carga de la responsabilidad con que se le comina*], the more so since whatever alteration in that which has been determined upon would

open up a breach in the public credit of the nation. And both [the executive and the Public Credit Administration] would deplore the inevitable results of the squandering [*derroche*] of this fundamental basis of organization and social happiness.[5]

Assessment of Infante-Madero Difference on State Debt Policy

Infante defended the Sucre administration against the *Fenix* charges in *Condor* in April 1828. On the Mining Bank question he took the charges at face value and asserted simply that not one peso had been taken from public funds under pretext of capitalizing the bank and that it was well financed as a result of government economies. He gave figures on the capital of the bank to prove his point. On the charge that only friends of the Sucre administration were permitted to use government paper to purchase state-owned haciendas, he noted that the language of the June 12 decree clearly made this option available to all citizens. If friends of the administration were to take advantage of the offering under the decree, it was done for the purpose of encouraging other citizens who may have lacked "a spirit of enterprise and confidence" to take advantage of the decree themselves.[6]

On the charge that the Sucre administration had caused the decline in the value of the billetes by preventing prompt interest payments, Infante insisted that this was not the cause of their drop in value, that through the first third of 1828 interest payments on all billetes in circulation were current. The payments that were not made were those into the sinking fund. Since the revenues assigned by law to public credit were inadequate, the executive had the right to make allocations and set priorities.

In Infante's reply, there were "many reasons" why the billetes lost their value, the first being that they were a novelty in Bolivia. Madero had been cautioned that this would happen but "with very good intentions he wanted to create the billetes [and] his beautiful theories convinced the Congress to pass the law." The results not only justified the earlier fears but were the principal reason why Madero resigned, admitting "that his calculations were completely flawed, in his whole system." Infante cited also the political uncertainty caused by the revolution against Bolivar in Peru and the profusion with which Madero used billetes to indemnify claims as the other factor causing the real value decline of the billetes. It was "to raise the value of the billetes that the June 12 decree, which originated in the Ministry of Government, was issued, permitting them and the vales to be made negotiable for public property and redemption of censos held by the public welfare establishments." Infante proceeded to describe the process whereby the billetes and vales were amortized in property purchases and redemption of censos rather than through payment out of the sinking fund, as "giving a twist [giro] to public credit that was very distant from the mind of its creator [Madero]."

Here, Infante alluded to a difference in socioeconomic philosophy concerning the purposes of state debt policy in a society such as Bolivia. He said that Madero's concept was designed to create a society of savers in a capital-scarce environment. Madero's plan might apply to a society where the control on luxury consumption was necessary for the society's overall well-being. But Bolivia was far from being in that situation; the problem was a general absence of wealth, not a false conception of what it was. He attacked in particular Madero's focus on the popular classes. Trying to transform day workers (jornaleros) into savers was an irrelevant task because they were not economically active enough in the first place. What Bolivia urgently needed was a raising of the level of economic activity before it concerned itself with curtailing the spending habits of people. Madero's concept of funded state debt was the financial equivalent of laws that attempted to regulate personal expenditures. He did not want to "disparage the financial knowledge of Señor Madero because we do not know if the sumptuary laws he would like to establish in Bolivia might one day be advantageous, [but] in a country where there is so little luxury [currently] . . . it would be up to the government to foment it in order to create the incentives [*necesidades*] that would make our working class less indolent." By "incentives," Infante apparently meant creating wealth in certain social strata by focusing marginal growth activity there so that other (lower) strata could eventually be set into economic motion as a consequence.

Infante's rationale for using state debt to augment the power of a landowning class, as opposed to the state-sponsored popular savings class aimed at by Madero's funding program, was justified because it was seen as the most efficient way to increase the economic productivity of the country. The entrepreneurs who were ready to take advantage of state debt to get rid of censos and to purchase haciendas should be rewarded for the contributions their activities stood to make to the marginal economic product of the country. Such was the philosophy underlying the June 12 decree; it was the marginalist ethic of a free market economy.

Whereas Infante defined the economic problem as basically a mechanical one of freeing wealth from colonial constraints, Madero's philosophy defined the economic problem psychologically and socially. Madero (and Aguirre) recognized that for centuries investment flows in Bolivian society had been socially regulated by the practices of the Catholic church. Censos were at once symbols of economic value and of social trust: the capital that slowly, steadily accumulated in them had simultaneously protected the continuity of families over generations, expressed Catholicized feelings of faith and authority, and fueled investment in the domestic economy. If the institutions that had channeled wealth for centuries were swept away by liberal reforms, and replaced by nothing more than a mechanical raising of the level of economic activity in a free market context, Madero predicted dire social consequences. His concerns anticipated the questions that other Latin American "conservatives" asked themselves in the face of the rapid secularization of the methods of credit and mobilizing capital: "What would safeguard private wealth from the anarchistic excesses of such a revolutionary act? What would preserve the economic foundation of society if the Catholic, authoritarian heritage that had shaped it were itself destroyed?"[7] Would not the investment generated by the new secular arrangements lead to forms of growth based on a lack of confidence in society, for example, production for the foreign sector as opposed to the domestic sector, or production of luxury goods as opposed to wage goods that could be shielded from the "anarchistic excesses" of the new society? Would not the mechanical conception of the free market produce what developmental economists today call "socially disarticulated" growth?[8]

In order to maintain socially coherent investment flows, Madero felt that it was necessary to cast the state into the role of fiduciary agent for the savings wealth of the citizens, to define and create wealth on the basis of a trust relationship of the kind that the church had fomented through its "banking" activities in the colonial period. It was the only way to ensure that not just more economic activity but activity that built up the economic foundations of society resulted from investment flows, that for example investors continued to invest in the domestic economy as opposed to seeking "safe" enclaves for their capital in consumption, landholdings, speculation, or foreign sector investment. Madero believed that fiduciary state debt could make confidence in society and the state the underpinning of the capital accumulation process. To allow floating rather than funded state debt paper to fill the void in the capital formation process left by the dismantlement of the church's "banking" role would signal the death of the socially coherent growth model. To permit the vast structure of censos to become in fact a market for state debt paper was to destroy the economic foundations of Bolivian society.

In the balance of the nineteenth century, Bolivia's patently, socially disarticulated style of growth, marked by an elite agrarian appropriation process linked to the enormous growth of the mineral export industry, appears ample confirmation of Madero's fears. The role of state debt policy that originated in the June 12 decrees has been all too conspicuous in this pattern of socially disarticulated growth.

State Debt and the Growth of the Rural Land Market in the Nineteenth Century

Large quantities of state debt paper were channeled by the Sucre administration into the purchase of state-owned haciendas and into the redemption of censos held against rural properties. How was the rural future of Bolivia affected by these events? In the first place, did the new owners of haciendas bought with state debt paper, or freed from censos burdens by state debt paper, behave any differently from haciendas unaffected by state debt paper transactions? Were they, as might be imagined, any more inclined to collect rent from service tenants as opposed to relying on income from demesne production? Were they more prone to sell off parts of the hacienda to raise income? Were they less aggressive in expanding hacienda borders in order to increase output?

Or did the haciendas affected by state debt paper obey by the same cycles of stasis and partition that governed other haciendas in the nineteenth century? If a case study can be taken as evidence, the answer is that they did.

Leon Galindo was a Colombian (New Granadian) colonel who was a close friend of Sucre. He held the position of prefect of Potosi in the later stages of the administration. Galindo received from Sucre 8,300 pesos in treasury vales and used them to purchase the hacienda of Chullpas in Cochabamba. Its record in the nineteenth century was typical of the haciendas' cycle in Cochabamba: they continued as static wholes until the early 1870s when they underwent drastic partitioning into smaller units. Between 1830 and 1871, there were relatively few changes in hacienda boundaries by virtue of either partition or new acquisitions; a pattern of stasis prevailed, and it was as true of the Galindo hacienda as of the other 728 haciendas in Cochabamba. Although there was some movement in the market for haciendas because sales prompted by Sucre's June 12 decrees, and some partitioning due to inheritance arrangements, there were no signs at all of any instability in hacienda tenure. Between 1871 and 1929, however, 374 divisions of haciendas into small parcels for sale were recorded in Cochabamba. The Galindo hacienda also exemplified this cycle of partitioning. The year 1870 marked a rough watershed in the internal economies of the hacienda system of Cochabamba; service tenantry began to be replaced by sharecropping.[9]

Clearly the purchases of haciendas with state debt paper accelerated the privatization process by eliminating state leasing systems and censos. But it is probably safe to assume that whatever attitudinal differences may have existed between the hacienda owners who used state debt paper to buy their properties and redeem censos and those who did not were smoothed out by the socioeconomic factors that constrained hacienda performance in the course of the nineteenth century. It has been argued that hacienda behavior in the nineteenth century in all of Latin America was molded by either internal feudalism or external market forces. The historiography of the nineteenth-century hacienda in Latin America, Bolivia included, is roughly divisible into these two perspectives. The early 1970s marked a shift from the former to the latter.[10]

The market in state debt paper was created largely by the June 12 decrees. The focus was on redemption of censos and purchases of properties belonging to the state and to welfare. These state debt paper transactions were relatively more intense in La Paz (censos) and Cochabamba (hacienda purchases) than in Chuquisaca and Potosi. The latter two were the largest repositories of billetes, making the low level of transactions in them even more conspicuous. Thus the June 12 decrees discovered and accentuated underlying departmental differences in the haciendia-censos systems, as well as political differences.

We can assume therefore that the structure and role of censos was dismantled more quickly in La Paz and Cochabamba than in Potosi and Chuquisaca. It was argued here that the lack of incentives to eliminate censos in the mining districts circling Potosi derived from the fact that there were fewer of them, given the tendency of the Catholic Church to establish its censos (especially loans) in more dynamic agrarian areas where they performed a developmentalist, credit function. Haciendas in the Potosi area furthermore were not economically dynamic and therefore less in need of censos credit at a time when this form of credit was active among other haciendas. By the same token, censos in the form of family trusts would have been logical parts of this hacienda system.

Chuquisaca appears to have been an extension of the Potosi pattern. Langer's study confirms the fact that the hacienda system stretching across the Chuquisaca-Potosi border was owned by silver miners as consumers of their recreational and familial value rather than as investors in their profit-making potential. "Income from the mines still far exceeded that of the haciendas and though many of the [hacienda] administrators received a percentage of the net profit on the most important crops as an incentive to maintain production, they usually did not have enough influence to dictate any significant changes in the management of the estates. . . . Properties remained relatively neglected and the obligations of the hacienda peons . . . were not too severe." Langer also notes that the silver mining elite with its roots in the colonial period continued during the first half of the nineteenth century to exercise political and social prestige by "owning a multitude of haciendas that dotted the countryside." In this sort of an atmosphere, what use was there for securing vales and billetes to negotiate the redemption of censos? On the contrary, given the rentier mentality of these landowners, whose entrepreneurialism remained focused on the mines, the continuation of whatever censos there were on their haciendas would have posed no problem and in fact would have facilitated the maintenance of the haciendas within families. By the same token (but more speculatively), Langer's observations throw some political light on why the billetes were heavily concentrated in Chuquisaca and Potosi. The ownership of funded debt paper, in preference to the vales, would have corresponded to the aristocratic impulse, cited by Langer as characteristic of the silver elite, to control the government by controlling many of the positions in the state bureaucracy; in this case it meant seeking to control the government by controlling the Public Credit Administration where the funding project was lodged. (Madero's contacts were forged mainly in Potosi and Chuquisaca.) Langer analyses at length the efforts made during the balance of the nineteenth century by the silver elite to maintain control over the state by controlling national finances while the rising tin elite in La Paz sought to achieve control over the state through commercial predominance. The predominance of the nontransacted billetes in Chuquisaca and Potosi, in contrast to the more transacted billetes and vales in La Paz and Cochabamba, mirrored these political strategies.[11]

The greater commercialization of the hacienda systems in La Paz and Cochabamba would by contrast help to explain the larger use of state debt paper to redeem censos there as obstacles to economic efficiency. Herbert Klein's study of the relatively high level of agrarian capitalism that was characteristic of the La Paz hacienda system would reinforce this conclusion.[12]

With regard to Cochabamba, it is true that the decline in the Potosi market reduced the profitability of those haciendas. Brooke Larson and Gustavo Rodriguez Ostria have described the hacienda system in Cochabamba as being in the throes of a decay into feudalism by the early nineteenth century, as a result of the collapse of the Potosi market for their products. They placed the origin of this decay in the late colonial period and traced it until the late nineteenth century.[13] If such were the case, it helps explain the relatively nonaggressive use of state debt paper to eliminate censos on rural properties in the Cochabamba system. Jackson concedes the possibility of a continuing, relatively high level of censos in the Cochabamba system which ensured that the haciendas stayed whole and in family control for most of the century. Thus Jackson argues that the colonial hacienda with its structure of censos existed in the Cochabamba system until the late nineteenth century when it underwent a parcelization process because of changes in the national economy caused by the dismantlement of protection. But Jackson still rejects the feudal thesis expounded by Larson and Rodriguez Ostría. He shows that the decline of the Potosi market for Cochabamba wheat was by no means absolute and that the Cochabamba haciendas continued to produce until the late nineteenth century for the markets in southern Peru and northern highland Bolivia. Jackson's work amply demonstrates the continuation of innovative, entrepreneurial behavior by the Cochabamba hacendados. It was true, however, that state debt paper was used more in Cochabamba to purchase haciendas from the state than to redeem censos, at least in comparison to the pattern of use in La Paz. It may have been also true that censos continued at a relatively higher level in Cochabamba than in the La Paz hacienda system. Unfortunately, the model of agrarian capitalism developed by Cushner and used by Jackson to analyze the Cochabamba hacienda system did not include the elimination of censos on rural property among its criteria for identifying the capitalistic hacienda.[14]

What is true of both the La Paz and the Cochabamba systems is that as censos were eliminated, and as debt paper was used in the purchase of haciendas, the owners increased their equity in the haciendas, thereby making them mortgageable. Thus the long cycle of secularization of hacienda credit that played itself out in all of the Latin American countries during the course of the nineteenth century did so with a head start in Bolivia, especially in the La Paz–Cochabama systems, thanks to Sucre's early secularization of censos and their subsequent disentailment through the June 12 decrees. This process eventually reached into the hacienda systems of Chuquisaca and Potosi. In the second half of the century the liens and loans held against haciendas in all of Bolivia were held predominantly by commercial banks.[15]

In addition to these general observations concerning the linkages between state debt paper and the hacienda-censos system as it emerged from the colonial period, what can be said about the contribution of state debt to the expansion of the hacienda system at the expense of Indian communal lands, a process that unfolded over the course of the nineteenth century? What effect did state debt policy have on the balance between the haciendas and the Indian communal lands? What is the connection between the Sucre administration's failure to fund the internal debt and the massive use of state debt paper to buy Indian communal lands in the late 1860s?

After the overthrow of Sucre in June 1828, the internal debt of Bolivia underwent several expansions and consolidations. Of the 2,995,306 worth of funding paper that was issued, in 1830, 1,853,502 remained in circulation. Of the 613,700 in vales issued, 187,433 remained in circulation. This stock was augmented over the next two decades. Following Bolivia's defeat by Chile in the battle of Ingavi, President José Ballivián in 1843 demobilized the military and used a new 3 million peso issue in state debt paper bearing a 6 percent interest to pension off officers and soldiers. Following the example of Sucre's June 12 decrees, the new debt paper was made negotiable for state fiscal property—jobs and lands purchased from the state. This paper sold at 30 percent of its face value. It was extensively used by debt entrepreneurs, who bought it cheaply from the military retirees and negotiated it over to the state at par for the purchase of state lands. Even more ominously, some of the debt paper was used to purchase Indian communal lands. The eclipse of the funding role of state debt paper was not complete, however; echoes of Madero's funding plan existed in Ballivián's efforts to establish a *caja militar de ahorros* (a military fiduciary fund) in which military savers contributed two reales per month with the pool being used to purchase state debt paper yielding 6 percent interest per year. This fund started with a capital of 1,000 pesos and reached 200,000 pesos in several years, with most of it in the 6 percent state debt paper.[16]

In a futile effort to fund the internal debt, congressional laws passed in 1844 and again in 1850 consolidated the floating debt paper left over from 1826 into the new 6 percent paper. But state funds were lacking to meet interest and amortization payments and they were suspended in 1852, effectively forcing the debt paper back into the rural land acquisition market where it fueled the private appropriation of Indian communal lands in the 1860s.[17]

During the Sucre period, state-initiated transactions involving state debt paper did not immediately affect Indian communal lands. There were three main reasons why they did not. First, the elimination of censos on rural properties and the turnover of state-owned haciendas to private owners provided enough room for fleshing out the hacienda system without the necessity to encroach on communal lands. (Neither censos nor state-owned haciendas existed in sufficient volume for this to continue to be true in the second half of the nineteenth century.) Second, the Sucre administration was constrained by Bolivar's various decrees which sought to "compose" communal lands over to individual Indian owners, as part and parcel of the plan to eliminate their tributary status and to convert them into taxpaying freeholders. Although Sucre suspended these decrees, it was not in order to interpose the state as the seller of the communal lands. It was rather to maintain the Indian communal lands intact as the base for ongoing payment of the tribute, given the failure of the direct taxation program to take effect. The third factor was the tributary nexus between the Indian communities and the state, a nexus that continued to exist in Bolivia from early in the colonial period, when the communal lands were organized by Spanish Viceroys as tributary unities (and as reservoirs of mita labor), well into the second half of the nineteenth century.

The colonial tribute merged the concepts of a tax and a rent in the payments to the state by Indians organized into the communal lands. They paid the tribute as a form of assurance from the state of their absolute dominion over the communal lands and as a guarantee of their unrestricted access to them. During the early republican period, communal Indians continued to envisage the tribute payment as part of a reciprocal pact with the state; they developed production structures to generate a surplus specifically to pay the tribute on this basis. The tribute was an inherent part of the "moral economy" of the indigenous rural sector. The republican state, by continuing the tribute, led the Indians to believe that no essential changes had occurred in their mutual understanding: they paid the tribute, the state protected the communities. In fact, subtle change was making itself felt on the side of the state: the Indians living on the communal lands were beginning to be seen as tenants living on state-owned lands, and the tribute was increasingly seen as a rent which the state at its discretion might suspend in favor of auctioning off these lands to its preferred customers. This thinking crystallized in the notorious decrees issued by President Mariano Melgarejo in 1866, which gave the Indians a limited time to pay for individual titles to their portions of the communal lands after which they would be sold off at state auctions for debt paper.[18]

Silvia Cusicanqui has argued that this sell-off of community lands by President Melgarejo initiated a vast, speculative expansion of the feudal haciendas. In making this argument, she employed Antonio Mitre's division of the nineteenth century into the neocolonial and export-led growth periods, the protectionist and liberal phases, respectively.[19] According to this framework, the colonial regime continued in Bolivia from 1825 until 1870. Although silver exports stagnated during this period, the absence of foreign commerce in the highlands meant that silver continued to circulate and to stimulate native production for the mining centers; trading circuits dependent on the mining economy and developed during the colonial period remained largely intact. State policies continued to be those of the colonial government. The tribute on the Indians and the commitment to the protection of their communal lands were both maintained. In the mining sector, the state continued to require that all ore be sold to official mining banks, which paid for it in a progressively debased currency. Native artisans and manufactures were favored by these policies since the debased currency made foreign goods too expensive to import. The state exercised a monopoly over such exports as there were (guano and copper), continued to collect diezmos taxes, and operated a complex tariff system.

According to the Cusicanqui-Mitre scheme, in the early 1850s a new generation of silver miners appeared, backed by Chilean capital. They bought heavily into the silver mines, modernized them, and allied themselves with large import-export merchants. These miners were much less tied to the colonial economy than their predecessors. Their major objectives were to open Bolivia to foreign trade and capital; to eliminate the state monopolies, including the one in the mining sector; to eliminate the debased currency in favor of a revalued monetary unit that would make foreign imports more competitive in Bolivian markets; to transform the agrarian structure in the direction of more modern, capitalistic production methods by the imposition of a single tax on landowners and abolition of

Indian communal lands; to build railways from the mineheads to the Pacific; and to press for the passage of free trade legislation. This movement toward free trade and dismantling of the colonial economy and state remained largely centered in the Potosi silver/commercial structure until the late 1870s, when a diversification of foreign capital in the mining industry, propelled by the rise of tin mining and eclipse of the Chilean-dominated silver boom, signaled a shift in the liberal leadership to a La Paz–based commercial structure. This new leadership had a distinctly anti-Chilean tincture but an even more aggressive free trade stance and a wider alliance with foreign capital, especially British and, later, North American. This La Paz–based, tin-producing leadership completed the work begun by the silver miners of southern Bolivia.

Cusicanqui was trained in the feudal historiography of the rural sector of Bolivia that originated in the 1930s, based on a Marxist perspective. Her work, however, is revisionist in that it purports to establish the expansion of the feudal hacienda in the *second* half of the nineteenth century— the period of rapid economic growth resulting from the opening of the national economy to international trade and capital. According to her theory, this growth occurred in two distinct phases, both marked by huge sell-offs of Indian communal lands. The first was initiated by President Mariano Melgarejo in his decree of February 20, 1866, which after a grace period placed Indian communal lands in state auctions. The great bulk of auctioned sales of communal lands occurred in the Department of La Paz, but all of the departments in the country experienced auctions of the Indian communal lands. Cusicanqui's study focused on the auction sales held in La Paz (Mejillones) from 1866 through 1869, when 356 communal holdings were auctioned off to private bidders. The majority of payments (75.6 percent) were made in depreciated state debt paper and the rest in currency (most of it debased currency).[20] The second stage of communal land sales was initiated by the Law of Ex-Vinculación promulgated in October 5, 1874. Cusicanqui did a quantitative analysis of these sales of 33,401 hectares of Indian communal lands in the province of Pacajes in the La Paz department. These sales constitute for her the first phase (1881–1900) in a wave of selling of communal lands that she sees reaching its peak in the 1920s.

Cusicanqui attributes the expansion of the feudal latifundia in Bolivia in the second half of the nineteenth century to the motivations of those who bought into the communal Indian lands; she posits furthermore a continuity of motivation between the purchasers of the earlier Melgarejo period and those in the later period beginning in the 1880s. She argues that these buyers constituted a class of capitalistic bourgeoisie based in the burgeoning export-import economies that were being fueled by the silver and tin booms. This bourgeoisie bought agrarian properties as a cushion against downturns in the import-export business, especially against falloffs in world mineral prices. By a cushion she means owning the agrarian properties as something that could be sold as needed and as a steady source of income from rent. The entrepreneurial and capitalistic purposes of this class were focused on the mines and merchant economies; the agrarian properties served as a safety net for their fortunes. Hence a feudalistic, rentier mentality permeating agrarian ownership coexisted in the same people with a capitalistic, entrepreneurial attitude toward investments in the import-export-related economies. They were two sides of the same coin of Bolivia's integration into the international trading system.

Of particular note in Cusicanqui's thesis is the major emphasis that she gives to the role of depreciated state debt paper in the state auctions of Indian communal lands under Melgarejo. She argues that the survival of the feudal system resulted in large part from the use of debt paper in the purchase of the communal lands. The fact that these lands could be bought on the cheap using state debt paper simply encouraged a rentier kind of mentality toward the purchased properties as opposed to more of an entrepreneurial one. In this respect, she argues that the Bolivian case simply replicated the Spanish case reported by Herr, where the creation of a large latifundia system in the countryside resulted from the disentailment sales involving large amounts of vales reales in payment. However, Cusicanqui's reference to Herr is problematical since, as we saw, Herr was at great pains to show that the disentailment sales benefited not the rising capitalistic bourgeoisie but rather the agrarian oligarchies already in place in Spain's rural structures. Cusicanqui wants to argue that the liberalism of the rising bourgeois was responsible for the feudalistic stagnation of the agricultural sector in Bolivia. Herr, of course, adamantly rejects such a thesis in the Spanish case; his perspective was a liberal as opposed to a Marxist one.[21]

Cusicanqui's thesis has been challenged on three basic grounds (although not on the grounds of her characterization of the role of state debt paper, which is my main concern with her argument). First, the historiographic tradition that it derives from describes the Bolivian rural structure as being "feudal" without explaining the dynamics of the internal economy of the "feudal" hacienda.[22] Her approach is thus committed to a passive peasantry model which has been seriously questioned by new ethnographic scholarship (methodologically stimulated by Thompson and his major exponents among revisionist historians working in the Bolivian rural field, Tristan Platt and Erick Langer). This scholarship ascribes rational decision-making behavior, rooted in the Andean strategic experience and surviving within ostensible feudal settings, to the nonelite rural populations in the second half of the nineteenth century.[23] Even such a book as Brooke Larson's, avowedly committed to the concept of the strategic peasant, is overwhelmingly implicated in the passive peasantry historiography as far as her central interpretations concerning the behavior of the Cochabamba hacienda system are concerned.[24]

Second, new analyses of the population compositions and productive structures of the Indian communal lands have suggested a considerable amount of vibrancy and growth well into the late nineteenth century. If true, it certainly belies the picture of the Indians as hapless victims of feudalization. Based on his counting of the numbers of Indians living and working on communal lands as opposed to those working as colonos on haciendas, Erwin Grieshaber has demonstrated a relative decline of the former and increase in the latter, suggesting that it was not the communal structures that entered into crisis in the second half of the nineteenth century but the feudal haciendas themselves.[25] His thesis is given considerable weight by Tristan Platt's work on the communal lands in northern Potosi, which he shows to have remained extraordinarily dynamic and market-oriented until they lost state backing and opted for insurrectional activity in the late nineteenth century; expansion of feudalistic hacienda does not appear as a relevant factor in this cycle.[26]

Third, it appears that the state-initiated sales of Indian communal lands produced different configurations from region to region, as opposed to any monolithic expansion of feudal haciendas. In Sucre (formerly Chuquisaca) the silver elite living in the capital city did vigorously carve out whole new haciendas from communal lands that were put up for sale. But equally, it appears that a breakdown of Indian communal relations changed the strategic equation for Indians and prompted many of the sales of communal lands, often to other Indian buyers and urban mestizos, not hacienda owners.[27] In the Yungas, the haciendas crystallized vis-à-vis the Indian communities well before the period of communal land sales that started with Melgarejo's decrees.[28] In Potosi, the state in 1902 abandoned all efforts to implement sales of Indian communal lands because of the enormous resistance behaviors mounted by the Indian ayllus.[29]

In the case of Cochabamba the active land market that developed in the late nineteenth century was characterized by a radical parcelization process. Rodriguez Ostria argues that this process paralleled the extension of haciendas and that furthermore it was the sale of corporate Indian lands that acted as the catalyst for these parallel processes.[30] The existence of such a nexus in the Cochabamba land market has been called into question by more recent research.[31] This research has shown, for example, that Indians did not sell all of their communal lands but only a portion of them. Active markets in small parcels developed in places where there were no Indian communal lands. On the one hand, it appears that haciendas themselves were subject to the parcelization process. On the other, the small parcels land market in Cochabamba was shaped by the onset of an economic crisis (occasioned by the loss of protected markets incident to Bolivia's entry into the international economy) and a resultant factor shifting that was required to produce for smaller markets. Jackson's own work reinforces the view that the land market in Cochabamba was driven more by market-sensitive behavior than by state-initiated sales of Indian corporate lands. He also demonstrates how the change in debt structure on rural properties, from censos to bank mortgages, enormously influenced the land market by forcing parcel sales to pay the debt and by forcing sales of foreclosed properties.[32]

The expansion of the feudal hacienda that Cusicanqui described therefore appears to have been confined to the northern altiplano of La Paz, where it is true that large haciendas became territorially dominant over Indian communal lands only after the period of land sales began. This expansion is particularly vivid in the cases of Viacha and Pacajes.

After making allowances for the limitations of Cusicanqui's thesis, a question can still be posed with regard to its domain of most apparent validity: the Department of La Paz. What is the validity of her premise that the role of state debt paper in the rural land market fostered the growth of the feudal hacienda? What difference did the role of state debt paper make in the alteration of land tenure patterns? How did the debt-for-land swaps transacted during Sucre's administration figure into these later debt-for-communal-land swaps? By examining the differences between the land sales initiated under Melgarejo and those that flowed from the law of Ex-Vinculación of 1874, it is possible to pursue these questions because state debt paper figured significantly in the land market created by Melgarejo whereas it did not play a role in the land markets created pursuant to the 1874 law. Can motivational differences be observed between the buyers who used state debt paper and those who did not? Is Cusicanqui's premise of a continuity of bourgeoisie motivation valid?

Melgarejo's decrees were rooted ideologically in the propositions that the communal Indians were tenants on state lands and that the tribute was nothing more than a rent paid to the state. The state had the right to sell the lands and to dispense with the tribute when it saw fit. By way of justification, it was argued that the Indians, by becoming *colonos* (serfs) on feudal haciendas, would be protected from abuses practiced against them by local state officials and corrupt priests. The underlying idea was that of the patrimonialist state—the state as distributor of the communal lands, not individual Indians as sellers of the lands in an open market. As distributor of the lands, the state could choose to accept its own depreciated debt paper as the form of purchase.

The overwhelming majority of the purchases under the Melgarejo decrees were made by individuals who were personally linked to the caudillo-president rather than those who were hacienda owners or miners or merchants.[33] The former included Melgarejo's mistress, his sister, and, predominantly, military officers to whom state debt paper had been pledged by the president. The behavior of these new owners of Indian communal lands was loose and variable. Some tried to convert the Indian lands and Indian tributaries on them to a hacienda regime, but most seem to have been content with asking their own tribute from the Indians in kind and in service, leaving the communal organization virtually intact.

Clearly, a rentier mentality prevailed rather than an entrepreneurial mentality. This group of purchasers was not, as Cusicanqui suggests, a capitalistic group of state creditors using their control over state debt paper to push the state into selling communal lands to them as part of a dependent bourgeoisie economic strategy. Rather they were state cronies who preempted the appearance in the land market of a more economically motivated group of purchasers. Given their position as favorites of the president—or those due personal favor or as individuals in need of coaptation within the clientalist system of caudillo politics—they represented the Latin American counterpart of precisely the class of purchasers described by Richard Herr in the Spanish case: individuals who benefited from the process of wealth being transferred within the Spanish "redistributive" economy to the monarchy, the church, and the military. Whereas the wealth was redistributed more systematically in Spain via taxes, tithes, tariffs, and patronage, as well as through the vales reales, in the case of Melgarejo the mechanism focused exclusively on depreciated state paper made negotiable for Indian communal lands. But both groups were state clienteles. They were subsidized by different redistributive mechanisms (the one monarchical and corporatist, the other caudillistic and coaptative), but in both cases they were larger holders of state debt paper, by choice or position, than were capitalistic groups operating, in Herr's phrase, outside of the "administered economic flows" of the redistributive state.[34]

The patriomonalist ideology underlying the Melgarejo sales was invoked by spokesmen for the rising, Potosi-based silver mining–commercial groups in the Constituent Assembly that was called in 1871 following Melgarejo's overthrow. The cronyism and caudillism were condemned, but the same paternalistic concept remained; the Indians were better off away from the ayllus and under the tutelage of feudalistic haciendas. The state therefore was morally obliged to eliminate the ayllus. This thinking led to the formation of the Conservative Party a few years later. These spokesmen in the Congress were eclipsed, however, by a liberal group of landowners and miners who argued the inalienability of the communal lands and attacked the legitimacy of the 1842 law asserting state proprietorship. They asserted that Melgarejo had sold off land in state auctions that did not belong to the state. They argued the superiority of the productive capacity of the Indians' communal lands vis-à-vis feudal haciendas, but they advocated the division of communal lands into individually owned and worked Indian parcels, on the grounds of greater efficiency. The more idealistic of these legislators hoped that by converting communal lands to individual Indian ownership, the Indians would come to constitute a rural yeoman class that would form a rural branch of the national citizenry, yeoman who would dot the countryside, working their individually owned plots and producing a surplus for the towns. This was the hoped-for result of the abolition of the communities. The law was predicated, in the pamphlet literature of the day, on the view of the Indian as freeholder: "He would join the other classes of society, would mix with them, and bring an end to that engulfing power of class distinctions that erodes the foundations of our nationhood."[35]

These noble sentiments led to the voiding of all of the purchases made under Melgarejo's decrees and to the return of the lands to the communities. The Law of Ex-Vinculación passed in 1874 conceded the right of landownership to the Indians, provided for the parceling of communal lands among them on an individual ownership basis, and abolished the ayllu as a juridical entity.

The politics of the communal land sales changed significantly in the late 1870s. Bolivia lost the War of the Pacific which broke out in 1879 against Chile. The military became thoroughly discredited, paving the way for the creation of a genuinely civilian-controlled government in 1880 that effectively represented the coming to political control of the silver-mining elite (which ceded political dominance to the tin-mining elite in 1900) and the beginning of a long cycle of civilian politics that lasted until the 1930s. The ideology of the 1874 law was changed from its yeoman model of the Indian as freeholder as a result of this political reorientation. The immediate occasion for the shift away from the yeoman model was the need to finance the war from the sale of the community lands.

The ideology of the land sales after 1880 was supplied by Ladislao Cabrera, the minister in Campero's cabinet who was assigned the particular task of raising money for the war. He expected to do so by activating land sales under the 1874 law. But in order to acquire individual titles to communal lands, the Indians would be expected to pay ten times their yearly tribute obligation. Those who refused to pay would be forced to sell their land, and the new proprietor would have to pay 10 percent of the value of the property to the state. The latter scenario was the preferred one, as Cabrera made clear in a memorial. His goal was "to put the wealth of the communal lands into circulation, to hand it over to intelligent and capitalistic landowners." These new owners would not be the state cronies of the Melgarejo period, armed with debt paper to purchase the communal lands, nor yet would they be yeoman Indians; they would be "intelligent and capitalistic."[36]

Cabrera's brand of liberalism expressed the positivistic, social-Darwinistic philosophy which became current toward the end of the century in Bolivia and most other Latin American countries. The pastoral and somewhat romanticized liberalism that permeated the 1874 law was replaced by a "scientific," anti-indigenous, materialistic interpretation of that law's purpose. The Indians were perceived now as incapable of learning new agricultural techniques, of learning Spanish, of discarding old customs. Hence they were obstacles to progress and liabilities to the state. If the Indians were backward, it was their own fault; better they should die out than to have them weigh down the nation. The famine of 1878 was lauded by positivists as part of a selection process that would soon "if not erase the Indians from the national scene completely at least reduce them to a minimal expression."[37]

Those purchasers of the Indian communal lands in the 1880s in the La Paz Department consisted primarily of merchants, miners, and hacienda owners who extended the borders of their haciendas or acquired ones where they did not have any. Conspicuously absent were the state cronies who dominated the purchases in the period 1866–69. The new buyers paid in cash, in the new bolivianos which took the place of the debased pesos that had dominated circulation until the monetary reforms of the early 1880s. Most of the sales were of whole Indian communities, not parcels. A small number of buyers accounted for a large proportion of the communal lands purchased. Most of the lands were purchased directly from the Indians with no state mediation. The contracts typically specified that the Indians would agree to accept the status of colonos on haciendas in exchange for the buyers' commitment to let them stay on the land. It is easy to demonstrate that the balance of hacienda land compared to communal land shifted decisively in certain areas of La Paz Department as a result of these land sales.[38]

The purchasers of the communal lands under the 1880s law were thus a more economically motivated group than their predecessors in the late 1860s. The great bulk of these purchases occurred in the immediate environs of La Paz or close to the trade routes to the city. Grieshaber's close analysis of the behavior of this group showed that their motives included strategies for diverting food production to La Paz in the event that trade was cut off from the Pacific during the war with Chile; for taking advantage of population increases and increased indigenous markets for altiplano hacienda production; and for exploiting a perceived increase in value for altiplano haciendas that might have been caused partly by inflation. Finally, labor-intensive altiplano haciendas required little capital investment and turned a small steady profit, much like an investment in a mortgage note. As such, the purchased haciendas served as a hedge against inflation and afforded investors a means of preserving the value of their capital.[39]

Vis-à-vis the Indian communities, there was a harder edge on the hacienda expansion that took place in the years 1880–85 compared to that of the period 1866–69. Armed with depreciated state debt paper, the crony buyers of the earlier period were able to intercept the hacendados, merchants, and miners as purchasers of the communal lands and in effect to shield the communal lands from them—thus to supply to the hacienda expansion process a softer, more paternalistic, and more feudalistic quality that interfered less with communal structures. Clearly more entrepreneurial plans were at stake in the purchases in the later period, when the market in communal land was *not* mediated by state debt paper. The difference here was between state auctions of communal lands with privileged buyers and privately negotiated contract sales between Indians and purchasers, with the state's role in the latter being limited to supplying the legislative framework for the sales.

We saw how the caudillistic politics of the 1860s was exemplified by cronies of the president dumping state debt paper in the rural land market. The "intelligent capitalistic landowners" who dominated the land market of the 1880s were characterized by the *absence* of state debt paper as a factor in their motivation to purchase the Indian communal lands. The removal of state debt paper from the rural land market and the substitution of open transactions between buyers and Indian sellers for state auctions were both part of a reaction against the caudillistic politics and cronyism of the Melgarejo period. The introduction of the free market mechanism into the rural land market was accompanied by monetary reform (the substitution of the debased currency by the new fiat boliviano); fiscal reform (the elimination of the tribute and replacement by a single tax structure on all privately owned land and substitution of silver export taxes for the tribute as the mainstay of state revenues); and the entry of the Bolivian economy into its export-led growth phase (replacing the era of protection of the national economy with all of its complex internal trading circuits). All were part of a broad modernization program based on the rejection of the "pre-modern" past.

But Bolivian liberalism morally deteriorated at the same time. What was the relevance of the state's debt policy to this regression of liberalism into the social Darwinism defined by a highly cruel and racist attitude toward the Indians? What happened to the benign yeoman model of individual rural landowners, including the Indians, as its most important constituent part? Did the action of state debt paper in the rural land market pave the way to the moral deterioration of the yeoman model? We find that, to some extent, it did.

In the first place, state debt paper in the rural land market worked against the yeoman concept of the Indian because it was predicated on the concept of the state as seller of the communal lands and as such denied the Indian his status as ultimate owner. In order to vent state debt paper into the rural land market it was necessary to invoke a theory of the state as the owner of the communal lands and the Indian as tenants; Indians as the designated sellers would not likely accept depreciated state debt paper in payment for their communal lands. Ironically, however, it was the removal of state debt paper from the rural land market, and the elimination of the concept of the state as seller, that exposed the Indians to an even more invidious attack on the yeoman model. It took the form of deliberately conceiving the unregulated rural land markets as parts of a selection process that would eliminate Indians as owners in favor of Cabrera's "intelligent (i.e., white) capitalistic landowners."

This is certainly not to argue that the action of state debt paper in the rural land market was more congenial to the emergence of the yeoman landowning class than open markets operating in the absence of that paper. Although this debt paper shielded the market for some time from the entry of capitalists armed with positivistic theories degrading the Indians, the debt paper was itself mortgaged to a particular patrimonialist ideology of the state that was itself incompatible with the emergence of the Indian yeoman. If it was not the "intelligent capitalists," it was state cronies that blocked the yeoman model. But the debt analysis presented here can still provide perspective on the question of the degeneration of the yeoman model into the social Darwinism of Cabrera and provide some consideration of why liberalism took this untoward turn. The problem was not the role of state debt paper in the land market but rather the role of nonfunded, floating debt paper in the land market.

At this juncture, we return to the thesis pursued here: the emergence of floating debt paper was itself a result of the failure to fund the state debt in the immediate postindependence period. It is possible to speculate that the yeoman potential of the Indian would have been strengthened if funded paper had been substituted for the floating debt paper in the rural political economy, particularly if we recognize that instead of dismantling the tributary system it could have been made the basis for converting the Indians into citizen savers.

Madero's funding paper was intended to prevent the development of a privileged class of state creditors (in whom wealth was increasingly concentrated by the uses to which they put state debt paper) by creating instead a broader class of funding paper holders (citizen savers) receiving annuity payments at low interest rates but over an indefinitely long period of time. The original holders of the funded debt in Bolivia were not holding it in order to raid state wealth or to redeem censos or to gain control over state policy. They were holding it because it was assigned to them as titles of public credit in compensation for losses suffered during the wars for independence—inherently a better procedure for building up a fiduciary debt than that of putting the debt into the hands of people who bought it at auction and had no stake in the state's taking responsibility for making good the war damages suffered by citizens. Admittedly, the core of the class pushing the concept of the funded debt as opposed to floating debt was the émigré community linked to Madero and his followers in the Congress and to the silver-commercial elites based in Potosi. But it was expected that the funding paper would expand to include the middle and lower income groups and provide the basis for the creation of popular *cajas de ahorros*. This expectation is reflected in Infante's use of the term *day laborers* (jornaleros) to describe the range of billetes holders that Madero was trying to create on top of the original holders of the internal debt.

This pattern might easily have been extended to the Indians living on the communal lands. By using the mechanism of funding paper, the tributary system could have been transformed into an involuntary savings organization and then a voluntary one. The notably successful caja de ahorros established by Ballivián provided a model. The surprisingly liquid cajas de ahorros, which already were in place in the Indian communities, could easily have been converted to funding paper capital.[40] This approach would have required the Indians to save a certain amount every year (in lieu of tribute payment) by buying state funding paper. The growth of Indian capital would have put them into a position eventually to purchase communal lands and to invest in them as individual owners.

This scenario is not as farfetched as it might seem at first; seeing the tribute system as an embryo of a capital accumulation process, and as a symbol of trust between state and Indians paying it, is in fact what it was, notwithstanding the Darwinistic, liberalist rhetoric picturing it as a retrograde, colonial vestige. The tribute system contained elements of a reciprocal relationship between the state and the communal Indians; it was really a "mutual pact" which guaranteed group access to defined lands in exchange for paying the tribute (and providing labor services in the colonial period). In this sense the tribute acted as a state-guaranteed shield against the encroachment of private owners on these lands. Nor was the tribute the economically sterile arrangement it is commonly thought to have been. It was a dominant source of state revenue until the second half of the century. Dating back to the colonial period, it played a major role in monetizing the indigenous economy: in order to pay the tribute the Indians had to raise cash crops and provide goods and services to cities and the army in order to get access to metallic currency. The monetary circuit that existed in the colonial period between the royal cajas and the tributary Indians and then in the early republican period between the state treasuries and these Indians is well documented.[41] The tribute mutually engaged the Indians and the state in a dynamic economic interaction as well as a moral obligation; it was after all the disappearance of the tribute that coincided with the marginalization of the Indian population.

By using the mechanism of funding paper to transform the tributary system into a savings organization, the already positive elements in the state-Indian tributary relationship could have been vastly extended, with consequences for the role of the state different from those that followed from the state opting to extend its floating debt to the rural sector. By transforming the tributary system into a state-sponsored savings organization, the funding paper might have expanded the agrarian surplus via the accumulation of indigenous capital rather than extracting the surplus by forcing the Indians to become colonos on haciendas. It also would have expanded the fiduciary responsibilities of the state in its relationship to the rural Indian population. Madero's concept of not just quantitatively increasing the levels of economic activity but of strengthening the articulation between economic activity and the integration of Bolivian society would have come full circle with the extension of funding into the rural indigenous sector. By sponsoring socially coherent economic growth in the rural sector, the state would not have played broker to the disarticulation of the indigenous rural society in the name of the accumulation of the surplus by "intelligent and capitalistic" white landowners.

5

Normative and Historiographic Dimensions of Internal State Debt

IN THE PRECEDING CHAPTERS I have pursued the thesis that the existence of floating debt in Bolivia has distorted and obscured state-citizen relations. I argued that funded debt would have expanded those relations and made the state's role in society more accountable. The distinction between funded debt and floating debt has not been drawn in the historical writing on Latin American state debt, although certain recent trends in that historiography have opened up areas of debt policy analysis in which the need to make this distinction is apparent. The usefulness of this distinction is also apparent from the standpoint of nineteenth-century normative debate about state debt, as it applies to the peripheral states. Consideration of these two areas will serve to put the Bolivian debt experience as it has been analyzed here into a broader perspective. It will also perhaps allow the reader to judge the validity of the case that I have advanced for funded debt.

The Nineteenth-Century Normative Debate on Internal Debt

In the eighteenth and nineteenth centuries the subject of a state's internal debt was hotly debated by mercantilists and laissez-faire theorists. Mercantilists believed that the state's internal borrowing activities produced wealth; laissez-faire economists saw these activities as an interference in the natural (free market) economy. At the heart of this debate was the question of whether funded state debt was appreciably different from floating state debt. The additional question of whether funded state debt undermined the democratic state or broadened the democratic base of the state was addressed.

Berkeley's famous phrase that public debts were a "mine of gold" reflected the mercantilist belief that they were vital sources for augmenting the wealth of the state. Three continental writers with mercantilist leanings—Voltaire, Condorcet, and Melon—developed this view of public debt. They held that the public's investment in state debt activated funds that otherwise would remain idle. Further, interest payments on the state debt were essentially internal transfers that involved no primary burden. In Melon's oft-quoted phrase, public debts were the debts "of the right hand to the left," unlike debt owed to foreigners which did drain off wealth.[1]

Classical British economists—Smith, Hume, and Ricardo—who remorselessly characterized public debt as part and parcel of specious mercantilist doctrines of the state were particularly brutal toward internal transfer theory of the debt. Their common position was dictated by a belief that loan proceeds encouraged states to make unproductive and wasteful expenditures, thereby dissipating capital. Of the three, Hume was the most sensitive to the political power that holders of large state debt would acquire. They would gain unaccountable control over the state by having its various forms of revenue mortgaged over to them. The political survival of the democratic laissez-faire state, for Hume, required the extinction of the state debt, by one means or another.[2]

James Steuart agreed with Hume that public debt might lead to a "swelling of monied interest [that] threatened the tranquility of the state." But he argued that in these situations care should be taken "to establish a sinking fund . . . or the plan of borrowing on determinate [terminable] annuities." Steuart's insight was that the "tranquility" of the state was threatened by the development of floating, maneuverable debt charged ad hoc against the states' revenues while the creation of funded debt could act as a shield against this contingency. For Steuart, funded public debt would strengthen the state against intrusive creditors.[3]

Henry Adams, C.F. Banstable, and P. Leroy-Beaulieu were the so-called neoclassical writers on the public debt. They were less doctrinaire than their classical predecessors (mercantilism was a moot issue for them), but they shared their deep suspicion that public debt encouraged wasteful state expenditures and should be kept to a minimum necessary to finance demonstrably useful public works. Of the three, Henry Adams was perhaps the most suspicious of state debt and the most obtuse to Steuart's insight into the political advantage of funding.

Adams wrote that the public debt "comes to be of general convenience when of such form and character as to serve the purpose of investments, as the basis of contracts." Short-term debt was best: "The presence in the community of a moderate amount of such paper, which may be quickly and quietly bought and sold, is of great commercial convenience and this fact insures its acceptance on favorable terms." State financiers should "fashion the public contracts under which a debt is held as to meet the demands of commercial transactions." He felt that the best debt policy was the "clear and simple" one. He was particularly suspicious of long-term debt (annuity debt was repugnant to him) and especially dubious about "involved scheme[s] of funding" such as the one Alexander Hamilton adopted in recognizing America's revolutionary debt.[4]

Adams felt, then, that short-term state debt was commercially convenient in limited amounts while long-term debt, particularly funded debt, was inimical to a democracy. For him the key to self-government was the exercise by the people of complete control over state expenditure. The "evil of the funding system" was that it "allowed the public servant to veil the true meaning of his acts." Ordinarily, people cannot scrutinize state acts "except as they touch the pocket of the voters through an increase in taxes." A state that finances its expenditures out of long-term loans can "for a time administer its affairs independently of those who must finally settle the account. . . . A loan calls for no immediate payment from the people but produces vast sums for the government." Funded loans "by the promise of a perpetual annuity induce the holders of money to intrust it to the state. The administration is satisfied, since its necessities have been relieved without exciting the jealousy of the people; the lenders are satisfied, since they have secured a good investment for their capital and are not bothered with its management; while the people are not dissatisfied because of their profound ignorance of what has taken place."[5]

This logic is of dubious relevance to the situation of the Latin American states after independence. The precise challenge facing these fledgling states was whether they would be able to "administer their affairs independently" or would be dominated by creditors, domestic and foreign. Adams's qualms about a funded state debt being antidemocratic reflected more a North American's free market–based fear of European statism than the realities of the state dependency on the periphery of the world economy. Steuart's "mercantilistic" perception of the special advantage that funding gave the state in terms of avoiding manipulation by powerful creditors is more pertintent.

To a great extent, the weakness of the democratic base in Latin America has resulted from the existence of a floating, maneuverable, and secretive state debt with a powerful foreign branch that began to develop in the second half of the nineteenth century.[6] In Latin America funded state debt is the only alternative to the concentration of wealth and political power among creditors negotiating short-term debt for control over state revenues and state policy. By shifting their state debt from a floating to a funded basis, it will be possible for the Latin American states to begin building a democratic infrastructure.

Latin American Fiscal Historiography

Commenting on Peruvian writing in economic history, Heraclio Bonilla observed that "nobody has ever paid adequate attention to the internal debt. . . . [It] was always seen as either being of no significance or as the expression of the immorality of government leaders and bureaucrats."[7] Views on state borrowing in the domestic sector in the first half of the nineteenth century in Latin America broadly reflected this judgment. Given the weakness of money markets, state borrowing in the domestic sector was thought to be limited to small sums loaned out at high interest on a temporary basis. Moreover, the floating, internal debts carrying over from the revolutionary period were seen as impenetrable mazes that were juggled at the margins in the name of policy. Thus, all that the particular administrations in Venezuela and Colombia needed to mount their debt "policies" in the years from 1826 to the 1850s (when they returned to foreign borrowing) was to have a few "experts in short-term loans and [in the] manipulation of the bewildering variety of internal debt."[8]

The historical importance of debt policy has been brought out in four new approaches to the study of the fiscal history of Latin America. These new approaches were reacting against the oversimplification of the understanding of fiscal policy that resulted from the traditional twin historiographic images of the nineteenth century: the one of the first half of the century as a conflict between the liberal, free trade groups and the temporarily triumphant conservative, protectionist forces, the other of a correlation between economic and political modernization that came about in the second half of the century when repressed liberal groups gained control over the state. In the first instance, neomercantilistic protectionist regimes were seen as vehicles for preserving the social and political power of old colonial elites; they arose specifically to displace liberal free trade ideologies that surfaced briefly in the period 1820–30. After midcentury,

liberal free trade coalitions arose to erase the vestiges of the colonial state
and to orient the state toward external commodity markets and toward
borrowing in the foreign sector rather than in the domestic sector; domestic sector borrowing was seen as part of the mechanism of colonialist
elites to orient the state inward.[9]

The four new historiographies that have displaced this classification of
state fiscal policies into conservative (reactionary) and liberal (progressive)
phases are: application of a dynamic fiscal process perspective to the state
finances in the colonial period; application of an institutionalist perspective to the early republican period; application of a political economy
perspective to the early republican period; application of a perspective
that traces the origins of modern monetary and credit systems back to the
early republican and late colonial periods. Each of these trends has opened
up new horizons of internal debt analysis.

With regard to the first trend, the background was supplied by Earl J.
Hamilton in his *American Treasure and the Price Revolution in Spain,
1501–1660*. He projected the image of a Spanish fiscal structure in the
New World that was tightly controlled from above and geared exclusively
to forwarding Crown interests in Spain and in the New World. Fiscal operations in the New World were supposedly concerned exclusively with extracting wealth for the royal coffers in Madrid, leaving only small amounts
on the margins for paying the local costs of administering the colonial
order. More recent scholars have begun to look for patterns within the
flow of remittances from America to Spain—patterns that challenge the
monolithic fiscal image projected in Hamilton's study. Statistical analyses
applied to bullion flows from America to Spain have revealed a more
complex picture, including the fact that the early mining boom in America inflated European prices and reduced the value of silver in Europe at
the time that mineral production in America began to decline because of
local factors.[10]

The stage was set, therefore, for new analyses stressing the complexity
of Spanish fiscal policy operation by the publication of Sanchez-Bella's *La
Organización Financiera de las Indias: Siglo XVI*.[11] This detailed institu-
tional-juridical analysis pays particular attention to the operational procedures of the Spanish treasury offices (cajas) in America, stressing not only
their innovative and eclectic borrowing from the preconquest indigenous
"fiscal" practices but also the rootedness of many of their tax procedures
in medieval Castilian practices. But Sanchez-Bella does not address the
real dynamics involved in the fiscal process of spending and taxing by the

cajas or the role of that process in reflecting and molding class relationships; she ultimately envisaged the cajas as bureaucratic entities, not as autonomous actors. She examined spending patterns in some detail and acknowledged that by the end of the eighteenth century they may have reached over 85 percent of the royal revenues. But she did not address the cajas' autonomous spending strategies and the conflicts that these clearly created between the cajas and Madrid. In particular, she did not identify elements of the cajas' debt strategy. She tended to be bound by the image of the cajas being under strict control not to make any expenditures (libranzas) that were not approved in advance by special grants and for which specific revenues were earmarked. The existence of any large floating debt in the colonial period is not recognized explicitly.

Two basic branches of fiscal historiography have developed out of Sanchez-Bella's work. The first focused on fiscal policy as a mirror (and molder) of class and race relations. Javier Tord and Carlos Lazo have applied a Marxist perspective to the analysis of fiscal policy in the Viceroyalty of Peru.[12] They believed that at that time the major population sectors were in a state of precapitalism. They argued, therefore, that it was largely through fiscal pressure that the social relations of production were maintained, including dependency relations to Europe. They analysed the "fiscal dynamics" of an increasing surplus extraction over time, including abundant time series data on tax yields in the areas of commerce, tribute, mining, and administrative service.[13] Unfortunately, they did not analyze spending patterns and did not address borrowing as a branch of the fiscal dynamics.

Sonia Pinto's *El Financiamiento Extraordinario de la Real Hacienda en el Virreinato Peruano* has begun to fill in this gap.[14] She concentrated on the extraordinary fiscal measures ordered by the Crown in the Viceroyalty of Peru to extract wealth to cover the increasing royal indebtedness. The focus of her work was one particular component of the *aportes extraordinarios*: voluntary donations and loans (*servicios* and *préstamos*). Loans were accepted as part of the servicios; the principal was returnable with interest usually in a two-year period. The servicios were donations in specie and kind given to the Crown out of feelings of loyalty or expectation of some privilege in return. Her study included the four servicios occurring during the period 1575–1650, and she addressed the questions of amounts raised, proportion of loans and donations within each servicio, and source of the amounts given or loaned by regional location and by social strata. She demonstrated the gradual eclipse of the loan component by donations. It set the stage for an analysis of the subsequent eclipse of servicios as royal patriotism declined and caja fiscal strategies became tied more locally, notwithstanding the late Bourbon, centralizing reforms.

The second branch of fiscal historiography stemming from Sanchez Bella's work applied an autonomous fiscal process perspective to the cajas and included some preliminary work on debt management in the colonial period. John TePaske has adopted the revisionist view that the spending priorities for the cajas in the American empire were (1) to provide for local needs, (2) to provide for imperial or viceregal needs, and (3) to ship whatever was left over to Spain. This perspective emphasized the role of the cajas in retaining ever larger portions of revenues for local and regional expenditures to the extent that the elements of an essentially autonomous fiscal process in America can be identified. TePaske's work on Upper Peru is a convincing demonstration of this thesis of fiscal autonomy, one that is reinforced by Herbert Klein's work on the overall fiscal process within the newly formed Viceroyalty of Rio de la Plata.[15] These studies do not identify the process whereby servicios were replaced by an autonomous debt policy pursued in order to finance local expenditures. In their three-volume collection of data on the spending and collection patterns of royal cajas in Upper Peru, Peru, Chile, and the Rio de la Plata, however, the groundwork has been laid for isolation of debt management policy in the colonial period, including not only the tracking of loans over time but also the identification of debt disguised as other categories of income, for example, deposits on call (depósitos), a particularly dynamic category in the caja income stream.[16]

The thesis of fiscal autonomy has also been convincingly demonstrated by Kenneth Andrien in his book *Crisis and Decline; The Viceroyalty of Peru in the Seventeenth Century*, which contains many references to the growth of a large floating debt held against the Lima caja, totaling an estimated 3.5 million pesos in 1662.[17] Unfortunately, Andrien does not isolate debt management as part of the caja strategy of fiscal autonomy. The main exception is the large state debt owed to the miners at Huancavelica, which receives considerable analysis. Another exception is the extended analysis given to the issuance of annuity paper (*juros de heredad*) by the cajas, a subject pursued elsewhere by the same author.[18] But on balance, it is debt owed to the caja that received more attention than debt owed by it.

The second major branch of recent internal state debt historiography has arisen from the application of a state-building, institutionalist perspective to the early republican period. This application has involved an effort to substitute archival research on the reform policies of the new states, including financial policy, for the heroic historiography that has dominated this period. This institutionalist perspective was applied first by David Bushnell in his study of the Santander government in Colombia in the 1820s, in which he made a deliberate effort to go beyond the larger-than-life figures of Bolivar and Santander in order to get into the actual state machinery. A second leading example of this approach—one that was patterned on Bushnell's—is William Lofstrom's study of the Sucre administration in Bolivia in the 1820s.[19]

Financial policy making in the Santander and Sucre administrations was pictured in these two studies as a pragmatic, deficit-financing enterprise. Each author believed that the choices were made as though they were governed more by cash flow problems than by political or ideological determinations. Whether it was treasury vales or public credit billetes, the essential thing, according to Lofstrom, was to find an "antidote to the gaps that appeared between revenues and running expenditures." Lofstrom did not perceive any political differences between the vales and the billetes, only technical ones. "Although the treasury vales and the billetes of Public Credit were different experiments to try to solve the same problem, that of government insolvency, in their development and eventual failure, they were very similar. . . . To resort to a combination of treasury bills and titles [billetes] of Public Credit to satisfy the urgent obligations of the government was the only alternative that remained to Sucre." Bolivia, he argued, was only following the example of Colombia as described by Bushnell.[20]

Indeed, Colombia experimented with various debt management techniques, including funding. Like Lofstrom, Bushnell put these decisions on a pragmatic policy-making continuum, although Bushnell separated the question of amortizing the internal debt from the question of new state borrowing more than Lofstrom. But he did not attach any decisive significance to the funding initiative. Judging from Lofstrom's and Bushnell's studies, Bolivia's and Colombia's internal debts were comparable except that Colombia's large foreign loan impinged on its internal borrowing position more than was the case in Bolivia, which did not go into the foreign sector. But Lofstrom's view of the debt question during the Sucre administration was affected by Bolivian liberalist historiography more so than Bushnell was affected by Colombian liberalist historiography.

Before Lofstrom addressed the Bolivian debt question extant during the Sucre period, an image of it had been generated by liberalist historiography.

This historiography was represented by José Delance, Casto Rojas, and Luis Peñaloza in three major works.[21] Although Delance was in a special category because he advocated protectionism over free trade, these authors projected a feudalistic-patrimonialist image of Bolivia's colonial period, one characterized by a heavy clerical mortmain structure on landownership and a fiscal policy whose only purpose was to enrich the state. Financial methods of the "modern" state were unknown; everything was "a grand patrimonial exploitation" done in the name of conquest and absolutism.[22] Bolivia would have to wait until the second half of the century to experience economic and political modernization. The republican economic and financial institutions adopted after independence merely carried forward the patrimonialist practices of the colonial period, and represented a victory by those who opposed independence in the first place over those who desired and fought for it.[23]

Typically, holders of this liberalist perspective marked the downfall of the Sucre administration in 1828 as the beginning of the triumph of the neocolonialist state in the republican period. For example, they pointed out that the administration that followed Sucre's debased the metallic currency that miners were legally required to accept from the state in payment for their silver ore, allowing the state to bleed the mining sector for its own benefit, just as it had done in the colonial period. That Sucre's own monetary policy "did not have for its exclusive object the fiscal enrichment of the state is proved by the fact that the adoption of debased metallic currency did not start until 1829," after his government had been replaced.[24]

This liberalist historiography as applied to the debt question during the Sucre administration had two features. First, Madero's plan for the state's recognition of internal debt was a victory for the colonialist forces, particularly loyalist and émigré elements bent on sabotaging Sucre's reforms, who disguised themselves by joining the ranks of the other holders of the internal debt—the patriotic population that suffered losses during the struggle for independence. The state was forced to recognize debts inherited from the colonial period, which it felt it should pay "in spite of all logic and right" and despite its lack of income to meet running expenditures. Madero's motivation in recognizing this debt was considered "natural" since, in the liberalist historiography, those who were against independence in the first place managed to exert political control over the republican states in the immediate aftermath of independence. Madero's

policy embodied the perpetuation of the "colonialist spirit" that deliberately rewarded the enemies of the republic.[25]

Second, the loan vales of the Sucre administration and the billetes of
the Public Credit Administration were seen as indistinguishable parts of
the depreciating state debt paper that began to circulate in Bolivia in the
late 1820s as a means of purchasing state haciendas cheaply and liquidating tax and censos obligations.[26] At least Costa Rojas recognized that the
model for the billetes was the British method of funding, but he drew no
significance from this fact; the billetes were bound to head in the same direction of pilfering wealth as the loan paper, given the inertia of colonial
practices that steered all branches of the fiscal process toward the enrichment of the state and its clients. The billetes were made worthless in his
analysis by overpayment to Spanish holders of the internal debt. He
"proved" his point by quoting a statement by Sucre to this effect, without
indicating that this statement was designed by Sucre's advisers to justify
his own loan program by discrediting the funding program.[27]

Lofstrom's analysis reflects the liberalist historiography in various ways.
He attributed the failure of direct taxation to the machinations of a colonialist elite trying to preserve its privileges under the old system.[28] And, as
we saw, he lumped together the funding and the loan paper, following, in
effect, the deterministic analysis of Delance, as carried forward by Peñaloza
and Costa Rojas.

Lofstrom's analysis was much less simplistic than these three works. He
recognized that the same economic liberalism heralded by the liberalist
historians led to a debt policy that served to enrich a particular clientele
and to destroy the state's role in guaranteeing a welfare system. He did not
point out, however, that the forces of economic liberalism operated through
the Sucre-Infante debt policy, based on highly negotiable short-term loan
paper, which was what destroyed the funding policy that *would* have protected the state's roles in maintaining the welfare system and in preventing
an unfair concentration of landownership. Failure to make this distinction
was only partly because of the influence of liberalist historiography on
Lofstrom's analysis. It was also a product of his style of analysis, which
deemphasized political analysis in favor of the technical, institutionalist
perspective.

The third and most recent of the debt historiographic trends sought to
apply a political economy perspective to early state finances in order to dis-
cover relationships between state debt management and the formation of

class systems. The idea that state debt management was dictated by pragmatic policy-making decisions under conditions of insolvency was rejected
in favor of portraying those decisions as elements in the state's collabora-
tion with a rising commercial bourgeoisie, foreign and domestic. Tulio
Halperin-Donghi, in his analysis of state finances in the early republican
period in Argentina, made the arresting observation that the uncertainty of
the state's financial situation developed after 1815, not because of cash
shortages but rather because of the state's overidentification with Buenos
Aires commercial houses. These houses "imposed" credit lines on the state
in order to trade them for huge tax breaks and special licensing arrangements. Thus it was not state insolvency but the capitalization of a commercial class that drove state debt in Argentina.[29]

In recent work, the political economy perspective has been brought to
bear on the specific question of management of existing internal debt and
on attempts to consolidate it in order to see if privileged classes can be
identified. The leading work deals with Peruvian state finances in the first
half of the nineteenth century. Peruvian consolidations were portrayed as
vehicles for the enrichment of a dominant commercial class, much like the
process that Halperin-Donghi identified in the case of Argentine debt
floats. Alfonso Quiroz, in *La Deuda Defraudada: Consolidación de 1850
y Dominio Económico en el Peru*, argues that in the first half of the nineteenth century, Peru's internal state debt created two classes of state creditors. One class was composed of those with claims on the state who did
not ever get paid—small ranchers, mining owners, rural proprietors. They
received depreciating state paper without guarantees. The privileged creditors of the state lent at high interest and were paid punctually because
they had leverage as future suppliers of credit. This group included foreign
commercial houses that invested in state vales or made advances against
future fiscal income in customs and the mint and domestic commercial
houses that, as administrators in the administrative service tax field, advanced loans to the state. Quiroz argues further that the colonial aristo-
cracy joined forces with the rising privileged class of state creditors as it
tried to reconstitute itself after independence by forging new political and
economic alliances. It pressed for recognition of the floating state debt
held over from the late colonial period and the period of armed struggle.[30]

Quiroz argues that given the unequal distribution of wealth, internal
debt should provide a mechanism for redistribution and for guaranteeing
the rights of investors who put their confidence in the state. These purposes have been defrauded in Peru's internal debt because the consolida-

tions were selective, fomenting speculation that has benefited privileged sectors unconnected with the original debt. His analysis showed how the 1850 consolidation debt paper ended up in the hands of the commercial bourgeoisie, domestic and foreign. The consolidation translated guano proceeds into capital gains for the commercial class in Lima in prejudice to the impoverished class of state creditors—miners, ranch owners, state employees, rural proprietors. The underlying problem, it might be observed, was not consolidation per se but the failure to employ annuity paper instead of commercial paper (vales) as the form of the consolidated issue.

Another Peruvian author, Javier Tantaleán-Arbulu, analyzed the memoirs of state financial ministers of Peru. He also gathered data on the evolution of the internal indebtedness of the Peruvian state from the early 1820s through the consolidation of 1850. His book, *Política Económica-Financiera y la formación del Estado; Siglo XIX*, describes the increasing complexity of the internal debt and the stages of the state's effort to amortize it.

In the 1830s Arbulu argued that the caudillo state synthesized an alliance between large landowners in the interior and the commercial elites in Lima. The hacendados acted as an extension of the state in collecting the tribute and in recruiting Indians for caudillo armies. The commercial elites acted as banks of credit for the state fisc. When the tribute fell short of running expenditures, the state sold debt paper to the commercial elites. These elites, through these loans, "negotiated" their participation in the financing of the state, unlike those who paid the tribute tax or passive state creditors holding depreciating state debt paper originating in the colonial and revolutionary periods. So the "internal debt could be converted into a resource for capitalization at their service and therefore as a method for capital accumulation." Arbulu largely confirmed Quiroz's analysis of the 1850 consolidation as a tool whereby the state channeled guano profits into the pockets of commercial elites, landowners, financiers, and politicians.

This shared conclusion concerning the consolidation is ratified by Paul Eliot Gootenberg in his *Between Silver and Guano: Commercial Policy and the State in Post-Independence Peru*. His analysis is based, however, on the thesis that commercial elites in the protectionist period preceding the liberal period in Peru were forced to lend money to various caudillo states until this system bankrupted them. The shift to a liberal, free trade regime was designed deliberately by a new commercial elite to bring foreign lenders into state debt in order to protect itself from the forced loans that had bedeviled their predecessors under the old state debt system. The earlier commercial elite had tried to save itself by selling the state on a policy of amortizing all of its outstanding internal debt. The new commercial elite, by contrast, established itself by selling the state on the policy of consolidating internal debt. Gootenberg's analysis of the difference between "amortization politics" and "consolidation politics" is provocative and original.

The final branch of fiscal historiography attempted to place state debt in the 1820s in the context of structural shift from mercantile economies to capitalistic economies and the attendant beginnings of modern monetary and banking systems in Latin America. This perspective is most notable in the work on Argentina and Mexico, although these two historiographies contain different emphases reflecting the different financial conditions of the two countries in this period.

Argentine scholarship has emphasized the role of state debt in the banking and monetary perspective. Argentina had the first genuine bank in Latin America and the most sophisticated funding experiment. It was the earliest state to attempt to shift from metallic to fiat currency. Argentine historiography has emphasized the role of state debt paper as a precursor of paper money. This historiography has been molded by Emilio Hansen's *La Moneda Argentina*, which followed by twenty years the publication of another key work, Agustin de Vedia's *El Banco Nacional: Historia Financiera de la Republica Argentina, 1818–1854*. More recently, the placing of state debt in the context of the early foundations of the monetary and banking system of Argentina was emphasized in Jorge Difrieri, *Moneda y Banco en la Republica Argentina*, Sergio Bagú, *El Plan Económico del Grupo Rivadaviano, 1811–1827*, and Miron Burgin, *The Economic Aspects of Argentine Federalism, 1820–1852*.

Mexican debt historiography of the 1820s places less influence on the beginnings of a monetary and a banking system and more on the development of the state's role in financing the underlying shift from a mercantile economy to a capitalistic one. This historiography has benefited from the financial crisis, characterized by the extraordinary foreign indebtedness of the Mexican state, that developed in the 1970s. This crisis prompted a wave of scholarship focusing on the origins of state indebtedness in the colonial and early republican periods.

One branch of this research, led by Masae Sugawara, located the antecedents of state debt and subsequent borrowing practices in the spillover of Spanish debt management policies into New Spain in the period 1780–1809.[31] This research showed how Mexican state debt management was largely an extension of the Spanish Consolidación de Vales Reales and how it was intimately shaped by the process of disentailing church wealth. Other parts of the empire were much less affected by the Consolidación process than was Mexican state debt, but their state debts were closely linked nevertheless to the disentailment of church wealth and Mexican debt historiography is an essential reference point.

A second branch of Mexican debt historiography in the past fifteen years was associated with the research of Marcello Carmagnani and Carlos Marichal.[32] Their premise was that the later state debt of Mexico could be tied to the evolution of a particular credit system with roots in the late colonial and early independence periods, when banks did not exist significantly in Mexico. This lack caused state debt paper to serve as a basis of commercial contracts and transactions. Questions revolved around the functions of credit in the late colonial–early republican period, relations of credit to circulation and to production, and origins and sources of credit. From this perspective, debt management occurred within the evolution of a credit system that was linked not to an industrial process but rather to a process of mercantilizing the productive structure. The credit system was formed at a preindustrial stage of capitalism in which commercial capital and state debt played essential credit-supplying roles. Credit expansion depended on the growth of state debt. The value of this historiography is that it revealed how the state debt policies were molded by the need to finance the growth of developing mercantile economies in a precapitalist stage when banks did not really exist.

The Mexican historiography is a valuable contrast to the Argentine in that it shows the function of the state indebtedness within a developing precapitalist commercial economy and emphasizes the pressures to commercialize state debt within a mercantile framework. These pressures ultimately foreclosed the opportunity to fund Mexican state debt. Argentine historiography reflects a different and more financially sophisticated state financing situation in the 1820s. It was more monetaristic and more attuned to efforts to shift state debt from commercially redeemable debt instruments to irredeemable paper money and the concomitant creation of a funding system as an alternative to the commercialization of public debt. Argentine historiography emphasizes the (potential) fiduciary function of state debt in disseminating titles of public credit among the citizenry rather than its commercial function.

Notes

ABBREVIATIONS

CO   *Colección Oficial de Leyes, Decretos, Ordenes, Resoluciónes Que Se Han Expedido Para El Regimen De La Republica Boliviana.* Vol. 1, 1825–26; vol. 2, 1827–29. La Paz, 1834.

DRB   Vicente Lecuna, ed., *Documentos Refentes a la Creación de Bolivia.* 2 vols. Caracas, 1975.

GRM   Colección Gabriel René-Moreno. Biblioteca Nacional de Bolivia.

MH   Archivo del Ministerio de Hacienda, 1825–28. Archivo Nacional de Bolivia.

MI   Archivo del Ministerio del Interior, 1825–28. Archivo Nacional de Bolivia.

RAR   *Redactor de la Asamblea de Representantes; Legislatura del Año de 1825.* La Paz, 1914.

RAC   *Redactor de la Asamblea Constituyente de 1826.* La Paz, 1917.

CHAPTER 1

1. Frank Dawson, *The First Latin American Debt Crisis*; Carlos Marichal, *A Century of Debt Crisis in Latin America.*
2. Elena Bonura, "El Crédito Publico Bajo La Administración de Juan Manuel de Rosas," 195–96.
3. Richard Ehrenberg, *Capital and Finance in the Age of the Renaissance*, 32–42.
4. Henry C. Adams, *Public Debts: An Essay in the Science of Finance*, 41.
5. Ehrenberg, *Capital and Finance*, 35–41; Adam Smith, *The Wealth of Nations*, 859–81.
6. Sergio Bagú, *El Plan Económico Del Grupo Rivadaviano, 1811–1827*, 174–75.
7. Hargreaves, *National Debt*, 1.
8. Ibid., 23–24.
9. Clara Garcia Ayluardo, "El Comerciante y el Crédito durante la Epoca Borbónica en la Nueva Espana"; Marichal, "El Nacimiento de la Banca Mexicana en el Contexto Latinoamericano." Cf. Donald Stabile and Jeffrey Cantor, *The Public Debt of the United States.*

10. Alfonso W. Quiroz, *La Deuda Defraudada: Consolidación de 1850 y Dominio Económico en el Peru*, 52; Luis Peñaloza, *Historia Económica de Bolivia*, 2:395.

11. Peñaloza, 396.

12. Ibid., 397.

13. Ibid., 402.

14. Quiroz, *La Deuda Defraudada*, 19, 29–30.

15. Tulio Halperin-Donghi, *Guerra y Finanzas en los Origenes del Estado Argentino, 1791–1856*, 76 ff.

16. Ibid., 151, 153–54.

17. Nikita Vallenilla, "Banca y Estado Venezolano, 1830–1911," 1:210–11.

18. Marichal, "El Nacimiento."

19. Halperin-Donghi, *Guerra y Finanzas*, 109–10.

20. Ibid., 102–3.

21. Vicente Lopez, *Historia de la Republica Argentina*, 1:457–69; Juan Carlos Pereira Pinto, *Temas de Historia Económica y Social Argentina durante el Siglo XIX*, 88–94.

22. Jorge A. Difrieri, *Moneda y Banco en la Republica Argentina*, 37.

23. Bagú, *El Plan Económico*, 174–75.

24. Ibid., 298–99.

25. Miron Burgin, *The Economic Aspects of Argentine Federalism, 1820–1852*, 49–54; Difrieri, *Moneda y Banco*, 58–61; Bonura, "El Credito Publico," 196–97. On emphyteusis policy, see Bagú, 159, 167, 179–81, 351–76, esp. 308–9, for prohibition of land sales for debt paper.

26. Difrieri, *Moneda y Banco*, 60.

27. For the text of the September 20, 1780, cedula, see Masae M. Sugawara, "Los Antecedentes Coloniales de la Deuda Publica de Mexico," 215–21. On the origins of the vales reales initiative, see Jaime Vicens Vives, *An Economic History of Spain*, 585–86.

28. On phases in the market discounting of the vales, see Sugawara, *La Deuda Publica de España y la Economía Novohispaña, 1804–1809*, 7; Richard Herr, *Rural Change and Royal Finances in Spain*, 84, 101–2, 110, 112–13, 118. On the 1794 vales issue decrees, see Sugawara, "Antecedentes," 247–50.

29. On the Caja de Amortización decrees, see Sugawara, "Antecedentes," 289–93.

30. For the texts of the September 24 and 25, 1798, decrees, see ibid., 296–97.

31. For the text of the August 30, 1800, decree, see ibid., 328– 50.

32. Francisco Carrasco, *Represetación al Rey Sobre Amortización* (1765); Gaspar Melchor de Jovellanos, *Informe de la Sociedad Económica de esta Corte al Consejo de Castila en el Expediente de Ley Agraria* (1795).

33. See Sugawara, "Antecedentes," 193, for citation of the decree of August 21 and 24, and 191–92 for the decrees of March 11 and 23.

34. Vicens Vives, *An Economic History of Spain*, 34–36.

35. Ramos Tamames, *The Spanish Economy*, 24–25, quoted at 25.

36. Herr, *Rural Change*, 720–22.

37. Ibid., 721–23.

38. Ibid., 550–55.
39. Ibid., 751–52.
40. Ibid., 744. On caciquismo, see 723, 745.
41. Sugawara, *Deuda Publica*, 7.
42. On the decrees of November 28 and December 26, 1804, see ibid., 13–26.
43. Ibid., 11; Arnold Bauer, "The Church in the Economy of Spanish American Censos and Depósitos in the Eighteenth and Nineteenth Centuries."
44. Sugawara, *Deuda Publica*: "Representación Contra la Consolidación de Vales Reales del Ayuntamiento de Ciudad de Mexico," 28–29.
45. Ayluardo, "Comerciante," 27; German Comenares, "Censos y Capellanías: Formas de Crédito en una Economía Agricola," 123; Asuncion Lavrin, "El Capital Eclesiastico y las Elites Sociales en Nueva España"; John F. Schwaller, *Origins of Church Wealth in Mexico; Ecclesiastical Revenues and Church Finances, 1523–1600.*
46. Margaret Chowning, "The Consolidación de Vales Reales in the Bishopric of Michoacan." See also Bauer and Ayluardo as cited in my bibliography.
47. Susana B. Liberté, "Notas Sobre la Consolidación de Vales Reales en el Río de la Plata, 1806–1809."

CHAPTER 2

1. John TePaske and Herbert S. Klein, *The Royal Treasuries of the Spanish Empire in America*, 2:178–82.
2. Liberté, "Notas Sobre la Consolidación," 316, 319.
3. Ibid., 315.
4. José Maria Delance, *Bosquejo Estadístico de Bolivia*, 177–81, 201.
5. Carlos Sempat Assadourian, *El Sistema de la Economía Colonial; El Mercado Interior y Regional y Espacio Economico*, 129–30, 132–33.
6. Ibid., 161, 130–31.
7. John TePaske, "The Fiscal Structure of Upper Peru and the Financing of Empire," 71, 76–77; Sempat, *El Sistema*, 140.
8. TePaske, "The Fiscal Structure," 77, 79–80, 83.
9. Ibid., 77; Sempat, *El Sistema*, 143–45, 146–47, 154.
10. Herbert Klein, "The State and the Labor Market in Rural Bolivia in the Colonial and Early Republican Period," 98–99; Tristan Platt, "Estados Tributarios y Libre Cambio en Potosi durante el Siglo XIX"; Kenneth J. Andrien, *Crisis and Decline: The Viceroyalty of Peru in the Seventeenth Century*, 30–31; Karen Spalding, "Kurakas and Commerce: A Chapter in the Evolution of Andean Society"; TePaske "The Fiscal Structure," 76.
11. Javier Tord and Carlos Lazo, *Hacienda, Comercio, Fiscalidad y Luchas Sociales en Peru Colonial*, 204–7.
12. Klein, "The State and the Labor Market," 98–104.
13. Magnus Morner, *The Andean Past: Land, Societies, and Conflicts*; Andrien, *Crisis and Decline*, 72–73.

14. Andrien, *Crisis and Decline*, 21–22; Robert G. Keith, *Conquest and Agrarian Change: The Emergence of the Hacienda System on the Peruvian Coast*, 135.

15. Herbert Klein, "The Structure of the Hacendado Class," quoted at 198.

16. Ibid., 192–95, 198–99, 205.

17. Gabriel Reyes Martinez, *Finanzas de las 44 Diocesis de Indias*, 34.

18. Schwaller, *Origins of Church Wealth in Mexico*, 2–5.

19. Reyes Martinez, *Finanzas*, 92, 234.

20. Ibid., 57; Schwaller, *Origins of Church*, 83–84.

21. Bolivia National Archives: MI, t. 10, no. 7; William Lofstrom, *The Promise and Problem of Reform*, 140–41; Dalence, *Bosquejo Estadístico*, 202–3.

22. Schwaller, *Origins of Church*, 111–13.

23. Reyes Martinez, *Finanzas*, 34–35.

24. Ibid., 54–57, 150, 192, 211; Daniel J. Santamaría, *Iglesia y Economía Campesina en el Alto Peru, Siglo XVIII*, 14.

25. Morner et al., *Compraventas de Tierras en el Cuzco, 1825–1869*, 51.

26. Bauer, "The Church in the Economy," 718.

27. Santamaria, *Iglesia y Economía*, 14.

28. Morner et al., *Compraventas*, 52; Lofstrom, *Reform*, 145–46.

29. Bauer, "The Church in the Economy," 32; Brian H. Hammett, "Church Wealth in Peru: Esates and Loans in the Archdiocese of Lima in the Seventeenth Century," 115.

30. Rosario Jiminez, *Mineria en Bolivia, 1826–1848*, 1, 11–20.

31. Andrien, *Crisis and Decline*, 32.

32. Lofstrom, *Reform*, 139–40.

33. David Brading, *Haciendas and Ranches in the Mexican Bajo, 1700–1860*; Enrique Florescano, ed., *Haciendas, Latifundios y Plantaciónes in America Latina*.

34. Morner et al., *Compraventas*.

35. Lofstrom, *Reform*, 137–18, 141–43.

36. Cochabamba: MI, t. 9, no. 1, January 10, 1826 ; La Paz: MI, t. 27, no. 7, December 31, 1826.

37. Morner et al., *Compraventas*, 10, 51, 55, 59, 62.

38. Tord and Lazo, *Hacienda, Comercio, Fiscalidad*, 211–12; Santamaria, *Iglesia y Economía*, 5, 14; Reyes Martinez, *Finanzas*, 35.

39. Valentine Abecia, *El Criollismo de la Plata*; Gabriel René Moreno, *Ultimos Días Coloniales en el Alto Peru*.

40. Charles Arnade, *The Emergence of the Republic of Bolivia*; Sabino Pinilla, *La Creación de Bolivia*; Juan R. Cabrera, *La Guerra de los Quince Anos*.

41. Lofstrom, *Reform*, 278–80.

42. Ibid., 143–44.

43. *Condor*, August 17, 1826, no. 37, 4.

44. Sucre to Bolivar, June 25, 1825, DRB, I, 256–58; Sucre Address to the Deliberative Assembly, August 6, 1825, DRB, I, 283–92; Sucre to Esteños Bolivar's secretary, November 8, 1825, MI, t. 1, no. 3. Quotation is from the last.

45. Decree, December 11, 1825 CO, 71–73.

46. Lancaster teacher from Buenos Aires: Infante to Church Government, December 13, 1826, MI, t. 19, no. 8.

47. Lofstrom, *Reform*, 91–94; *Encyclopedia Universal Ilustrada* (Barcelona, 1925), vol. 28, part 1, 1400, cited originally by Lofstrom.

48. Potosi decrees: DRB, II, 47–51.

49. 70 article code: DRB, II, May 14, 1826, 130–39.

50. Infante to Church Government, Chuquisaca, December 13, 1826, MI, t. 19, no. 8.

51. Infante to Church Government, February 9, 1826, MI, t. 19, no. 8.

52. *Condor*, October 12, 1826, no. 46, 2–3.

53. Decree, December 11, 1825, CO, I, 71–73.

54. Terrazas to Jerónimo Valdez, March 4, 1824, MI, t. 1, no. 5.

55. Terrazas to Antonio Maria [*sic*] Sucre, February 25, 1825, MI, t. 1, no. 5.

56. Terrazas to Sucre, July 21, 1825, MI, t. 1, no. 5.

57. Terrazas to Sucre, December 21, 1825, MI, t. 1, no. 5; Permanent Delegation to Sucre, April 15, 1826, MI, t. 4, no. 1, and November 18, 1825, MI, t. 1, no. 2.

58. Infante to Constituent Congress, August 3, 1826, MI, t. 19, no. 1, and July 31, 1826, t. 19, no. 8.

59. Regular convents count: MI, t. 10, no. 7; cf. Lofstrom, *Reform*, 26.

60. Sucre decree: CO, I, 173–75.

61. Esteños to Sucre: November 8, 1825, MI, t. 1, no. 3.

62. Congressional law: CO, I, 334.

63. Decree, December 11, 1825, CO, I, 71–73. Cited also in note 53.

64. Terrazas to Infante, January 31, 1826, MI, t. 10, no. 7.

65. *Condor*, April 6, 1826, no. 19, 1.

66. Terrazas to Infante, January 25, 1826, MI, t. 10, no. 7.

67. Terrazas to Sucre, March 7, 1825, MI, t. 1, no. 5.

68. Diezmos auction decree cited in Madero to Cochabamba Prefect, March 1, 1827, MH, t. 17, no. 1.

69. CO, I, 276–77, for clavería incorporation law. On Sucre's decrees converting claveria employees and limiting their functions at diezmos auctions, see Madero to Infante, April 14, 1827, MI, t. 15, various numbers, containing clavería notories' petitions to Madero for relief from Sucre's decrees.

70. On debate on clavería and diezmos: RAC, September 12, 1826, 532–37.

71. On Olañeta's defense of his own patriotism: *Expresión de Casimiro Olañeta*, GRM, March 10, 1826, M416, XI, cat. no. 1464.

72. On clavería "monster": ibid., 535–36.

73. Thirty-eight parish reports on revenues from births, marriages, burials, all broken into Indian and mestizo categories: Terrazas to Infante, April 24, 1826, MI, t. 10, no. 7. Representative endowment packages of obras pías, capellanías, corfradías, plus municipal rents and taxes, for orphanages, schools, poorhouses in Cochabamba: MI, t. 9, no. 1.

74. Infante to Constitutive Congress, December 19, 1826, MI, t. 19, no. 1.

75. Albert O. Hirschman *Exit, Voice and Loyalty; Responses to Decline in Firms, Organizations and States*, quoted at 86.

76. Olañeta to Bolivar, October 19, 1825, in *Memorias de General O'Leary*, ed. Daniel O'Leary, 11:21. On Olañeta's defense of his own patriotism, see Ola-

ñeta, *Expresión de Casimiro Olañeta*. For rebuttal of émigré charges that royalist collaborators were favored for state appointments: *Condor*, May 18, 1826, no. 25, 2–3. On provocateurs in the émigré community: Sucre to Dean Funes, August 2, 1826, Argentine National Archive, document no. 542/97, Sucre-Funes correspondence.

CHAPTER 3

1. For Madero's biographic details, see Edmund Temple, *Travels in Various Parts of Peru*, 2:18, and Lofstrom, *Reform*, 94. On Madero's predilection for Argentine institutions: J.B. Pentland, *Report on Bolivia, 1827*, 138. On Sucre's appointment of Madero and reasons: Sucre to Bolivar, March 9 and 27, 1826, DRB, II, 64 and 82, respectively. On the creation of the new portfolios provisionally under Infante's supervision: decree by Geraldino, secretary of war, DRB, II, 6. On the order separating treasury and interior, and appointing Madero minister of treasury: CO, I, March 31, 1826, 176.

2. For the experiments in public credit leading to the establishment of the Caja Nacional under the Pueyrredón administration: Lopez, *Historia de la Republica Argentina*, 3: 457–69. For the treatment of the same from a monetary perspective, Pereira Pinto, *Temas de Historia Económica y Social Argentina durante el Siglo XIX*, 88–94. On concepts of political economy adopted by the Rivadavia administration and derived from Puerrydón's earlier funding initiatives: the "Santiago Wilde Plan" in Bagú, *El Plan Económico del Grupo Rivadaviano*, 131–37. On Madero's role in the Rivadavia reforms and commitment to funding: Bagú, 131–37. The rationale for shifting away from customs revenues is contained therein. See also Bagú, 32–33, and Difrieri, *Moneda y Banco*, 54 ff. The Wilde Plan contained the rationale for the substitution of direct taxes for indirect taxes. For the debate in the Executive Junta on this question, see Bagú, 216–24. The plan for funding the public debt and amortization strategy is described by Difrieri, 25–61, and Burgin, *Economic Aspects*, 48–76, and documented in Bagú, 33–39, 177–84, 298–308. The emphyteusis policy is documented in Bagú, 159, 167, 179–81, which contain texts of Rivadavia's letters and speeches on the subject. The congressional debate over emphyteusis on May 18, 1826, is reported in Bagú, 351–76.

3. Carlos Ortiz de Zeballos, *Mision de Ortiz de Zeballos en Bolivia*, Pando to Ortiz, November 22, 1826, 86. On Bolivar's insistence on Santa Cruz's appointment to the La Paz prefectureship, see Sucre to La Paz Prefect, October 12, 1825, Pedro Grases, ed., *Archivo de Sucre*, 7:151–52.

4. On Madero's return to the Congress of its direct taxation bill, see Madero to Congress, July 12, 1812, and July 26, 1826, in DRB, II, 211–12 and 225–27, respectively. For Bolivar's three decrees, see CO, 1825, 66–71. The text of the law of December 11, 1825, leaving the recognition of the debts of the Spanish government in Alto Peru to the future determination of Congress is referenced in Madero's decree of April 26, 1826, which set up procedures for the documentation of the internal debt and the framework for indemnification: DRB, II, 114–15.

5. On Madero's exclusive responsibility for the drafting of the public credit bill, see Pentland, 38. On Sucre's reluctant acquiescence, see Sucre to Galindo, August 31, 1827, in Blanco Galindo, ed., *Cartas del General Antonio José de Sucre a Leon Galindo*, 165–66. On the indemnification emphasis in the public credit approach of the Pueyrredón administration, see Lopez, 461–63. On Madero's trip to Buenos Aires, see Infante to the Argentine Foreign Minister, September 9, 1826, DRB II, 266.

6. Reference to the issues of 1815 and 1820 is made in *Condor* no. 76, May 11, 1827, 3. The "money in hand" quotation is from *Condor* no. 25, May 18, 1826, 4.

7. For the prediction of a rapid fall in the market value of Madero's notes, see *Condor* no. 118, March 6, 1828, 2. On the conditions of the Argentine bank note issue and Sucre's pessimistic evaluation, see Periera Pinto, 85–91, and Sucre to Bolivar, December 4, 1826, DRB II, 296–97. On the disparaging remarks made by Sucre about the Public Credit Program in Bolivia, see Sucre to Galindo, August 31, 1827, in Galindo ed., *Cartas*, 165–66.

8. On Sucre's hope to pay the gratification from the proceeds of the loan: Sucre to Bolivar, August 20, September 20, and December 27, 1826, DRB II, 251, 271, and 306, respectively. See 271 also for reference to using loan funds to finance the expedition to Havana. For Sucre's sharing of Bolivar's opposition to paying gratification out of a loan raised abroad: Sucre to the Constituent Congress, May 25, 1826, DRB, II, 158. For Sucre's particular objection to a foreign loan for this purpose: Infante Circular to the Departments, March 16, 1827, MI, t. 69, no. 11; cited also in note 19 below.

9. For the text of the loan law, CO, I, 339. For the October 23, 1826, congressional discussion, RAC, 677–78. For the substitution of "hipoteca" for "garantia": RAC, November 16, 1826. For the interpretation that the loan would be more heavily discounted if it had been intended for the domestic market, Aguirre (minister of treasury) to prefect of La Paz, November 20, 1827: MH, t. 17, no. 2.

10. For the debate in Congress of the public credit bill: RAC, 681, 690–91, 720–23.

11. For Aguirre's comments, see RAC, 722. For the public auction decree from which Madero's quotations are taken: DRB II, 138–8, Resolution of May 15, 1826. I have extrapolated Madero's philosophy behind his funding from two sources: Infante's characterization of Madero's views in *Condor* (see chapter 4) where he specifically criticized Madero's concern with turning jornaleros into savers, and the emphasis on popular savings as an antidote to a luxury spending in the Santiago Wilde Plan (Bagú, 216–24), which was a critical document in political economy that underlay the financial reforms of Rivadavia. Madero's signature is on it.

12. For the text of public credit law: CO, I, 354–360. For the sections on the sinking fund: Chapter 1, art. 6 and Chapter 3, arts. 21–22. On the Departmental Treasuries' obligations to the amortization offices: Chapter 3, arts. 17 and 18.

c13. For Madero's draft bill of particulars for émigré indemnification, see RAC, 850–52. For laws of December 15 and 17, 1826: CO, I, 375–76 and 376–77, respectively. Law of January 11, 1827, CO, II, 85–86.

14. Articles 3 and 9 of the December 15 and 17 laws, respectively, placed stric-

on the negotiations of billetes for "capital belonging to churches, convents, religious brotherhoods, obras pías, and any other public establishments."

15. For an accounting of the departmental revenues and expenditure in 1826: MH, t. 5, no. 4. Same for the use of intradepartmental transfers to cover deficits. Costs of military garrisons as a percentage of departmental revenues are computed from this document. For the total military costs in 1827 (1,083,705 pesos): *Condor*, June 19, 1828. For a description of the revenue decline in 1826 and specifically the shortages in the collection of direct taxes: *Condor*, April 15, 1827, 2. On the 70,000-peso cost for readying Voltigeros for evacuation: Sucre to Bolivar, September 19, 1827, DRB, II, 458.

16. On the decree of February 1, 1827, opening subscriptions to the loan: CO, II, 102–3. On the weakness of domestic bidding: Lofstrom, *Reform*, 467–68. On Sucre's abandonment of the foreign loan and the subscription format in favor a domestic loan float: Sucre to Bolivar, May 19, 1827, DRB, II, 436. On Sucre's effort to arrange a loan in Peru: Sucre to Santa Cruz, December 24, 1826, DRB, II, 295–96.

17. On Infante's notification to Madero of the loan decision including the reference to the favorable reception in La Paz: Infante to Madero, March 18, 1827, MI, t. 19, no. 7. The subsequent massive use of vales in the La Paz Department to cancel out liens and mortgages supports the inference that Sucre and Infante received advice in La Paz to make their loan vales usable for this purpose. On slowness in organizing the Public Credit Office in La Paz: Lofstrom, *Reform*, 481. On Madero's rejection of Infante's bringing this matter to his attention, on the ground that the executive had no authority over the Public Credit Offices: Madero to Infante, May 12, 1827, MI, t. 15, no. 7.

18. For text of Infante's original loan instructions to the La Paz prefect dated March 12, 1827: MI, t. 69, no. 11.

19. For text of loan circular: MI to Prefects of Cochabamba, Potosi, Chuquisaca, Oruro, La Paz, March 16, 1827, MI, t. 69, no. 11.

20. On the Oruro project: Esteños to Sucre, November 12, 1825, MI, t. 1, no. 3.

21. On debate in Congress on state hacienda sell-off to capitalize the Mining Bank: RAC, July 20, 1826, 308–15.

22. For quotation by Carpio: ibid., 310.

23. For Olañeta, "dead hands": RAC July 27, 1826, 333. For Molina, "different placement": RAC, July 20, 313.

24. For arguments against the sell-off: RAC, July 20, 308–15, passim, especially Gutierrez and Bozo.

25. For La Paz Welfare Board complaint against the sell-off: referred to in the debate, RAC, 310–15; also (July 27), 332–34.

26. Gutierrez, Bozo Callejo statements warning of effects of the sell-off on public establishment endowments: RAC, 310–15, and Gutierrez and Bozo, 332–34.

27. For arguments in favor of the sell-off: Carpio, Molina, Olañeta, RAC, 308–15 passim.

28. For Infante remarks, RAC, July 27, 333.

29. For Infante's chastising of Madero: Infante to Madero, March 12, 1827, MI, t. 19, no. 7. For Madero's reply: April 4, 1827, MI, t. 15, no. 7. For Infante's

contention that the decision to make loan vales negotiable for state property and censos was made after he and Sucre returned to Chuquisaca: *Condor*, no. 118, March 6, 1828, 2.

30. Madero to Infante, March 7, 1827, MI, t. 15, no. 7.

31. A typed copy of this letter from Sucre to Madero exists in the Bolivian Archives and was consulted by Lofstrom and quoted from by him, with the source given as Bolivian National Archives, Gabriel Moreno Collection, MS Copies, VI. This classification does not presently exist in the Gabriel Moreno Collection. Completely by accident, I encountered the copy of the letter tucked away in the Prensa Peruana section of the Gabriel Moreno Collection, in the *Telégrafo de Lima* (Peruvian newspaper), January 10–July 1826, where it still is as far as I know. The original of the letter, in Sucre's hand, is, according to the information on this copy, in the library of Andres La Mar in Buenos Aires, to whom it was given by Juan N. Madero, the son of Sucre's minister of the treasury.

32. On Madero's refusal to sign the decrees as originally drafted: *Condor*, no. 7, December 22, 1827, 2, note 24. For text of the June 22, 1827, decrees, CO, II, 130–35.

33. Sucre to Bolivar, May 19, 1827, DRB II, 436–37. For "forbearance" quotation: Sucre to Bolivar, September 19, 1827, DRB II, 458.

34. On failure of the citizens to take advantage of the June 12 decrees and the relevant quotations: *Condor* no. 118, March 6, 1828, 2. The writer is undoubtedly Infante. On the difficulties encountered by the military vales holders in selling them and Sucre's impatience: Sucre to Bolivar, September 19, 1827, DRB II, 458.

35. For the text of the law of December 30, 1826: CO, I, 400–401. For Madero's interpretation of "bienes nacionales" in the December 30 law: see his decree of May 13, 1827, CO, II, 125. For Infante's different interpretation: Infante to the La Paz Prefect, May 16, 1827, MI, t. 19, no. 11. For Infante's orders to sell a hacienda to an independence fighter's widow for billetes, even if the hacienda generated income for welfare establishments: Infante to the Prefect of Cochabamba, May 8, 1827, MI, t. 69, no. 11. For the actual registration of the sale of this particular hacienda (Zuiaquiabi) to the widow (Juana de Dios Banbeyto) for 19,200 in billetes: MH, t. 9, no. 9, "Accounting of . . . Billetes of Public Credit Deposited in the Treasury for One or Another Reason, Submitted by the Prefect of Cochabamba to MH, November 24, 1828."

36. On Alarcón's endorsement of 1,900 bonds over to Geraldino: MH, t. 10, no. 10, "Accounting of Vales Which Have Been Distributed, Endorsed, or Moved to Other Departments" submitted to MH by the Public Treasury of the Department Chuquisaca, January (n.d.), 1828. For the registration of Alarcón's purchase of the Zacabamba hacienda in Chuquisaca: MH, t. 10, no. 10, "Accounts of Individuals Who Have Made Their Payments in This Office in Notes of Public Credit to Pay Their Pre-1825 Debts, in Billetes to Buy Properties and to Redeem Mortgages, and in Vales for the Same Purposes." On the earlier appraisal of the Zacabamba Hacienda at 90,000 pesos: *Fenix* (Lima newspaper) January 13, 1828, in GRM, Prensa Peruana.

37. This whole reconstruction of the Fernandez affair in terms of the underlying conflict between the congressional law concerning the Mining Bank and the

June 12 decrees is based on Infante to the Prefect of Potosi, October (n.d.) 1827, MI, t. 19, no. 17; copy also in MI, t. 19, no. 16. For the text of the congressional order conveying the proceeds from the sale of public haciendas to the Mining Banks: CO, I, 255.

38. Aguirre to Infante, January 3, 1828, MI, t. 20, no. 10.

39. For the registration of Geraldino's purchase of the Zacabamba hacienda for haberes, vales and billetes: MH, t. 9, no. 9, "Accounting of Military Haberes Cancelled for the Sale of Public Property and the Redemption of Mortgages; of Loan Bonds Amortized for the Same Purposes; of Billetes of Public Credit Deposited in the Treasury for One or Another Reason," submitted by the Prefect of Cochabamba, November 25, 1828. On Aguirre's use of the Geraldino purchase to illustrate the difficulties in arranging for financing of welfare establishments losing their endowments by the operation of the June 12 decree: Aguirre to Infante, January 19, 1828, MI, t. 20, no. 10.

40. On the accounting of the debts dating from the colonial period—back taxes, obras pías in arrears, back tribute collections—amounting to 90,799 pesos: MH, t. 10, no. 10, submitted by the Treasury of Chuquisaca, February 15, 1828. On the uses made of government paper in Chuquisaca, MH, t. 10, no. 10.

41. On the uses made of government paper in Cochabamba: MH, t. 9, no. 9.

42. On the amortization of state debt paper in Potosi, MH, t. 10, no. 14: "Accounting of Loan Vales Amortized until April 1828 through the Purchase of Properties and Redemption of Censos under the June 12 Decree," submitted November 30, 1828, and, same file and date, "Accounting of Billetes of Public Credit Which Have Entered the Treasury for Purchases of Properties, Redemption of Censos in Accord with the June 12 Decree, and in Liquidation of Pre-1825 Debts."

43. On the amortization of state debt paper in La Paz: MH, t. 10, no. 11, La Paz Treasury to the Prefect, April 11, 1828. On the turnover of billetes from the treasury to the welfare establishments pursuant to Sucre's order: MH, t. 12, no. 2. This also itemizes billetes amortized in the treasury through January of 1828.

44. On Infante's conveyance of Sucre's instructions to turn over 50,000 in billetes to the two welfare establishments: Infante to the La Paz Prefect, February 7, 1828, MH, t. 12, no. 2.

45. On Infante's qualified praise of the Prefect, MH, t. 17, no. 1, Infante to Prefect of Cochabamba, February 2, 1827. Lofstrom incorrectly stated that "public institutions whose property was purchased and whose 'censos' were redeemed by proposed vales would become vales holders; the Government would service and eventually redeem them, therefore maintaining the institutions income" (469). On Aguirre's correct statement that the vales once returned to the treasuries did not bear interest, and his parallel argument that the treasuries could not escape financial responsibilities for the financing of the welfare establishments: Decrees of December (n.d.), 1827, CO, II, 226.

46. On the total amount of billetes put into circulation in 1827 and their distribution by department: MH, t. 9, no. 3, January 8, 1828; reprinted in *Condor* no. 113, January 31, 1827. For Infante's case that interest payments were kept current through the first payment period in January and the quotations: *Condor* no. 113,

March 6, 1828, 2–3. On the case that they were current through September 3: *Condor* no. 100, November 1, 1827, 3.

47. MI, t. 5, no. 2: Ministry of Hacienda Circular, December 28, 1827.

48. On the allegation of Madero's laxity in issuing billetes to the public during the absence of Sucre and Infante from Chuquisaca: *Condor* no. 118, March 6, 1828, 2. On one clerical error involving 10,000 pesos made in the La Paz issue of the billetes: La Paz Treasury to the Prefect, April 28, 1828, MH, t. 10, no. 11. On the attempted recall of the billetes in Cochabamba: Geraldino to MH, January 3, 1828: MH, t. 9, no. 9. On Aguirre's "austerity" circular, MI, t. 5, no. 2, December 28, 1827.

49. Cochabamba Prefect (Geraldino) to MH, January 3, 1828: MH, t. 9, no. 13. On the arrearage allowed to develop in military salaries, Lofstrom, *Reform*, 488.

50. For the last-minute postponement in Potosi and Aguirre's reaction, see Lofstrom, 484–85. For the Potosi figures on total interest paid through the third payment period in September, 1828: Potosi Treasury to MH, November 30, 1828: MH, t. 10, no. 14.

51. MH to Prefect of La Paz, November 20, 1827: MH, t. 17, no. 2.

CHAPTER 4

1. *El Peruano de Lima*, no. 31, October 17, 1827, GRM, Prensa Peruana, F-125, 2–9.

2. Text of the first *Fenix* article: *Condor* no. 7, December 22, 1827, 1–4, with 35 footnotes of rebuttals and clarifications supplied by the *Condor* editors.

3. The second *Fenix* article: GRM, Prensa Peruana, *Fenix*, January 13, 1828, a handwritten copy, 14 pp.

4. Sucre to Bolivar, August 20, 1826, DRB, II, 251.

5. Public Credit Administration (President Callejo) at Chuquisaca to MI, September 3, 1827, MH, t. 5, No. 5.

6. For Infante's rebuttal of the second *Fenix* article: *Condor* no. 118, March 6, 1828, 2–3.

7. Richard Hyland, "A Fragile Prosperity: Credit and Agrarian Structure in the Cauca Valley, Colombia, 1857–87," 386.

8. Alain de Janvry, "Social Articulation in Latin American History."

9. Robert H. Jackson, *Liberal Land and Economic Policy and the Transformation of the Rural Sector of the Bolivian Economy: The Case of Cochabamba, 1860–1929*, 203, 209–11.

10. On systemic feudal thesis in Bolivian historiography: Brooke Larson, *Colonialism and Agrarian Transformation in Bolivia*; Silvia Rivera Cusicanqui, "La Expansión del Latifundio en el Altiplano Boliviano; Elementos para la Caracterización de Una Oligarquía Regional"; Gustavo Rodriguez Ostría, *Expansión del Latifundio y Supervivencia de las Comunidades Indigenas*; Gustavo Rodriguez Ostría, *La Acumulación Originaria de Capital en Bolivia, 1825–1885; Un ensayo sobre la Articulación Feudal-Capitalista*. On the internal economy perspective on

the hacienda: Erick D. Langer, *Economic Change and Rural Resistance in Southern Bolivia*; Jackson, *Liberal Land Policy*; Jackson and José M. Gordillo, "Mestizaje y el Proceso de Parcelización en la Estructura Agraria de Cochabamba"; Jackson, "Markets, Peasantry, and the Formation and Fragmentation of the Hacienda in Cochabamba, Bolivia," 44.

11. Langer, 37, 59, 218.

12. Herbert Klein, "The Structure of the Hacendado Class in Late Eighteenth-Century Alto Peru."

13. Larson, *Colonialism*, and Rodriguez Ostría, *Expansión*, as cited in note 10 above.

14. Jackson, *Liberal Land Policy*. See his use of Cushner's model, 323–24. See also his review of Larson's book where he took account of the structure of censos on Cochabamba haciendas and its effect on stability of hacienda tenure in the post-independence period: Jackson, "Markets, Peasantry," 44. He implied that censos continued to hold haciendas together during most of the nineteenth century much as they had in the colonial period but observed that this proposition "needs to be tested through a systematic examination of the records of hacienda sales, and the contracts which established censos on given properties."

15. Jackson, *Liberal Land Policy*, 192–202, esp. 194; Hyland, "A Fragile Prosperity," 279.

16. Peñaloza, *Historia Económica*, 2:279, 399–400; Casto Rojas, *Historia Financiera de Bolivia*, 80, 147; Caja de Ahorros, ibid., 130, 148.

17. Peñaloza, *Historia Económica*, 2:402.

18. Tristan Platt, *Estado Boliviano y Ayllu Andino*, 41–42.

19. Cusicanqui, "La Expansión del Latifundio"; Antonio Mitre, *Los Patriarcas de La Plata; Estructura Socioenonomica de la Mineria Boliviana en el Siglo XIX*. See also Langer, *Economic Change*, 12–35, for an excellent account generally following Mitre.

20. Cusicanqui, 364.

21. Ibid., 362; Herr, *Rural Change*, 44–50.

22. Jackson's thesis was essentially that the survival of certain labor forms such as service tenantry, which had led some to conclude that they were "feudal," was due rather to the internal economy of the hacienda, the abundance of land, and labor and market conditions. In *Liberal Land and Economic Policy*, he analyzed service tenantry in the Cochabamba hacienda system in these terms; 47, 82, 324, and note 10 above. Jackson maintained that service tenantry continued to represent a rational economic choice by hacendados as it became necessary for them to diversify risks of production in the face of a decline in demand caused by the Potosi market collapse dating from the late colonial period. Jackson and Gordillo, "Mestizaje y el Proceso de Parcelización en la Estructura Agraria de Cochabamba," 18, 26n.11, made out this argument but the authors seemed to concede here that the increase in service tenantry reflected a growing "rentier" and "lethargic" mentality on the part of hacendados, which suggests a less marked rejection of the feudalization thesis than the position taken by Jackson in his other works cited above.

23. E. P. Thompson, "The Moral Economy of the English Crowd in the Eighteenth Century."

24. Jackson and Gordillo, 43.

25. Erwin Peter Grieshaber, *Survival of Indian Communities in Nineteenth-Century Bolivia*.

26. Platt, *Estado Boliviano y Ayllu Andino*.

27. Langer, *Economic Change*, 42–43, 65, 70.

28. Rodriguez Ostría, *Expansión del Latifundio*.

29. Ibid., 13; Platt 71, 94.

30. Rodriguez Ostría, 13.

31. Jackson and Gordillo, 20.

32. Jackson, *Liberal Land Policy*, 187, 191. On changing credit structure on haciendas: 192–202.

33. Rodriguez Ostría, 6, 17n.12.

34. Herr, *Rural Change*, 722.

35. As quoted in Langer, 19–20.

36. Cabrera quote in Gershieber, 237.

37. For social Darwinism and the quotation see ibid., 231–33.

38. Ibid., 241–50; Rodriguez Ostría, 9–10.

39. Grieshaber, 250, 253–57.

40. Ronald Escobedo Mansilla, "Bienes y Cajas de Comunidad en el Virreinato Peruano."

41. Platt, "Estados Tributarios," 98–143.

CHAPTER 5

1. James Buchanan, *Public Principles of Public Debt*, 17–18.

2. On Hume, see Hargreaves, *The National Debt*, 75, 103–4.

3. Steuart, quoted ibid., 85.

4. Adams, *Public Debts*, 158, 204.

5. Ibid., 22–24.

6. Carlos Marichal, *A Century of Debt Crisis*.

7. Quoted from preface to Javier Tantalean-Arbulu, *Politica Económica-Financiera y la Formación del Estado, Siglo XIX*, 19.

8. Malcolm Deas, "Venezuela, Colombia, Ecuador; The First Half-Century of Independence," 519.

9. Marcello Carmagnani and Albert Gallo, "As Tensões de Territorialidade: Os Poderes Regionais nos Estados Brasileiro e Mexicano: Una Analise Comparativa," 2:1080–81.

10. Julian B. Ruiz Rivera, "Remesas de Caudales del Nuevo Reino Granada en el XVII." On Hamilton's influence, see TePaske, "Fiscal Structure," 69–70, 83.

11. Ismael Sanchez Bella, *La Organización Financiera de las Indias*.

12. Tord and Lazo, *Hacienda, Comercio, Fiscalidad y Luchas Sociales en Peru Colonial*.

13. Ibid., 202–4.

14. Sonja Pinto Vallejos, *El Financiamiento Extraordinario de la Real Hacienda en el Virreinato Peruano: Cuzco, 1575–1650.*

15. John TePaske, "The Fiscal Structure of Upper Peru"; John J. TePaske and Herbert S. Klein, *The Royal Treasuries*; Klein, "Structure and Profitability of Royal Finance in the Viceroyalty of Rio de la Plata in 1790."

16. TePaske and Klein, *The Royal Treasuries.*

17. Andrien, *Crisis and Decline.*

18. Kenneth Andrien, "The Sale of Juros and the Politics of Reform in the Viceroyalty of Peru, 1633–1700."

19. David Bushnell, *The Santander Regime in Gran Colombia*; Lofstrom, *The Promise and Problem of Reform*; Lofstrom, *La Presidencia de Sucre en Bolivia.*

20. Lofstrom, *Presidencia*, 423.

21. Delance, *Bosquejo Estadístico de Bolivia*; Rojas, *Historia Financiera de Boliviana*; Peñloza, *Historia Económica de Bolivia.*

22. Rojas, 44.

23. Ibid., 13.

24. Peñaloza, 2:316.

25. Ibid., 2:258; Rojas, 78.

26. Peñaloza, 2:397–98; Rojas, 399–402.

27. Rojas, 78.

28. Lofstrom, *Reform*, 397–402.

29. Halperin-Donghi, *Guerra y Finanzas*, 105.

30. Quiroz, *La Deuda Defraudada.*

31. Mesae Sugarawa, "Los Antecedentes Coloniales de la Deuda Publica de Mexico." See 215–402 for Real Cédulas texts. See also Sugawara, *La Deuda Publica De España.*

32. Marcello Carmagnani and Enrique Florescano (eds.), *El Estado en las Economías de los Países Latinoamericanos*; Carmagnani and Alberto Gallo, "Os Tensoes de Territorididade"; Marichal, "El Nacimiento de la Banca Mexicana en el Contexto Latinoamericano."

Selected Bibliography

Abecia, Valentine. *El Criollismo de la Plata*. La Paz: Juventud, 1964.

Adams, Henry C. *Public Debts, An Essay in the Science of Finance*. New York, 1890.

Anderle, Adam. "Alternativos de le Formación del Estado de las Región de los Andes a Comienzos de Siglo XIX." In Annino et al., q.v., 31–42.

Andrien, Kenneth J. *Crisis and Decline: The Viceroyalty of Peru in the Seventeenth Century*. Albuquerque: University of New Mexico Press, 1985.

———. "The Sale of Juros and the Politics of Reform in the Viceroyalty of Peru, 1633–1700." *Hispanic American Historical Review* 62 (February 1982): 49–71.

Annino, Antonio, et al. *America Latino: Dallo Statto Coloniale allo Statto Nazione*. 2 vols. Milano: Angeli, 1987.

Arguedas, Alcides. *Historia General de Bolivia*. La Paz: Arnó Hermanos, 1922.

Arnade, Charles. *The Emergence of the Republic of Bolivia*. Gainesville: University of Florida Press, 1957.

Ayluardo, Clara Garcia. "El Comerciante y el Crédito Durante la Epoca Borbónica en la Nueva España." In Marichal and Ludlow, eds., q.v., 27–50.

Bagú, Sergio. *El Plan Económico del Grupo Rivadaviano, 1811–1827*. Buenos Aires: Instituto de Investagaciónes Históricas Facultad de Filosofía y Letras, Universidad Nacional del Litoral, 1966.

Bauer, Arnold J. "The Church in the Economy of Spanish America: Censos and Depositos in the Eighteenth and Nineteenth Centuries." *Hispanic American Historical Review* 63, no. 4 (1984): 707–37.

Benavides, Julio M. *Historia de la Moneda en Bolivia*. La Paz: Ediciones Puerta del Sol, 1972.

Bethell, Leslie. *The Cambridge History of Latin America*. Vol. 3, *From Independence to 1870*. New York: Cambridge University Press, 1985.

Bonura, Elena. "El Credito Publico Bajo La Administración de Juan Manuel de Rosas." *Nuestra Historia* (Buenos Aires) 14, no. 28 (December 21, 1981): 195–205.

Brading, David. *Haciendas and Ranches in the Mexican Bajo, 1700–1860*. New York: Cambridge University Press, 1970.

Buchanan, James M. *Public Principles of Public Debt*. Homewood: Richard Irwin, Inc., 1958.

Buchanan, James M. and Flowers, Marilyn R. *The Public Finances*. 5th ed. Homewood: Richard Irwin, 1980.

Burgin, Miron. *The Economic Aspects of Argentine Federalism, 1820–1852.* Cambridge: Harvard University Press, 1946.

Bushnell, David. *The Santander Regime in Gran Colombia.* Newark: University of Delaware Press, 1954.

———. *Reform and Reaction in the Platine Provinces, 1810–1852.* Gainesville: University of Florida Press, 1983.

Cabrera, Juan R. *La Guerra de los Quince Anos.* Santiago, 1867.

Carmagnani, Marcello, and Enrique Florescano, eds. *El Estado en las Economías de los Países Latinoamericanos.* Barcelona: Editorial Critica, 1984.

Carmagnani, Marcello, and Alberto Gallo. "As Tensões de Territorialidade: Os Poderes Regionais nos Estados Brasileiro e Mexicano: Una Analise Comparativa." In Annino et al., 2:1080–96.

Chowning, Margaret. "The Consolidación de Vales Reales in the Bishopric of Michoacan." *Hispanic American Historical Review* 69, no. 3 (1989): 451–78.

Comenares, German. "Censos y Capellanías: Formas de Credito en una Economía Agricola." *Cuadernos Americanos* 2 (1974).

Cusicanqui, Silvia Rivera. "La Expansión del Latifundio en el Altiplano Boliviano; Elementos para la Caracterización de Una Oligarquia Regional." In Florescano, ed., *Origines,* 355–86.

Dawson, Frank. *The First Latin American Debt Crisis.* New Haven: Yale University Press, 1990.

Deas, Malcolm, "Venezuela, Colombia, Ecuador; The First Half-Century of Independence." In Bethell, *Cambridge History of Latin America,* q.v.

de Janvry, Alain. "Social Articulation in Latin American History." In *Debt and Development in Latin America,* ed. Kwan Kim and David Ruccio. South Bend, Ind.: Notre Dame University Press, 1985.

Delance, José Maria. *Bosquejo Estadístico de Bolivia.* La Paz: Universidad Mayor de San Andres, 1975: reprint of 1851 edition.

de Vedia, Agustin. *El Banco Nacional: Historia Financiera de la Republica Argentina, 1818–1854.* Vol. 1, Buenos Aires, 1896.

Difrieri, Jorge A. *Moneda y Banco en la Republica Argentina.* Buenos Aires: Abeledo-Perrot, 1967.

Ehrenberg, Richard. *Capital and Finance in the Age of the Renaissance.* Translated from the German by H. M. Lucas. London: Jonathan Cape, 1928.

Escobedo Mansilla, Ronald. "Bienes y Cajas de Comunidad en el Virreinato Peruano." *Revista Intercional de Sociología* 32, no. 2 (October–December 1979): 465–92.

Florescano, Enrique. *Haciendas, Latifundios y Plantaciones en America Latina.* Mexico City: Siglo Veintiuno Editores, 1975.

———, ed. *Origines y Desarrollo de la Burguesía en America Latina 1700–1955.* Mexico: Editorial Nueva Imagen, 1985.

Galindo, Blanco, ed. *Cartas de General Antonio José de Sucre a León Galindo.* La Paz, 1911.

Gootenberg, Paul Eliot. *Between Silver and Guano: Commercial Policy and the State in Post–Independence Peru.* Princeton: Princeton University Press, 1989.

Grases, Pedro, ed. *Archivo de Sucre.* 7 vols. Caracas: Vicente Lecuna Foundation, 1980.

Grieshaber, Erwin Peter. *Survival of Indian Communities in Nineteenth-Century Bolivia.* Ph.D. diss., University of North Carolina, 1977. Ann Arbor: University Microfilms International, 1984.

Halperin-Donghi, Tulio. *Guerra y Finanzas en los Origines del Estado Argentino, 1791–1856.* Buenos Aires: Editorial de Belgrano, 1982.

Hammett, Brian R. "Church Wealth in Peru: Estates and Loans in the Archdiocese of Lima in the Seventeenth Century." *Jahrbuch für Geschichte von Staat, Wirtschaft, und Gesellschaft Lateinamerikas* 10 (1973): 113–32.

Hansen, Alvin. *Fiscal Policy and the Business Cycle.* New York: W.W. Norton, 1941.

Hansen, Emilio. *La Moneda Argentina.* Barcelona: R. Sopenal, 1916.

Hargreaves, E.L. *The National Debt.* London, 1930; reprinted New York: A.M. Kelley, 1966.

Harris, Seymour E. *The National Debt and the New Economics.* New York: McGraw-Hill, 1947.

Herr, Richard. "Hacia el Derrumbe del Antigo Regimen: Crisis Fiscal y Desamortación Baja Carlos V." *Moneda y Credito* 118 (September 1971): 27–100.

————. *Rural Change and Royal Finances in Spain.* Berkeley: University of California Press, 1989.

Hirschman, Albert O. *Exit, Voice, and Loyalty; Responses to Decline in Firms, Organizations and States.* Cambridge: Harvard University Press, 1970.

Hyland, Richard. "A Fragile Prosperity: Credit and Agrarian Structure in the Cauca Valley, Colombia, 1857–87." *Hispanic American Historical Review* 62, no. 3 (1982).

Jackson, Robert H. *Liberal Land and Economic Policy and the Transformation of the Rural Sector of the Bolivian Economy: The Case of Cochabamba, 1860–1929.* Ph.D. diss., University of California, Berkeley, 1988.

————. "Markets, Peasantry, and the Formation and Fragmentation of the Hacienda in Cochabamba, Bolivia." *Peasant Studies* 16, no. 1 (Fall 1988).

Jackson, Robert H., and José M. Gordillo. "Mestizaje y el Proceso de Parcelización en la Estructura Agraria de Cochabamba." *Revista Latinamericano de la Historia Económica y Social* 10 (1989): 15–37.

Jimenez, Rosario. *Curatos en Bolivia, 1800–1923.* Vol. 4, *Fuentes de Historia Social Americana.* Lima, 1978.

————. *Mineria en Bolivia 1826–1848; Documentos.* Lima: Biblioteca Andina, 1979.

Keith, Robert G. *Conquest and Agrarian Change: The Emergence of the Hacienda System on the Peruvian Coast.* Cambridge: Harvard University Press, 1976.

Klein, Herbert J. "The State and the Labor Market in Rural Bolivia in the Colonial and Early Republican Period." In Spalding, ed., q.v., 195–206.

————. "The Structure of the Hacendado Class in Late Eighteenth-Century Alto Peru: The Intendency of La Paz." *Hispanic American Historical Review* 60, no. 2 (1980): 191–212.

_____. "Structure and Profitability of Royal Finance in the Viceroyalty of Río de la Plata in 1790." *Hispanic American Historical Review* 53 (August 1973): 440–69.

Langer, Erick D. *Economic Change and Rural Resistance in Southern Bolivia.* Stanford: Stanford University Press, 1989.

Larson, Brooke. *Colonialism and Agrarian Transformation in Bolivia.* Princeton: Princeton University Press, 1988.

Larvin, Asuncion. "El Capital Eclesiastico y las Elites Sociales en Nueva España." *Mexican Studies* 2 (Winter 1985): 1–28.

Liberté, Susana B. "Notas Sobre la Consolidación de Vales Reales en el Río de la Plata, 1806–1809." In *Investigaciónes y Ensayos* 6–7 (January–December 1969): 295–322. Buenos Aires: Academia Nacional de Historia.

Lofstrom, William Lee. *La Presidencia de Sucre en Bolivia.* Caracas: Academia Nacional de la Historia, 1987.

_____. *The Promise and Problem of Reform: Attempted Social and Economic Change in the First Years of Bolivian Independence.* Ithaca: Cornell Dissertation Series, June 1972.

Lopez, Vicente. *Historia de la Republica Argentina.* 3 vols. Buenos Aires: Editorial Argentina, 1970.

Marichal, Carlos. "El Nacimiento de la Banca Mexicana en el Contexto Latinoamericano: Problemas de Periodización." In Marichal and Ludlow, eds., q.v., 231–65.

_____. *A Century of Debt Crisis in Latin America: From Independence to the Great Depression, 1820–1930.* Princeton: Princeton University Press, 1989.

Marichal, Carlos, and Leonor Ludlow, eds. *Banca y Poder en Mexico, 1600–1925.* Mexico City: Grijalbo, 1986.

McFarlane, Anthony. "Económica/Política y Política/Económica en Colombia, 1819–1850." In Annino et al., *Statto*, 187–208.

Millington, Thomas. "Bolivian Public Expenditure and the Role of the Decentralized Agencies: A Test of the Wilkie View." In *A Statistical Abstract of Latin America*, ed. James W. Wilkie, 547–66. Los Angeles: UCLA Latin American Center Publications, 1981.

Mitre, Antonio. *Los Partiarcas de la Plata: Estructura Socioeconomica de la Mineria Boliviana en el Siglo XIX.* Lima: Instituto de Estudios Peruanos, 1981.

_____. *El Monedero de los Andes.* La Paz: Hisbol, 1986.

Moreno, Gabriel René. *Ultimos Días Coloniales en el Alto Peru.* La Paz: Editorial Juventud, 1970.

Morner, Magnus. *The Andean Past: Land, Societies, and Conflicts.* New York: Columbia University Press, 1985.

_____. et al. *Compraventas de Tierras on el Cuzco, 1825–1869.* Lima: Instituto de Estudios Latinoamericanos de Estocolmo, 1984.

Navarro, Gonzalez. "Tipología del Liberalismo Mexicano." *Historia Mexicano* 32 (October–December 1962): 198–225.

Ortiz de Zeballos, Carlos. *Misión de Ortiz de Zeballos en Bolivia.* Lima: Ministerio de Relaciónes Exteriores del Peru, 1956.

Ouneneel, Oriz, and C.J.M. Bijleveld. "The Economic Cycle in Bourbon Central Mexico: A Critique of the Recaudación de Diezmos Liquidos en Pesos." *Hispanic American Historical Review* 69, no. 3 (1989): 478–530.

Peñaloza, Luis. *Historia Económica de Bolivia*. 2 vols. La Paz, 1953.

Pentland, Joseph Barclay. *Report on Bolivia, 1827*. London, 1974.

Pereira Pinto, Juan Carlos. *Temas de Historia Económica y Social Argentina durante el Siglo XIX*. Buenos Aires: Editorial Cologuio, 1975.

Pinilla, Sabino. *La Creación de Bolivia*. La Paz: Universidad Mayor de San Andrés, 1975.

Pinto Vallejos, Sonia. *El Financiamiento Extraordinario de la Real Hacienda en el Virreinato Peruano: Cuzco, 1575–1650*. Santiago: Centro de Estudios Humanisticos, Universidad de Chile, 1981.

Platt, Tristan. "Estados Tributarios y Libre Cambio en Potosi durante el Siglo XIX: Mercado Indígena y Lucha de Ideologías Monetarias." In *Annino* et al., 98–143.

———. *Estado Boliviano y Ayllu Andino*. Lima: Instituto de Estudios Peruanos, 1982.

Quiroz, Alfonso W. *La Deuda Defraudada: Consolidación de 1850 y Dominio Económico en el Peru*. Lima: Instituto Nacional de Cultura, 1987.

Reyes Martinez, Gabriel. *Finanzas de las 44 Diocesis de Indias*. Bogota, Colombia: Ediciones Tercer Mundo, 1980.

Rodriguez Ostría, Gustavo. *Expansión del Latifundio y Supervivencia de las Comunidades Indigenas*. Cochabamba: Universidad Mayor de San Simon, Instituto de Estudios Sociales y Economicas, 1983.

———. *La Acumulación Originaria de Capital en Bolivia, 1825–1885: Un ensayo sobre la Articulación Feudal-Capitalista*. Cochabamba: Universidad Mayor de San Simon, 1979.

Rojas, Casto. *Historia Financiera de Bolivia*. La Paz: Universidad Mayor de San Andres, 1977; reprint of 1912 edition.

Ruiz Rivera, Julian B. "Remesas de Caudales del Nuevo Reino Granada en el XVII." *Anuario de Estudios Americanos* 34, 241–71. Seville, 1977.

Sanchez-Bella, Ismael. *La Organización Financiera de la Indias*. Seville: Escuela de Estudios Hispanoamericanos, 1968.

Santamaria, Daniel J. *Iglesia y Economía Campesina in el Alto Peru, Siglo XVIII*. Occasional paper #5, Latin American and Caribbean Center, Florida International University, 1983.

Schwaller, John Frederick. *Origins of Church Wealth in Mexico; Ecclesiastical Revenues and Church Finances, 1523–1600*. Albuquerque: University of New Mexico Press, 1985.

Sempat Assadourian, Carlos. *El Sistema de la Economía Colonial: El Mercado Interior Regional y Espacio Económico*. Mexico: Editorial Nueva Imagen, 1983.

Smith, Adam. *The Wealth of Nations*. New York: The Modern Library, 1937.

Spalding, Karen. "Kurakas and Commerce: A Chapter in the Evolution of Andean Society." *Hispanic American Historical Review* 53 (November 1973): 581–99.

————, ed. *Essays on the Political, Economic and Social History of Colonial Latin America.* Newark: University of Delaware Press, 1982.

Stabile, Donald R., and Jeffrey A. Cantor. *The Public Debt of the United States; An Historical Perspective.* New York: Praesor, 1991.

Sugawara, Masae M. "Los Antecedentes Coloniales de la Deuda Publica de Mexico." *Boletín del Archivo General de la Nación Mexico* 8, nos. 1–2 (1967): 109–402, Real Cedulos Texts: 215– 402.

————. *La Deuda Publica de España y La Economía Novohispaña, 1804–1809.* Mexico: Instituto Nacional de Anthropologia y Historia, 1976.

Tamames, Ramos. *The Spanish Economy.* New York: St. Martins, 1986.

Tantalean-Arbulu, Javier. *Politica Económica-Financiera y la Formación del Estado, Siglo XIX.* Lima: Centro de Estudios Para el Desarrollo y Participación, 1983.

Temple, Edmund. *Travels in various parts of Peru including a year's residence in Potosi.* 2 vols. Philadelphia, 1833.

TePaske, John J. "The Fiscal Structure of Upper Peru and the Financing of Empire." In Spalding, ed., q.v., 69–94.

TePaske, John J., and Herbert S. Klein. *The Royal Treasuries of the Spanish Empire in America.* 3 vols. Durham: Duke University Press, 1982.

Thompson, E.P. "The Moral Economy of the English Crowd in the Eighteenth-Century." *Past and Present* 50 (1971): 76–136.

Tord, Javier, and Carlos Lazo. *Hacienda, Comercio, Fiscalidad y Luchas Sociales en Peru Colonial.* Lima: Biblioteca Peruana de Historia Economía y Sociedad, 1981.

Vallenilla, Nikita Harrier. "Banco y Estado Venezolano, 1830–1911." In Annino et al., q.v., 1:209–43.

Vicens Vives, Jaime. *An Economic History of Spain.* Princeton: Princeton University Press, 1969.

Index

Abascal, Fernando (viceroy of Peru), 46–47

Adams, Henry (classic text on debt), 4, 131–32

Aguirre, Miguel Maria: Bolivian cabinet member, 67; supports funding law, 75; replaces Madero, 93; questions uses of debt paper, 93–94, 94–95; monitors billetes in Cochabamba, 100; lowers price floor on vales, 101–2

Alarcon, Pedro, 90–92, 94, 104

Alcabalas, 14

Andrien, Kenneth, 136

Annuities, 20, 75, 132

Argentina: consolidates internal debt, 7, 15, 17, 18; customs revenue of, and debt, 15–16, 18; emphyteusis policy of, 17–18; nationals of, in Sucre administration, 67–70; funding law of, influences Bolivia, 75–76; class structure of, influences debt, 140; debt historiography of, 142–43

Articles of Confederation, 10

Audiencia (Upper Peru), 46

Augustinians, 40, 55

Ayacucho (battle of), 54

Badajoz, 50

Bagú, Sergio, 142

Ballivián, José, 115

Banks: absence of, in Latin America, 1, 5, 8–9, 15; role of, in British funding, 8; role of, in U.S. funding, 11; in Venezuela, 15; replace church credit, 45, 114–15; in Mexico, 143

Banstable, C.F., 131

Beaterios, 48–49

Billetes de credito publico: different from bonds, 7; political significance of, 16; slow appearance of, in La Paz, 38; and Bolivian funding law, 72, 74–76; restrictions on use of, 76–77; as obstacle to Sucre's loan, 78; and Mining Bank, 81; and June 12 decrees, 85–89; loss of public confidence in, 88, 100–101, 105, 108–9; transactions in, 93–98, 112; concentration in Potosi and Chuquisaca, 112; liberal historiographic view of, 139

Bolivar, Simon: approves Sucre's creation of Bolivia, 47; period in Bolivia, 47; views on education, 49–50; decrees on state welfare institutions, 53; decrees on nationalizing convent wealth, 57; decree to reduce parish income from diezmos, 58–59; decree recognizes émigré claims, 71; *El Fenix* attacks on, 104, 106

Bolivia: absence of European debt in, 1; population of, 34–35; Bolivar's constitution for, 47, 50; legislative entities of, in 1825–26, 48; internal debt of, 71; foreign debt of, 71, 72

—Upper Peru: effects of Consolidación de Vales Reales on, 31–34; administration of, 34; internal and external economies of, 34–35; decline of mining industry in, 35–40; outbreak of revolution in, 46; educational structure of, 48–49; patronato in, 54; state bonds history in, 72

Library of Congress Cataloging-in-Publication Data

Millington, Thomas.
    Debt politics after independence: the funding conflict in Bolivia
/ Thomas Millington.
        p.   cm. — (University of Florida social sciences monographs;
no. 79)
    Includes bibliographical references and index.
    ISBN 0–8130–1140–X
    1. Debts, Public—Bolivia—History.   2. Fiscal policy—Bolivia—
History.   I. Title.   II. Series: University of Florida monographs.
Social sciences; no. 79.
HJ8572.M55   1992   92–3776
336.3′4′0984—dc20   CIP